Dynamics of North Bengal Economy: Colonial to Post-Colonial Period

(Recasting Economic Transformation, Political Agitation and Power-Relationship)

Dynamics of North Bengal Economy: Colonial to Post-Colonial Period

(Recasting Economic Transformation, Political Agitation and Power-Relationship)

Editors
I. Sarkar
Anil Bhuimali

ABHIJEET PUBLICATIONS
NEW DELHI 110002

ABHIJEET PUBLICATIONS
4658-A, First Floor, Ambika Bhawan,
21 Ansari Road, New Delhi 110002
Phone: 011-23259444
E-mail: abhijeetpublication@gmail.com

DYNAMICS OF NORTH BENGAL ECONOMY: COLONIAL TO POST-COLONIAL PERIOD

First Published 2021

ISBN 978-81-950909-9-0

PRINTED IN INDIA

Published by J.K. Singh for Abhijeet Publications, New Delhi-110002, Lasertypeset by Abhijeet Typesetters, New Delhi and Printed at Milan Enterprises, New Delhi.

Dedicated to

Late Professor Amlan Dutta,
Former Vice-Chancellor, University of North Bengal
and
Late Professor P.C Sarkar, Former Professor of Economics, University of North Bengal
Whose blessings and ideals have ever been instrumental in shaping our academic career.

Introduction

The idea behind the collection of the essays incorporated in the present book titled *History of North Bengal in the Making (Recasting Economic Transformation,and Power-Relationship) - Pre-Colonial to Post-Colonial Period* goes back to the beginning of the first decade of this century. Both of us decided to fill up the minimum gap of the historical writings on North Bengal and ultimately we planned to collect few articles on economic aspects on this region. Instantly we received responses from different scholars and academicians and the issues and concerns of the them in the long run prompted us to compile altogether and so to say the presentation of this book is out of such a background. We know there are other areas which are still untouched and could not be covered in this small volume and we hope to take another venture at the earliest.

The themes examined in this work reflect a common desire to understand historical and economic processes over the time and from the perspective of agitation and power-relationship which through the ages facilitated the economic transformation of North Bengal. Through this attempt, we believe, the present book will perhaps demonstrate not only some of the fascinating chapters that dictated the course of the history of North Bengal and at the same time may stimulate other scholars for further academic investigation.

The thireen contributions included in this collection are from the scholars who are reputed and recognized in their respective field and the readers might get clues to develop ideas from their own stand point.

In this opportunity, however, we would like to thank all the contributors for their unstinted sympathy and timely responses with their writings. Abhijeet Publications, New Delhi has responded to our request for its publication and we are very much thankful for the gesture.

I. Sarkar
Anil Bhuimali
01.01.2021

Acknowledgements

The book titled *Dynamics of North Bengal Economy: Colonial to Post-Colonial (Recasting Economic Transformation, Political Agitation and Power-Relationship)* is a collection of thirteen articles which are intended to deal with one another having an objective to explore different economic aspects and historical narratives on North Bengal in consonance with the new trend and perspectives of modern research. Some articles may invite debates and controversies but in the long run, we hope, they may unfold and create some space for further researches. Fact remains that, such a research work cannot be accomplished without the help of different individuals and fellow researchers who showed interest all along for the completion of the book. In this regard, we are deeply indebted to all the scholars who could not but respond positively by contributing articles based on their respective field of studies. We are extremely grateful to a few colleagues and friends of the University of North Bengal elsewhere who ever showed curiosity, support and encouragement for the publication of the book. We must also acknowledge the inspiration and guidelines of some outstanding personalities and scholars who have directly or indirectly encouraged us very often in many critical situation of our academic career. Mention may be made of late Professor Amalendu De, Former Gurunanak Professor of History, Jadavpur University, late Professor Pijush Kanti Saha, former Vice Chancellor, University of North Bengal, late Ajitesh Bhattacharya, Former Lecturer, Department of Bengali, Balurghat College, late Professor P.C. Sarkar, Department of Economics, University of North Bengal, who have all the time given us untiring guidance to create among us a taste of history and economics beside various branches of social sciences with special reference to North Bengal. Late Professor P.K. Bhattacharyya, Sir Jadunath Sarkar Professor of History, University of North Bengal, Professor Tapas Roy Chowdhury, Professor of History, University of North Bengal (Retd) and especially late Sri Nirmal Chandra Chowdhury, Pandapara, Jalpaiguri, who are all still recognized as the path finder in the study and research of regional history specially North Bengal and its neighboring regions. We must record here the name of Bhaskar Chanda, a former PG student of the Department of History, University of North Bengal, who has time and again co-operated with us to work out many important liabilities to bring out the final manuscript of the present book.

Thanks are also due to our family members namely Mrs. Ayesha Sarkar, Anjashi Sarkar and also Mrs Anita Bhuimali and Arumoy Bhuimali who have stood by us to withstand the stress related to this academic programme and gladly shared family burdens throughout the time of our engagement for this work. Needless to say, without their sacrifices and lovable company we would not have completed this book in the present form.

We are also especially thankful to J.K Singh and his associates of the Abhijeet Publications, New Delhi, for their interest and willingness to take the responsibility of its publication.

Last but not the least; despite all the help and inspiration of so many people and well-wishers, we are the only persons as editors to welcome warm remarks on its outcome which may encourage us for further research and study.

01.01.2021

Ichhimuddin Sarkar
Anil Bhuimali

Notes on Contributors

Adhikari, Madhab Chandra, Professor of History, Cooch Bihar Panchanan Barma University, West Bengal.

Basu, Nirban, Former Professor of History, University of Calcutta, West Bengal.

Bhuimali, Anil, Vice-Chancellor, Raiganj University, Uttar Dinajpur, West Bengal.

Das, Meenakshi, Freelance Writer and Researcher, West Bengal,

Das, Nupur, Secretary, Under Graduate Council, University of North Bengal, Darjeeling.

Das, Aniruddha, Associate Professor of History, Raiganj University, West Bengal.

Dey, Palash, Assistant Professor of History, Nur Mohammad Smriti Mahavidyalaya, Dhuliyan, West Bengal

Ghosh, Tirthankar, Assistant Professor of History, Kazi Nazrul University, Asansol, West Bengal.

Kibria, Gholam, Former Associate Professor of Management, Rangpur Govt. College, Bangladesh.

Mukherjee, Salil, Assistant Professor, Department of Commerce, South Malda College, Malda.

Mukherjee, Suman, Assistant Professor, Department of History, THLH Mahavidyalaya, Mallarpur, Birbhum, West Bengal.

R. Ranjit, IAS, District Magistrate (at the time of submission of the article)

Roy, Dulal Chandra, Assistant Professor of History, Kalimpong College, Darjeeling.

Sarkar, I., Former Professor, Department of History, University of North Bengal, Darjeeling.

Sen, Partha, Former Associate Professor of History, Islampur College, Uttar Dinajpur.

Contents

1

The Hill Economy of Darjeeling: Past and Present

Dulal Chandra Roy

Darjeeling is the most developed district in North Bengal. As per West Bengal Human Development Report, 2004, Darjeeling ranks 4th and its position is just next to that of Kolkata, Haora and North 24 Parganas. The other districts of North Bengal lack far behind in respect of such indices, for example, the position of Jalpaiguri is 10th, Koch Behar 11th, Dinajpur 13th and Malda 17th. The HDI has been calculated on the basis of three different indices—a) Health Index (comprises of longevity i.e. life expectancy), b) Income Index (comprises of per capita income, per capita consumption expenditure and population living above poverty line) and c) Education Index (comprises of literacy rate and school enrolment ratio). HDI is the average of the three indices. If we go by individual index, Darjeeling's position is even better in respect of Income Index where it ranks 3rd; its rank in Health Index is 4th and 5th in Education Index (Appendix-I).

Keeping in view the recent position of Darjeeling district in the state, the present work has been aimed at analyzing the hill economy of the district in its past and present perspectives. The work has been devised in two sections—*a)* the first section has been planned to analyze the hill economy of Darjeeling with the help of secondary data particularly census documents and gazetteers and *b)* the second section deals with the identification of the type of the hill economy of the district from the angle of personal experience and field survey.

SECTION—1

In order to know the origin of the district we need to go back to the period 1835 when the hill region (south of great Runjeet River, east of the Balasan, Kahail and little Rungit rivers and west of the Rungno and Mahananddi rivers) was donated to the East India Company by the Sikkim Puttee Rajah, Tsugphu Namgyal. The present shape of the district reminds us another incidence of 1865 (Sinchula Treaty) by which hill territory east of Teesta was ceded by the Bhutan Govt. to the British Govt. This created the present day Kalimpong subdivision.

At present the district comprises of four subdivisions (three in the hills—Darjeeling Sadar, Kurseong and Kalimpong and the other Siliguri in the plains) with the total geographical area of 3149 sq. Km. (Appendix-II). Out of the total geographical area of 3149 sq.km., only Siliguri-Naxalbari (367.98 sq.km.) and Kharibari-Phansidewa (480.06 sq.km.) are in the plains. As 73.07 percent areas are hilly, many a times we call the economy of the district as hill economy.

The economy of the district can better be discussed after categorizing it in four different periods :

Period—I : Before 1835

When British first occupied the territory, it contained only 100 souls (L.S.S.O'Malley, 1907; 35). This small number of aboriginals might have been engaged in collecting fruits and roots from the forest. "They appeared in the most simple, primitive stage, living in the midst of the vast, wild, magnificent forests, old as the hills themselves, and each family resides by itself, having no village or communities... From the forest they obtained fruits of numerous descriptions edible and otherwise useful; thus all other wants were supplied." (G.B. Mainwaring, 1875; ix). The economy may well be identified in the hunting and food gathering stage with primitive tribal character. G. C. Bagchi could find a sort of nomadic life among the inhabitants. "They lived in caves and bamboo huts in the midst of impregnable forests which covered the lower slopes of the mountains. As the aboriginals of the mountain forests, they lived in their splendid Himalayan isolotion as the free sons of the forests, the hearty yeomen of the land and the lords of the soil." (G. C. Bagchi in K. S. Singh ed., 1982, 303). The inhabitants lived in the forest and established a close relationship with the forest. Thus, the forest had sustained the inhabitants and there existed a 'symbiotic relations' between the forest and the inhabitants. Beside this, at the later stage, some sort of agriculture in and around the hut was also mentioned by some writers. But there was no village as such and the inhabitants never remained confined to any particular place for a long time. This type of cultivation may better be identified as 'shifting cultivation'. Risley wrote, "They do not form permanent villages, and merely remained longer than three years in one place, at the expiration of which they move into a new part of the forest, sometimes near, often distant, and there go through the labour of clearing the space for a house, building a new one, and preparing the ground fro a crop" (H. H. Risley, 1891, 13).

It may be noted that during this period there was no separated identity of Darjeeling but it was a part of Sikkim and was ruled by the Rajahs of Tibetan origin. Capital of the country was shifted four times—initially from Yoksam to Rabdentse and then to Tumlong and finally to Gangtok. But all these places were located in the northern part of the country bordering Tibet. The rulers, because of their Tibetan origin, were found to be less interested about the southern part of the country and perhaps felt politically safer in the northern part of the country. So this part (the present day Darjeeling) comprised of dense forest without any habitation as such.

Period—II : From 1835 to 1865

During this period by Darjeeling one can identify a small strip of hill territory, 24 miles long and about 5 miles wide (E.C.Dozey, 1922; 3) donated by the Rajah of Sikkim to the East India Company for the construction of sanatorium. Lt. General Lloyd and Mr. Grant were responsible in the work of handling over the territory between the two parties. But it was Dr Campbell, the first Superintendent of Darjeeling, who made the change in the hill economy by introducing tea plantation in the region. The first tea garden (Aluabari Tea Garden) was started in Kurseong in 1856. "By the end of 1866, i.e. only 10 years after the establishment of the industry on a commercial basis, there were no less than 39 gardens with 10000 acres under cultivation of tea" (L.S.S.O'Malley, 1907; 74).

Tea plantation changed the economic structure of the then society. Inhabitants no more found free land to move and practice shifting cultivation. Land, slowly but steadily, became a scarce factor and the people need to get permission from the authority to use land. The forest reservation policy restricted use of forest by the inhabitants. The tea plantation is labour intensive and needed huge amount of labour for its production. Demographic structure of the region got changed due to influx of huge number of migrants from the neighboring country. Two distinct types of economic activities could be marked : the aboriginals were more engaged in the forest based activities and settled cultivation while the new comers were given the work in plantation activities. Britishers also started settling in different places which necessitated human hands for their construction of houses, roads, etc. Natives helped the Europeans in accompanying them during different tours and travels and also helped them in day to day household activities.

Anyway, from their nomadic and shifting cultivation, people settled in basically garden based activities or agriculture.

Period—III : From 1865 to 1947

This period started with the annexation of the area east of Teesta from Bhutan through a war with a population of 3530 souls in the present day Kalimpong area. This area was actually taken over by the Bhutanese from Sikkim in 1700 and they ruled until it was annexed with British India in 1865. During the period 1865-1947, the geographical area of the district remained more or less stable to nearly 3149 sq. km.

Teesta being the demarcating line, the economy of the extended district could sharply be divided in two broad categories: *a)* the area to the west of Teesta (old Darjeeling) was basically tea plantation based settled economy, and *b)* the area to the east of Teesta (present Kalimpong) was terraced based settled agricultural economy.

By the time the Britishers left India there were as much 142 tea gardens having a geographical area of 63,059 acres which constitute more than 1/3 of the area under cultivation of the district. A distribution of tea gardens in 1942 over the district shows that there was absolutely no tea garden in Kalimpong police station while there were only six gardens under Gorubathan police station (Appendix-III).

In 1870, there were 56 gardens with 11,000 acres under cultivation employing 8000 labours and which increased to 113 gardens with 18,888 acres of land and 19000 souls in 1874 (L.S.S.O'Malley, 1907; 74). Beside the direct employment, inhabitants were also engaged in transporting, communicating and trading tea. Darjeeling tea became world famous and earned both domestic and foreign currency for the private individuals and to the government in the form of incomes and revenues.

Although the inhabitants on the east of Teesta were in close contact with the *Dukpas* of Bhutan during 1700-1865 but no influence of Bhutanese has been marked in the economic and social structure of the region. The British travelers, administrators in the region noted the century old shifting cultivation, food gathering and hunting habits of the inhabitants. But after 1865 due to sudden influx of population, the original inhabitants of the area were either cornered to limited geographical area or had to practice terrace based settled cultivation. This made a dramatic change in the socio cultural structureof the region. The process of expansion of tea garden remained restricted to the western bank of the Teesta while the eastern bank was confined to agricultural operation so as to feed the labour of the tea gardens.

The settlement of the Kalimpong track was conducted first in 1882 by Mr. Marindin, second in 1901-03 by C.A. Bell and third in 1919-21 by H.C.V. Philpot. As per these settlements, the raiyats need to take patta from the government against the payment of rent. The amount of rent varies on the basis of different types of land e.g. *panikhet, sukhakhet,* waste land (Appendix IV). Bell mentioned that out of the government estate area of 114216 acres, the raiyati area was 33809 acres and cultivable area was 32322 acres (C.A. Bell, 1905; 9). Thus more than 1/3rd area of the subdivision came under agricultural operation within a very short period of 40 years. British rule could change the economic structure of the region within a very short period which the *Dukpas* could not do during their long 160 years of reign.

Period—IV : From 1947 onwards

The first census under the free independent India was conducted in 1951 where industrial classification of workers was carried out. A cross section comparison of the workers helps us to know the nature of the economy but the basic limitation in this regard is change in definition and categorization of the workers. For example, 1951 census classified the population as total workers; it also classified workers in agricultural class and non agricultural class which got missed in the successive census documents; similarly categorization of marginal workers was done only for 1981 and 1991 documents. The available CD for 2001 census restricts to a few categories of workers and hence a number of items remained blank in the present work. Any way, we tried to make some sort of adjustments to show the basic nature of the hill economy with the help of post independent census documents.

Industrial classification of population for the district (Appendix VI) reveals that with the increase in population over the decades the percentage of workers to total population has decreased from 42.60 in 1961 to 29.76 in 2001 and this is more so for the females which decreased from 30.08 percent to 15.38 percent during the same period.

Among the workers, nearly 35 percent falls under the category of agricultural worker. Although its percentage has decreased from 40.40 percent in 1961 to 30.60 percent in 2001 but agriculture remained the single largest sector in absorbing the workforce of the district. It is interesting to note that females are depending more on agriculture than their counterpart of male workers. Engagement in agriculture was recorded to be 43.99 for the females while it was only 26.14 percent for the males in the census year 2001.

In absorbing the workforce, the non agricultural sector plays an important role for the district over the decades. Dependence on non-agricultural sector remains more or less the same (60 percent plus) and the females take almost equal share in absorbing themselves before 1981 but recently males dominate over the females in this category. It may well be inferred that the tea gardens in the western part of the district might have played a dominant role in absorbing the females in the past but at present they failed to complete with the males who are more engaged in non plantation activities.

Engagement of workers in agriculture is shown under two categories : cultivator and agricultural labour. As a percentage to total workers, cultivator comprises around 30 percent to 18 percent. Agricultural labour as separate class does not emerge as significant sector for both the males and the females (column 21 and 22). It may be noted that the proportion of cultivators has significantly been decreased from 37.47 percent in 1961 to 18.42 percent in 2001.

The second important sector next to cultivation is live stock, forestry, fishing, hunting, plantation, orchard and allied activities which absorb nearly 21 to 30 percent of total workforce. It may well be placed that plantation is the only dominating sector for the district in this category. It is most interesting to note that females surpassed the males in all the decades by more than double. The tea plantation absorbs proportionately more females than males. Beside this, the females are responsible for taking care the livestock as a subsidiary work along with their principal source engagement in the household activities.

The next five non-agricultural categories (*a.* mining, quarrying, *b.* manufacturing, processing, servicing and repairs in household industry, *c.* manufacturing, processing, servicing and repairs in other than household industry, *d.* construction, *e.* marginal workers) do not play any significant role in absorbing workforce of the region. (Column 26-40). Without going into the details, it may be recorded that their importance over the decades are on the rising side, although very negligibly.

Trade and commerce has emerged as the third sector of involvement of workers. Its role over the decades is increasing from 5 percent to 11 percent (data for the year 2001 is not available). But it is to note that this sector is absolutely dominated by the males while the females play almost no role in contributing in this category.

Transport, storage and communication is another sector which is dominated by the males (6.25 percent) and the females (0.42 percent) play very insignificant role (Column 44-46). The engagement of males has been doubled from 3.46 percent in 1951 to 6.25 percent in 1991.

The other services absorb nearly 15 percent of the workforce of the district is no less important for the economy of the district. In this sector also the males dominates over the females (Column 47-49). In 2001 a separate category under the heading other workers has been created to club all the individual items. As high as 71.48 percent workers are shown in this combined category. This loss of data is an incomprehensible loss for the researchers who are dealing with the secondary data.

SECTION–II

By now it has been established that the economy of Darjeeling in general is agriculture based. But within its broad agrarian and self sustained economic structure one can observe some elements of modern market oriented economy. The coexistence of these two economies in one economy has been identified as 'dualistic economy' by J.H. Boeke in his famous book *Economics and Economic Policy in Dual Societies*.

Dual economy is an important character of underdeveloped economy where the subsistent rural economy coexists with market based urban economy. Centered in the town, the market economy is ultramodern with all the amenities of life viz. communication, housing, water supply, electricity supply, educational institutes, banking facilities, shopping centres etc. On the other hand, the subsistent rural economy, with all the characters of an underdeveloped economy, is agriculture based and is located far away from the market place.

In Boek's economic dualism the modern capitalistic elements penetrates into the indigenous pre capitalistic sector. Here both the sectors coexist simultaneously without affecting the other sector. With the growing up of capitalism, the modern trade and commerce expands while the rural sector remains at its underdeveloped stage without any change in its basis subsistent nature.

In the hill economy of the district, one can notice a type of socio-economic dualism between the rural and the urban sectors. The rural economy is agriculture based and is basically pre-capitalistic one. The urban sector, on the other hand, is purely market based capitalistic economy with all the modern facilities of life.

In agriculture, people of Darjeeling cultivate two types of crops—food crop (paddy, maize and millet) and cash crop (ginger, cardamom, vegetables, floriculture). Food crop is used absolutely for domestic consumption and no part of it is sold in the market. The cash crop, on the other hand, is meant for the market. Food crops are cultivated with traditional seed, domestic manure, rain water, domestic capital, household labour and with indigenous technology. As a result productivity of the food crops are at low level. For cash crops, the farmers use HYV seeds, chemical fartilizer, hired labour, invest loaned capital, and adopt modern technology. As a result, the productivity of these crops is much higher than those of the food crops. The aged, uneducated and less informed land owners, located far away from the town, are more inclined to the food crops while the energetic, educated youths with modern outlook prefer to cultivate cash crops. The traditional system of mutual exchange of lablur (locally known as parma) is prevalent in the cultivation of food crops while it is totally replaced by hired wage labour in case of cash crops.

Beside the dual character within the agricultural sector, the hill economy of the district witnessess a sort of dualism between the rural and urban sectors.

As against no place to keep the vehicles in the main road under the municipal area, so many rural areas of the district are not at all connected even by kachha road. One needs to walk hours together to avail the facilities of motor able road. Doko still continues to be the popular method of carrying articles in the villages as against the modern vehicles in the urban areas. Agriculture remains the only source of earning in the rural areas while people can avail a variety of opportunities to accommodate themselves in the urban areas.

The multidimensional activities in the urban areas not only help the individuals to engage themselves but also help them to maintain their per capita income at higher level. As a result the urban sector has developed compared to the rural sector. Urbanites can avail the facilities of modern electronic devices (like TV, computer, mobile, internet etc.) while there is hardly any village which can avail any such facilities. The modern world has become a village in terms of accessibility and exchanging information but a good number of villages in the district are still without the bare minimums of life like drinking water, medical facilities, communication facilities etc.

Educational institutions have been centralized in the urban areas and it has purely been commercialised where a good number of people are engaged with the educational institutions both directly and indirectly (as teaching and non teaching staff, keeping students as paying guests, engaging vehicles, supplying articles etc.). Beside a few government aided primary schools, a large number of villages are without any educational institutions. It never emerges as a means of earnings to the rural people. Lack of educational institution is responsible for low rate of literacy among the rural mass and which is responsible for arresting economic development of the villages in the long run. It is as if English medium education is the only prerogative of the urban dwellers while the rural students are to start schooling only through their vernacular.

Trade, transport and commerce—the three sectors are absolutely captured by the urban people. The villagers are exploited twice— once at the time of selling their agricultural produce and once again when they go to buy the industrial products from the town. The quality products are not at all available in the rural areas and the maximum retail price as printed on the articles carry no meaning to them. The social infrastructure (like health care, education, training etc.) has been made available within the municipal area and 'water for all', 'education for all', 'health for all' remained simply as slogan for capturing votes of the rural villagers.

Financial institutions, like banks, are no more considered as service but become profit making institutions. Some such institutions (like Uttar Banga Kshetriya Gramin Bank, Regional

Rural Bank) are supposed to be located in the villages but they prefer to establish their branches in the town areas. Banks are extending their better services (ATM facilities) to only one section of the customers while no new branches have been opened in the rural areas in the recent past. Maha Loan Mela has been organized in the town to educate and facilitate the urbanites to take loan from the bank even for luxury consumables while the villagers are still in the clutch of the village mahajans and they are born in debt, live in debt and die in debt.

In the fields of information and communication, the urban areas of the district avail all types of modern facilities like internet, E-mail and are linked with the websites. But so many villages could not bring under the net of ratio and television service. Once somebody humorously commented, 'we can get the radio news two days after its broadcast.' This hints about the degree of remoteness and the type of information network of the rural areas.

Beside all these, a sort of social dualism has also been noted between the rural and urban sectors of the subdivision. The traditional dress of all the leading communities (Nepalese, Lepchas, Bhutias and Tibetans) has been replaced by the modern fashionable dress of the west (Appendix V). This is more so for the urban areas than the rural areas. Each of the communities has an identifying hat. But both the dress and the hat have become purely ceremonial and are during the occasions as ornamental to the community. The days old traditional culture remain the culture of the underprivileged class while advancement is connected with imitation of pop and rock culture of the west. The higher income group of the urban areas has changed their food habit in favour of either dry food or Chinese dish leaving their days old community food to be consumed only by the low income groups.

Epilogue

It has been seen by now that the district Darjeeling has some economic, social and geographical division all over. There are some differences in the degree of geographical development, differences in social customs and attitudes, between the traditional and imported social systems and differences in the structure and level of economic development where the modern capitalistic structure penetrates into the traditional pre capitalistic economy. The economy of the district can thus be identified as an example of 'Dualism'. Three types of dualism may be important to note : 'Geographical Dualism', 'Socio-Cultural Dualism' and 'Economic Dualism'.

Geographical Dualism

The present area of the district is due to the annexation of different geographical areas at different periods. The treatment of the central authority never remained uniform and separate polices had been adopted for the development of the newly annexed areas. As a result different geographical areas perform different level of development and the district witnesses a sort of 'Geographical Dualism'.

River Teesta divides the district in two separate centre of development. The eastern part is based on agriculture and is comparatively underdeveloped but self sufficient in the production of food grains. The western part, on the other hand, is plantation based and more monetized but depends on other areas for the supply of food grains. Proportion of forest to total geographical area is more in the eastern part than in the western sector. River Teesta divides the district in two separate geographical zones.

Geographical division is also evident between the urban and rural areas of the district. The rural sector is underdeveloped and pre capitalistic as it is basically nature dependent while the urban sector is capitalistic and is based on profit yielding activities. There is self sufficiency in rural areas while the cities have to depend on the outside world. Cities are dynamic and progressive while villages remained in their static and stagnant mode.

Socio-Cultural Dualism

Presence of two mutually exclusive non economic factors of different communities makes the districts a sort of Socio Cultural Dualism. It has so happened that the traditional culture and values are associated only with the villagers who are basically underprivileged economically. The modern culture and values are linked with the urban centres where incidentally the well to do persons reside.

The traditional culture, dress, food habit and overall life style are still preserved and maintained by the countrymen while the urbanities are more inclined to the western culture and life style. The nature and pattern of a society is closely linked with the nature and pattern of the economy which play a predominant role in giving the shape of the society.

Modern education is the prerogative of the urbanities while mass illiteracy with heavy dropout is the usual picture of the rural areas. In 1991 the overall literacy rate for the district was 49.17 percent but it was as high as 76.82 for the urban population. The percentages of literates with some of the major urban areas are : Kurseong (83.80), Darjeeling (83.04), Kalimpong (79.12) and Siliguri (74.23).

Economic Dualism

The coexistence of two different types of economies that are usually exclusive to two different types of economies is present in the district of Darjeeling. Subsistent village economy is the example of pre capitalist type where barter system still prevails in a number of cases. Mutual exchange of labour for both agricultural and non agricultural purposes limits the use of wage labour in the rural areas of the district. The urban economy, on the other hand, is capitalistic and is based totally on money. This market oriented urban sector is depended on outside world for the supply of daily necessities. The wide and multifarious connectivity of the urban economy makes the district economy nearer to the capitalistic pattern while the self sufficient agriculture based rural economy is characterized by pre capitalism. But before the Britishers came to this place, the economy was fully pre capitalistic one. So capitalism penetrates into the original pre capitalistic economy without destroying the later in its totality.

There is wide disparity between the agricultural and non-agricultural sectors of the district. As against 30 percent workers in the agricultural areas, the non- agricultural sector contributes nearly 70 percent of workers of the total workforce. Kalimpong is basically agriculture based while the area west of Teesta is dependent on tea and cinchona plantation. Agriculture is pre-capitalistic while plantation is capitalistic.

Cultivators and plantation workers contribute nearly equally (nearly 25 to 35 percent each) to the development of the economy but the contributions of other sectors (like mining, manufacturing, construction, trade and commerce transport, storage etc.) are very insignificant.

Time series data reveal that over the years all the sectors are not playing consistent and equal role in framing the shape of the economy. The sectors whose role has decreased over the years are agriculture and plantation but still they could retain their leading role in contributing the pattern of the economy. The emerging sectors which gained importance in the economy in recent years are manufacturing, trade, commerce and transport.

NOTES AND REFERENCES

1. G.C. Bagchi, (1982)—From Semi nomadic to Settled Agriculture. In K.S.Singh (ed.)—*Economics of Tribes and their Transformation*, New Delhi.
2. A. K. Banerjee, and others (1980)—*West Bengal District Gazetteers-Darjeeling*. Govt. of West Bengal.
3. C.A. Bell, (1905)—*Final Report on the Survey and Settlement of the Kalimpong Government Estate in the District of Darjeeling, 1901-03*, Bengal Secretariat Press, Calcutta.
4. E.C. Dozey, —*A Concise History of the Darjeeling District since 1835*. Reprint Jetsun Publishing House, Calcutta, 1989.
5. Govt. of India—*Census of India*, 1951.
6. —*Census of India*, 1961.
7. —*Census of India*, 1971.
8. —*Census of India*, 1981.
9. —*Census of India*, 1991.
10. Govt. of West Bengal—*West Bengal Human Development Report 2004*, Department of Development and Planning, Govt. of West Bengal, 2004.
11. G.B. Mainwaring, (1876)—*A Grammar of the Rong (Lepcha) Language as it Exists in the Darjeeling and Sikkim Hills*, Reprint Daya Publishing House, Delhi 1985.

12. L.S.S O'Malley, (1907)—*Darjeeling District Gazetters*, Reprint, Gyan Publishing House, New Delhi.
13. H.C.V Philpot, (1925)—*Final Report on the Survey and Settlement of Kalimpong Government Estate 1919-19021*. Bengal Secretariat Book Depot. Calcutta.
14. H.H. Risley, (1891)—*Tribes and Castes of Bengal : Ethnographic Glossary*, Vol. II, Reprint, Firma KL Mukhopadhyay, 1981.

Appendix-1: Human Development Indicators for the Districts of West Bengal

Name of districts	*Health*		*Income*		*Education*		*Human*	
	Rank	*Index*	*Rank*	*Index*	*Rank*	*Index*	*Rank*	*Index*
1	*2*	*3*	*4*	*5*	*6*	*7*	*8*	*9*
Darjeeling	0.73	4	0.49	3	0.72	5	0.65	4
Jalpaiguri	0.61	11	0.38	10	0.60	13	0.53	10
Kochbehar	0.50	14	0.41	7	0.65	10	0.52	11
Dinajpur	0.62	10	0.39	9	0.53	15	0.51	13
Malda	0.49	15	0.36	11	0.48	17	0.44	17
Murshidabad	0.57	12	0.29	12	0.52	16	0.46	15
Birbhum	0.53	13	0.27	13	0.61	12	0.47	14
Bardhaman	0.74	3	0.47	4	0.71	6	0.64	5
Nadia	0.65	9	0.41	7	0.66	9	0.57	9
North 24 Parganas	0.72	5	0.49	3	0.76	2	0.66	3
Hugli	0.77	2	0.46	5	0.67	8	0.63	6
Bankura	0.67	8	0.26	14	0.62	11	0.52	11
Purulia	0.61	11	0.18	15	0.55	14	0.45	16
Medinipur	0.68	7	0.45	6	0.74	4	0.62	7
Haora	0.77	2	0.53	2	0.75	3	0.68	2
Kolkata	0.82	1	0.73	1	0.80	1	0.78	1
South 24 Parganas	0.71	6	0.40	8	0.68	7	0.60	8
West Bengal	0.70	-	0.43	-	0.69	-	0.61	-

Source : West Bengal Human Development Report, 2004, Development and Planning Department, Govt. of West Bengal.

Appendix-II

Area of the district of Darjeeling over the census period

Year	*1901-1921*	*1931*	*1941*	*1951*	*1961*	*1971*	*1981*	*1991*
Area in sq.km.	3014.8	3130.1	3087.3	3107.2	3254.6	3075	3149	3149
Area in sq. miles	1164	1212	1192	1199.7	1199.7	-	-	-

The variations in the territorial figures are mainly due to differences in the survey methods. (Banerjee, A.K., 1980 : 3).

Appendix-III

Distribution of Tea Gardens in Darjeeling district in 1942

Name of PS	*No.*
Darjeeling	19
Jore Bunglow	16
Sukhiapokhri	9
Pulbazar	2
Rangli Ranliot	9
Kurseong	25
Mirik	5
Siliguri	27
Kharibari	11
Phasidewa	13
Kalimpong	0
Gorubathan	6
Total	141

Source : West Bengal District Gazetteers : Darjeeling 1980 : Edited by A. K. Banerjee and others, Govt. of West Bengal, Calcutta, p. 229.

Appendix-IV
Rent of different types of land during 1901-03

Class	*Terraced Rice (panikhet)*			*Dry Cultivation (sukhakhet)*			*Waste Field*			*Remarks*
1	2			3			4			5
	Rs.	A	P	Rs.	A	P	Rs.	A	P	
I	1	4	0	0	15	0	0	3	0	Rupees
II	1	0	0	0	13	0	0	3	0	5 to Rs 10
III	1	13	0	0	11	0	0	2	0	according to
IV	0	11	0	0	9	0	0	2	0	the Price.

Source : C.A.Bell, 1901-03; XXVII.

Appendix-V
Traditional dress of major communities of Darjeeling

Community	*Male*	*Female*	*Hat (for male)*
1	*2*	*3*	*4*
Nepali	Doura Saural	Choubandi Cholee/Faria	Topi
Lepcha	Dum Praa	Dum Dem	Thyaak
Tibetan	Chuba/Mongu	Chuba/Khuthung	Shyamo
Bhutia	Gho	Kira	Shyamo

Source : Field Survey in Kalimpong.

Appendix-VI

IndustrialClassificationofpopulation, Main Workers, non-workers of Darjeeling

Census	Total Population			Total Main Worker			Total non Worker		
Year	Person	Male	Female	Person	Male	Female	Person [Col. 2-5]	Male [Col. 3-6]	Female [Col. 4-7]
1	2	3	4	5	6	7	8	9	10
1951	445260	239018	206242	445260	239018	206242	-	-	-
	100.00	53.68	46.36	100.00	100.00	100.00			
1961	624640	335036	280604	266105	178969	87136	358535	156067	202468
	100.00	53.64	46.36	42.60	53.42	30.08	57.40	46.58	69.92
1971	781777	415442	366335	282442	203273	79169	499335	212169	287166
	100.00	53.14	48.86	36.13	38.93	21.61	63.87	51.07	78.39
1981	1024269	542567	481702	358590	264002	94588	665679	278565	387114
	100.00	52.97	47.03	35.01	48.66	19.64	66.99	51.34	80.36
1991	1299919	679323	620596	438248	317733	120515	861671	361590	500081
	100.00	52.26	47.94	33.71	46.77	19.42	66.29	53.23	80.58
2001	1609172	830644	778528	478851	359110	119741	1069730	427674	612056
	100.00	51.62	43.48	29.76	43.23	15.38	64.61	51.49	78.62

Sources : Govt. of India—Ceusus of India—1951, 1961, 1971, 1981, 1991, 2001.

Note:1. Percentages of main worker and non-worker are in proportion to the corresponding total.

2. Percentage figures in all types of workers are in proportion to their total worker.

3. In 2001 data on a number of items are not available. A separate category under the heading 'Other which cannot be compared with the other census periods.

4. Figures in the parenthesis indicate their corresponding percentages.

Non Agricultural Worker			*Cultivator*			*Agricultural Labour*			*Livestock, Foresty, Fishing Hunting, Plantation, orc & Allied Activities*		
Person Col.5+11	*Male Col.6-12*	*Female Col.7-13*	*Person Col.11+20*	*Male Col.12+21*	*Female Col.13+22*	*Person Col.11+17*	*Male Col. 12+18*	*Female Col.13+19*	*Person*	*Male*	*Female*
14	*15*	*16*	*17*	*18*	*19*	*20*	*21*	*22*	*23*	*24*	*25*
2424	164752	137672	134309	69700	64609	7929	4239	3690	598	327	271
7.92	68.93	66.75	30.16	29.16	31.33	1.78	7.71	1.79	0.13	0.14	0.31
8595	113783	44812	99703	59825	39878	7807	5361	2446	82236	46257	3597
9.60	63.58	51.43	37.47	33.43	45.76	2.93	2.99	2.81	30.90	25.85	41.29
0605	123875	46730	86054	60948	25106	25783	18450	7333	76172	39434	3673
0.40	60.94	59.03	30.67	29.98	31.71	9.13	9.08	9.26	26.97	19.39	46.4
1742	173516	58226	94728	65679	29049	32120	24807	7313	-	-	-
4.63	65.73	61.56	26.42	24.88	30.71	8.96	9.39	7.73	-	-	-

Mining & Quarrying			Manufacturing, Processing, Servicing, Repair in Household			Manufacturing, Processing, Servicing, Repair in other than Household			Industry		
Person	Male	Female	Person	Male	Female	Person	Male	Female	Person	Male	Female
26	27	28	29	30	31	32	33	34	35	36	37
-		-	-	-	-	-	-	-	-		
-	-	-	-	-	-	-	-	-	-		
-	-	-	4501	3671	830	4805	4729	76	3160		
		1.69	2.05	0.95	1.18	2.64	0.66	1.19			
90	85	5	4923	3683	1240	8802	8082	522	3371		
0.03	0.04	0.06	1.74	1.82	1.57	3.11	4.07	0.66	1.19		
-	-	-	4735	3827	908	-	-	-	-		
-	-	-	1.32	1.45	0.96	-	-	-	-		
63	60	3	2722	2057	665	28866	23684	5182	10525		
0.01	0.002	0.02	0.62	0.65	6.59	6.59	7.45	4.29	2.40		
-	-	-	15852	9880	5972	-	-	-	-		
-	-	-	3.31	2.75	4.99	-	-	-	-		
8040	206077	71963	108426	75085	33341	51782	36571	15211	92086	47160	4492
3.44	64.86	59.71	24.74	23.63	27.66	11.81	11.51	12.62	21.01	14.84	37.28
2307	265249	67058	88194	57871	30323	58350	35990	22360	-	-	-
9.39	73.86	56.01	18.42	16.12	25.32	12.19	10.02	18.67	-	-	-

2

Population Growth and the Economy of Darjeeling Hills (1835-1947)

Minakshi Das and Aniruddha Das

1. Introduction

Historically and from the administrative viewpoint the Darjeeling hills is constituted of the three hill subdivisions Darjeeling (Sadar), Kurseong and Kalimpong. The facts of history reveal that from a very meagre number of people there was a great leap in the number of people in the mid 19th century that is after the British occupation of Darjeeling. From the theoretical perspective Kuznets has defined modern economic growth as a sustained increase in population attained without any lowering of per capita product. Sometimes a growing population has been proffered as a net contributor to economic growth : *a)* because of its stimulating effect on demand and its risk reducing incentive to investment, *b)* because it provides for constant improvement of the labour force with better trained workers, and *c)* because population pressure may encourage technological innovation. Moreover, large population size permits economies of scale in production for large markets. (Nancy Birdsall : *Analytical Approaches to the Relationship of Population Growth and Development*, pp. 65-66). M.P. Todaro also subscribes to the same viewpoint. We presuppose that the population growth in the Darjeeling hill areas came as a boon to the development of the hill economy.

2. Location

Darjeeling the northern most district of West Bengal is located between 26031/ and 27013/ North latitudes and 87059/ and 88053/ East longitudes.[1] Of all the frontier districts of India the boundary of Darjeeling is most complicated. There is Nepal to the west, Sikkim to the north, Bhutan and Jalpaiguri to the east and Purnea, North Dinajpur and Bangladesh to the south. The area of the district according to the Surveyor General of India is 1160 sq. miles but according to the Director of Land Records and Surveys, West Bengal, 1200 Sq. miles.[2] The plains from which the hills take their rise are only 300 feet above sea level; the mountains ascend abruptly in spurs of from 6000 to 10000 feet in height. The two highest mountains in the world, Kanchanjanga in Sikkim, and Everest in Nepal, are visible from the town of Darjeeling.

3. Origin of the name of the district

The name probably had Tibetan origin means where *Indra's* thunderbolt or scepter rested, (Dorje—thunder bolt, Ling—place). Hence 'the place of the thunderbolt'. This was the name of a Buddhist monastery once situated on the top of Observatory Hill.[3] In Sanskrit, the name, derived from the word *'Durjay Ling'*, means 'Siva of invincible prowess, who rules the Himalayas.'

4. Brief History

Little is known about the early history of Darjeeling. The area was historically part of the kingdom of Sikkim. In 1780, the Gorkhas marched into Sikkim, annexed the Terai, advanced to the Teesta river and set off a conflict they had not bargained for. They had trodden on the toes of the East India Company, the war of 1814 was fought with Nepal, the tract ceded by the treaty of Titaliya in 1817, and the Raja of Sikkim was reinstated with his sovereignty guaranteed by the Company. Sikkim, including Darjeeling, became a buffer state between Nepal and Bhutan.[4] Ten years later the dispute broke out afresh. In 1828, another dispute occurred between Nepal and Sikkim. Two Officers, Captain Lloyd and Mr. Grant were deputed in

1828 to deal with the disputes. They however found the Darjeeling region very suitable as a sanatorium for British troops. The company negotiated with the king of Sikkim to lease the area starting in 1835. Dr. Campbell, a member of the Idian Medical Service and Lieutenant Napier were given the responsibility to found a hill station there. Thus in 1835 the king of Sikkim through a Deed of Grant gave a portion of the Darjeeling hills to the British for establishing a sanatorium. (See Annexure 1). This was an unconditional cession. But the government granted the Raja an allowance of Rs. 3000 as compensation and raised the grant to Rs. 6000 in 1846.

In 1839, Darjeeling got its first Superintendent, Dr. Campbell. He was given the charge of political relations with Sikkim besides, running the civil, criminal and fiscal administration, when he found time, he also acted as Postmaster, Marriage Registrar and Administrator of the station funds. Campbell built the district and laid the foundation of the, now multi-million dollar tea industry in 1841. Twenty-five years later, there were already 40 gardens in 10,000 acres with an out-turn of half a million pounds. Immigrants poured in. A road from Pankhabari was also laid-out.

In 1850 the Terai was annexed and a portion of the Sikkim hills bounded by Ramnan and Great Rangit on the north, by the Teesta on the East and by the Nepal frontier on the west also came under Darjeeling. The treaty put an end to the sufferings of the residents of Darjeeling, but the peace was interrupted by the incursions of the Bhutanese into the district. A large force was sent in the winter of 1864—ultimately the whole of the Dooars was occupied, the Kalimpong police circle was added. In the meanwhile Kurseong was developing and it was made head quarter of a new sub-division in 1891. Separated from the Kurseong sub-division, Siliguri was made a new sub-division in 1907. Kalimpong sub-division was created in 1917.

The Darjeeling area was a Non-Regulation district; thus acts and regulations did not automatically come into force in the district in line with rest of the country unless they were extended to it.5 After the 1905 Partition of Bengal, the area came under the jurisdiction of Rajshahi division. After the independence of India in 1947, Darjeeling became a part of the state of West Bengal.

5. Growth of Population

The Darjeeling district offers the most remarkable example of growth of population stemming mainly from immigration from outside.[6] At the time of the cession of the greater part of Darjeeling Sadar subdivision, the tract was almost entirely under forest and practically uninhabited. There were not even twenty resident families or households in that area containing a population of 100.

The decision of the Company to develop Darjeeling as a hill resort gave an opportunity to neighbouring peoples to immigrate and take part in the development. The original inhabitants, probably Lepchas, were rapidly outnumbered by settlers from Nepal and Sikkim. It was for Dr. Campbell's different developing activities that from a mere 100 souls in 1839 when he came, the population had shot up to 10,000 by 1849. In 1869 a rough census was taken of the inhabitants of this tract, the total was found to be over 22000.[7] From mid 19th century the Europeans both civil and military, traders, the Indian servicemen, doctors, advocates and the like found their way to the hills.

During 1901-11 there was a decline in the rate of growth of pupulation. Because there was only a limited area in which there was room for an increase in population. Reserved forests and the tea gardens extended over a considerable portion of the district. With the development of the area labour poured in and a phenomenal growth of population resulted. Then, all the land suitable for cultivation, within the area reserved for it, had been taken up; on the tea gardens. As it is, tea occupied a third of the cropped area and the tea gardens employed a labour force of 53000 or one-fifth of the total population of the district. As regarded ordinary cultivation, only one-third of the district was cultivable and thus it could not sustain a large agricultural population. Even in Kalimpong, where nearly half of the land was reserved for native cultivation, it was recognized that it had reached the limit of safety in some parts, and in such localities it had been founded necessary to prohibit further extension.

Between 1872 and 1881 the population had increased by 63.8% and during the next decade by 43.9%. The growth rate registered a drop to 11.6% during 1891-1901 and a further drop to 6.5% during 1901-11, which remained almost the same in the following decade. During 1901-11 most of the population growth took place in Kalimpong subdivision, which recorded a 19.3% rise in population, Sadar (Darjeeling) subdivision recorded 11.6% while Kurseong suffered a decrease of 8.8%. It appears that during this decade the growth of population by immigration was caused more by bringing waste lands into cultivation than by expansion of industry, trade, commerce or transport. During 1911-12 when the district recorded a 6.5% population increase, Kalimpong subdivision showed a higher growth, while Darjeeling (Sadar) showed a decline. During 1921-31 the district recorded a 13% growth in population, followed by a 17.7% increase in 1931-41. The population slowly rose—19,000 in 1911 grew to 27,000 by 1941. The following table gives a subdivision wise and thana wise distribution of population in the district in 1901 and 1931 as also the percentage variations between generations.

Table : 1

Subdivision wise and Thana wise Distribution of Population in Darjeeling District in 1901 and 1931 with Percentage Variation

District/Subdivision/ Police Station/Town	*Population*		*Percentage variation*
	1901	*1931*	*(1901-31)*
Darjeeling District	243117	319635	+28.31
DARJEELING (SADAR) SUBDIVISION	91953	119178	+29.61
Darjeeling	33808	44096	+30.43
Jore Bungalow	15472	21090	+36.31
Pulbazar	14062	18010	+28.08
Sukhiapukhri	9724	14179	+45.81
Rangli Rangliot	18887	21803	+15.44
Darjeeling (Town)	16924	21185	+25.18

KURSEONG SUBDIVISION	45187	51996	+15.07
Kurseong	32754	37689	+15.07
Mirik	12433	14307	+15.07
Kurseong (Town)	4469	7451	+66.73
KALIMPONG SUBDIVISION	41511	68203	+64.3
Kalimpong	34238	54841	+60.18
Gorubathan	7273	13362	+83.72
Kalimpong (Town)	1069	8776	+720.95

Source : Banerji, Amiya Kumar, et. al. : West Bengal District Gazetteers—Darjeeling, 1980.

5.1. Composition of the population

In the census 1891, it was found that out of the district population of 223314 persons, 88000 were born in Nepal.[8] The number excluded those whose parents or grandparents were born in Nepal. In 1901 it was found that 61% of the population was of Nepalese origin; 27% were tribes and scheduled castes; while the Bhutias formed 3% and the Tibetans 1% of the population. The remaining 4% was made up of people belonging to "upper" Hindu castes, Muslims and non -tribal Christians from the plains, and the Europeans. In 1931 people of Nepalese origin including the Sherpas and Limbus formed about 52%, the tribes and scheduled castes from Indian plains approximately 21%, the Lepchas and the Sikkimese Tibetans about 4%, the Bhutanese about 1% and the Tibetans about 1% of the total population. The rest of the population was made up of people belonging to "upper" Hindu castes, Muslims and non-tribal Christians from the Indian plains, and Europeans.

The Siliguri-Darjeeling railway line was opened in 1880-1881. It facilitated the growth of already existing Indo- Tibet, Indo-Sikkimese and Indo-Bhutanese trade thereby increasing employment potential in the tertiary sector of places situated on the railway line.

5.2. Distribution of population according to sex :

The table below shows the variation of sexes (females per 1000 males) in the district as a whole (with rural and urban break-ups) in 1901 and 1931.

Table : 2
Variation in Sexes (Females per 1000 Males) in Darjeeling District in 1901 and 1931

	1901	*1931*
Total	876	881
Rural	894	906
Urban	890	728

Source : Banerji, Amiya Kumar, et. al. : West Bengal District Gazetteers—Darjeeling, 1980.

5.3. *Rural and Urban distribution of population :*

The three municipal hill towns in the district are Darjeeling, Kurseong and Kalimpong. The following table indicates the rural and urban distribution of population in the district as also the percentage shares (shown within brackets) of rural and urban areas to the total district population in 1901 and 1931 from which the progress of urbanization will be apparent.

Table : 3
Distribution of Population in Rural and Urban areas of Darjeeling District in absolute numbers and in percentages in 1901 and 1931

	1901		*1931*	
Darjeeling	*Rural*	*Urban*	*Rural*	*Urban*
District	219871(90.44)	23246(9.56)	276156(86.40)	43479(13.60)
Sadar Subdivision	75028 (81.59)	16925 (18.41)	97993(82.23)	21185 (17.77)
Kurseong Subdivision	40718(90.11)	4469(9.89)	44544(85.67)	7451 (14.33)
Kalimpong Subdivision	40442(97.43)	1069(2.57)	59427 (87.14)	8776 (12.86)

Source : Banerji, Amiya Kumar, et. al. : *West Bengal District Gazetteers—Darjeeling,* 1980.

It will be seen that the urban populations of Kalimpong. Sadar and Kurseong subdivisions (in that order) fall below the district average. Darjeeling, Kurseong and Kalimpong became municipal towns in 1850, 1879 and 1945. After the establishment of the municipalities considerable amount of money was spent for the development of the areas as urban centres. Kalimpong was also growing as urban centre and it was also an entrepot market served by a communication network with Tibet, Sikkim and Bhutan. The waning of trade between India and Tibet has affected Kalimpong adversely.

The following table gives percentage variations of the district's rural, urban and total population between 1901 and 1941.

Table : 4

	1901-11	*1911-21*	*1921-31*	*1931-41*
Total	+5.31	+5.12	+12.85	+17.72
Rural	+4.47	+4.00	+8.68	+15.30
Urban	+14.89	+16.78	+51.48	+33.77

Source : Banerji, Amiya Kumar, et. al. : *West Bengal District Gazetteers—Darjeeling*, 1980.

6. Interrelation Between Demographic and Economic Growth

The rapid increase of population in the hills has made Darjeeling a real city. Many Tibetans and Chinese people have arrived in Darjeeling for trade purposes. Many more plainsmen have started settling in the urban areas.[9] The steady improvement in communications due to the building of Railway and roads also facilitated the immigration of population.[10]

The first major Nepali migration to India, as Leo rose writes, was into the virtually unpopulated areas in Darjeeling district in Bengal. The British who wanted a hardy labour force for their tea plantations facilitated the Nepali migration to Darjeeling. The Nepalis fitted admirably and became critical actors in the tremendous expansion of Darjeeling's economy from the mid nineteenth to the mid-twentieth centuries. By 1900 the Nepalis formed more than 50% of the total population in Darjeeling.[11]

Immigration (for various reasons) was the largest single factor in the growth of population of the district. But emigration from the district has always been relatively negligible. Moreover, the emigrees, in most of the times have left the district only temporarily. The table given below gives figures of immigration into and the emigration from the district from 1891 to 1951.

Table : 5
Immigration and Emigration : 1891-1951

Year	*Actual Population*	*Immigration*	*Emigration*	*Natural*
1891	223314	119670	962	104606
1901	249117	113588	802	136331
1911	265550	111269	6000	160281
1921	282748	101807	6000	186941
1931	319635	100700	3455	222390
1941	376369	95750	4120	284739
1951	445260	100311	6900	351849

Source : Banerji, Amiya Kumar, et. al. : *West Bengal District Gazetteers—Darjeeling*, 1980.

The Table : 5 shows how the immigrant population was being gradually substituted by their children born in Darjeeling. The emigrant population had been constantly representing those Indians who were born in the district whose parents were on pleasure tour, business and service. In 1947 according to the West Bengal Government 3315 Muslims left the State for Pakistan of whom 1385 later returned.

The following table gives information about the places from which immigration took place into the district in 1901.

Table : 6
Places of Origin of Immigration into Darjeeling District: 1901

Immigration

Year	*From Nepal, Bhutan Sikkim & Tibet*	*From Bengal districts*	*From other Indian States*	*From other countries outside India*
1901	80303	8725	34549	814

Source : Banerji, Amiya Kumar, et. al. : West Bengal District Gazetteers—Darjeeling, 1980.

6.1. Tea Industry :

As early as 1794 H T Colebrooke had pleaded for tea and coffee plantation in Bengal. In 1821 the tea plant had been discovered growing wild in Assam and in 1834 the Governor-General, Lord William Bentinck, had appointed a committee to advise on the introduction of tea culture in India.[12] The first trial of the tea plant at Darjeeling was made in 1841. The experiments continued. The first plantation was started in Kurseong in 1856 and another at Lebong near Darjeeling. In 1871 the number of tea estates, public and private, was 62, with an area of 12305 acres planted with tea. In 1891 there were 177 registered gardens with 45585 acres under tea and 242 square miles comprised in tea estates. Subsequently however the tea industry faced a crisis. Prices fell greatly between 1896 and 1901 and many gardens were no longer able to work at a profit. During 1901-11 the population showed a decline in the rate of increase. Between 1872 and 1921 the district experienced phenomenal growth, but between 1921-51 the happy period of expansion for an expanding market was over and the rate of growth during the period 1921-51 was very much less than half of the period 1872-1921. In the Kalimpong subdivision land was withheld from development under tea, government's policy being to reserve that area for forest and ordinary cultivation.[13]

From around 1856, immigration of population labour caused by the opening of tea gardens has been a major factor in the population increase of the district. It was revealed that in 1874 there were 129 Europeans employed as managers or assistant managers of tea gardens in Darjeeling and under them there were 1373 natives. The total number of labourers employed in all the gardens was 19424, while the returns of 1873 showed only 14019.[14] Evidently a decrease in the number of Europeans working in the tea gardens, it can be presumed at the same time that the number of the Indians or Nepalese increased. The main causes of the rapid increase of the population have been development of the tea industry and the influx of settlers to cultivate the wastelands of the district. The tea plantation workers are mainly the immigrants or the descendents of migrants form various parts of the country and even from the neighbouring countries. The entire work force of Darjeeling hills is exclusively of Nepalese origin.[15] By the middle of the 19th century Tea Industry had become the major economic activity in Darjeeling. The Darjeeling Himalayan Railway that was opened up in 1881 was practically aimed at carrying the tea to the plains. The rapid growth of

Tea Industry in Darjeeling hills has obviously resulted in the huge demand of labour force and the local inhabitants were found to be insufficient to solve this rising demand of labour. The result was an unexampled immigration.[16]

Table : 7

Tea Industry's Impact on Population Growth Darjeeling District: 1861-1921

Year	*No. of Tea Estates*	*Total area in hec. under tea*	*Total No. of all kinds of tea workers*	*Total of working force*	*Percentage of Col. 7- Col. 8*
1	2	3	4	5	6
1861	22	1317	2534	-	-
1871	56	-	8000	94712	8.45%
1881	155	11489	-	155179	-
1891	177	18462	-	155207	-
1901	170	20948	40451	155235	26.06%
1911	156	20853	39561	151604	26.09%
1921	168	23897	48710	174167	27.97%

The Table : 7 indicates that the total number of labourers was likely to fluctuate between 65000 and 75000. According to Census 1951, the total area under tea had been more or less constant since 1921. The permanent tea garden labour in Darjeeling had settled in family pattern.

6.2. Cinchona

In mid 19th century the first nurseries of Cinchona were tried at Senchal. Since the climate was too rigorous there, the plants had to be transferred to a milder climate at Lebong. The cultivation of Cinchona by private estates in the Darjeeling district was made possible through direct state encouragement by way of supply of seed at nominal rates. But it did not continue for long, being uneconomical. Preparation of the land for planting requires a great deal of labour. The total area under cinchona in the four plantations of Mangpu, Munsong, Rongo and Latpanchar in March 1949 was 4382 acres.[17]

The use of cinchona in the preparation of Quinine and the use of Quinine in the treatment of Malaria made cinchona economically profitable.[18]

6.3. Agriculture

Apart from tea industry general agricultural also had a great role to play in the growth of population. The early settlers were mostly agriculturists and Campbell gave them every encouragement to reclaim forestlands and settle down there, which also encouraged large-scale immigration to the newly reclaimed lands. In 1865 Kalimpong had a population of only 3530 persons. The number increased to 12683 in 1881 and to 41511 in 1901. The larger part of this population was composed of incoming agriculturists chiefly from Nepal. With the growth of settlements of plantation workers and agriculturists and of relatively well off white colour workers, the prospects of trade and commerce grew, which, again, attracted more immigrants.

The following table prepared from the data relating to agriculturists in the respective censuses, gives an account of total number of workers, agricultural workers in the district and their percentage to the total working force of the district.

Table : 8

Percentage of Agriculturists to total workers in Darjeeling District : 1901-1931

Year	*Total No. of all types of agricultural workers*	*Total No. of workers*	*Percentage of agriculturists to total working force (col. 2/col. 3%)*
1	2	3	4
1901	56029	155207	36.10%
1931	30175	129070	23.38%

Source : Banerji, Amiya Kumar, et. al. : *West Bengal District Gazetteers—Darjeeling*, 1980.

6.4. Railway

The construction of railways facilitated the trade. Many small trade centres were formed. Import and export of the commodities were also facilitated. The contact with the neighbouring areas and Nepal, Bhutan etc. neighbouring countries added a new dimension to Darjeeling's economy.

The construction of Darjeeling Himalayan Railway had begun in 1879 and the first 20 miles from Siliguri to Tindharia station was opened in March 1880 for the Viceroy's special train only. After a further 11 miles to Kurseong were completed, it was opened to the public on August 23 of that year. Construction up to Sonada was made on February 1, 1881, and Ghoom on April 14th, 1881 and finally on July 4th 1881 it reached Darjeeling, making a total of 50.75 miles.

In 1914, the Darjeeling Himalayan Railway (DHR) was further extended down south towards Kishanganj and close to the Nepalese frontier for jute traffic. Meantime the DHR was extended from Siliguri towards Sevoke by 10 miles and further to the north by 16 miles on Kalimpong road.

The purpose of the new railway was to reduce the transport rates of essential commodities (such as rice) to Darjeeling and to improve the economic viability of local industries such as tea production. In its first full year of operation the line carried 8000 passengers and 380 tons of goods. In 1885 a short extension for goods traffic was opened to the bazaar at Darjeeling. In 1905 traffic on the line continued to grow with 29,000 passengers and 31750 tons of goods. In addition to rice, flour and coal the line was bringing increasing numbers of tourists to the region.

O'Malley said that the downward traffic of Darjeeling hill section was principally tea, seed, potatoes, cardamoms, oranges, timber and fresh vegetables. The upward traffic of this section was principally rice and other food grains, flour, tea garden stores, oil, coal, cement, iron, salt, building materials, miscellaneous goods and general stores.

During the year 1919-1920, the railway carried 263000 passengers and 62000 tons of goods.[19]

Down the Teesta Valley line were carried wool from Tibet, and large quantities of oranges from Sikkim during the winter season with cardamoms, potatoes and timber. While the branch carried imports of food-grains, salt, piece goods, provisions and building materials.

The total number of passengers travelling during 1942-43 over the different sections of the Darjeeling Himalayan Railway was:—

Table : 9

Main line	308872
Teesta Valley Extension	35988

Source : Dash, A J : *Bengal District Gazetteers—Darjeeling,* 1947

The numbers of passengers to and from the following principal stations during the 1942-43 were :—

Table : 10

Stations	*To*	*From*	*Total*
Darjeeling	63147	101984	165131
Ghum	41436	50061	91497
Sonada	11062	16703	27765
Kurseong	44910	54069	98979
Riyang	2321	3539	5860
Siliguri Road and Siliguri	101207	95693	196900

Source : Dash, A J : *Bengal District Gazetteers—Darjeeling,* 1947

Table : 11

Year	*Main Line*		*Teesta Valley Extension*		*Kalimpong*
	No. of passengers (000's)	*Goods Tons (000's)*	*No. of passengers (000's)*	*Goods Tons (000's)*	*Ropeway Goods Tons (000's)*
1909-10	174	47	-	-	-
1919-20	263	62	34	29	-
1929-30	258	80	23	28	-
1934-35	240	76	12	30	-
1939-40	214	66	16	50	17
1940-41	206	57	15	43	15
1941-42	240	63	19	40	18
1942-43	309	63	36	38	14
1943-44	311	76	53	29	11

Source : Dash, A J : *Bengal District Gazetteers—Darjeeling,* 1947

6.5. Tourism

Urbanization through the establishment of a sanatorium

led to growth of employment opportunities and hence to population increase. The population of the urban area of Darjeeling district was subject to considerable seasonal variation. The most favourite summer resort of Eastern India, Darjeeling received large number of visitors in the towns of Darjeeling, Kurseong and Kalimpong. In the Autumn, in the months of September and October a smaller seasonal influx occurred. In the winter many people from the hills went down to the plains. It was difficult to estimate what the summer population was or the time it rose to, as the number of visitors varied from year to year. Trade depressions, military conditions had from time to time checked the flow of summer visitors.[20]

The first hotel was built in Kurseong, the second 'Darjeeling Hotel' in Darjeeling. By 1852, there were 70 European houses in Darjeeling town besides a bazar and a jail. Around 1898, Darjeeling assumed a unique political status when a Summer Secretariat of the Bengal Government was built there.

6.6. Education

The growth of population was also sustained by the growth of educational institution. On the other hand the growth of educational institutions removed one hindrance to the permanent human settlement in the hills.

The pioneers in the spread of education in the District were Christian missionaries and particularly those of the Church of Scotland Mission. When the British took over the district popular education was practically unknown. According to Census 1951, a few of the better classes had private tutors for their boys, in Buddhist monasteries novitiate monks were taught to chant Tibetan texts. The first attempt to reach the hill people by education was made about 1850 by the Rev. W. Start, a private missionary, who opened a school for the Lepchas. In 1873 a school for the Bhutias was also established.

Separate schools were there for the European and Anglo-Indian children. Although they allowed the Indian children if their parents could afford the fees. The earliest of the European schools in the district was the Loreto Convent for girls founded in 1846 and managed by the Loreto nuns who have their motherhouse in Dublin. In 1864, St. Paul's School was established in Jalapahar area. In 1889 St. Mary's College was started at Kurseong. St. Joseph's college, Mount Hermon, Victoria Boys' School, Goethals Memorial School etc. were other educational institutions meant for the Europeans.

In 1873 there were 25 Primary schools with 615 boys and girls receiving instructions. But in 1907 there were 70 schools of which 55 were both day and night schools with a roll of 2420 boys and 300 girls and an average attendance of 1880. In 1860- 61 there was only one school receiving government aid, which had a total attendance of 16 pupils. In 1904-05 there were altogether 142 schools with 3950 pupils. The total expenditure on education in the same year amounted to Rs. 38216 only.[21]

O'Malley observed that in Darjeeling the proportion of literate females rose during the decade ending in 1901 from 5 to 14 per 1000 (approximately 1 in 71)—a ratio surpassed by no other district in Bengal outside Calcutta. The schools for girls are the Diocesan Girls' School (Church of England), the Loreto Convent (Roman Catholic), the Queen's Hill School (American Methodist), all situated at Darjeeling and the Dow Hill Girls' School, maintained by Government, at Kurseong. Both the Maharaja of Cooch Behar and Burdwan took special interest in the field of education. Maharani of Cooch Behar and Maharajadiraj of Burdwan Bijay Chand Mahatap were the chief supporters of Maharani Girls' School.

6.7. Trade centre and Banking

The road system of the district as well as the Darjeeling Himalayan railway system facilitated trade. It had three categories trade with the plains, trade moving over the frontiers of Bhutan, Sikkim and Nepal and local trade within the district. The main commodities of trade are—paddy, gram and pulses, salt, sugar, wool, raw cotton, oranges, raw jute, iron and steel, kerosene, petrol, tobacco, coal, tea, marble stone etc.

While Marwari, Bengali and Behari bankers generally financed commodity markets and trade, branches of the Imperial Bank of India and Lloyds Bank provided general banking facilities in Darjeeling. The Imperial Bank opened its Darjeeling Branch in September 1922. It also provided funds for tea gardens in the district. A branch of Lloyds Bank was opened in 1935, which also provided funds for tea gardens and general banking facilities.[22]

The growth of population also facilitated trade. Coal was found in the Gondwana rocks running from near Pankhabari to Dalingkot. The Census 1951 mentions that the Bagrakot coal mine is still working. A labour force of not more than 50 persons was then employed on extraction of this coal.

Copper ores, chiefly chalcopyrite, occurred near Ranihat, on the western side of Mahanadi, at Peshok, on the left bank of the Teesta river east of Mangpu and in the neighbourhood of the Chel river.

The principal products of cottage industry in the district were blankets, woolen knitted articles, woven cotton and wool fabrics, kukris, various tools, pottery, bamboo products (baskets, mats, ghooms etc.) and ropes. In making a survey of cottage industries, the Kalimpong Industrial School deserves prominent mention. Large numbers of the carpenters working in the Darjeeling district and Western Duars have passed through this Industrial School and sometimes the specialized skill had become hereditary.

7. General Level of Prices

In 1871 the ordinary price of cheap rice eaten by coolies was Rs. 1-4 mound in the Terai and Rs. 2-4 a maund in the hills, while the other staple food of the people, Indian corn, was sold at Re. 1-8 a maund. In 1907, the price of these articles of food was 50% as great.

Table : 12

Coarse rice

(Prices in Rupees & paise per maund)

Year	*Rs.*	*Year*	*Rs.*	*Year*	*Rs.*	*Year*	*Rs.*
1871	2.3	1915	7.5	1927	9.5	1934	5
1903	3.4	1916	7	1928	9	1935	5
1907	6	1918	5	1929	8	1936	5
1910	3.8	1919	8	1930	6.7	1937	5
1912	5	1921	7.8	1931	4.5	1938	5
1913	6.7	1924	5.7	1932	5	1939	5
1914	5.7	1926	9	1933	5	1940	5.5

Source : Banerji, Amiya Kumar, et. al. : *West Bengal District Gazetteers—Darjeeling*, 1980.

The price of rice in Kurseong had hardly differed from the Darjeeling price. In Kalimpong the price had been slightly lower. From 1942 began a violent upward movement of prices corresponding to the famine prices, which developed in the rest of Bengal in 1943. Tea gardens procured rice for their labour forces often at very inflated prices. Locally grown supplies of maize and other grains with the rice that could be imported were sufficient to prevent the appearance of famine or scarcity conditions. Prices however soared and at times it was extremely difficult to buy rice or salt in the open market at any price. The price of rice reached its peak of Rs. 40 per maund in 1943; it gradually declined and under government control it was steadied and came down to Rs. 13-12 in 1945.[23] This stability was, however, short-lived.

8. Occupational Shifts

Occupational shifts experienced in the district between 1901 and 1931 are shown in the following table, which gives the intrinsic numbers of workers according to different categories as also their percentages (shown within brackets) to the total number of workers for the years 1901 and 1931.

Table : 13

Category of workers	*1901*	*1931*
Total workers	154489(100.00)	122904(100.00)
Cultivators	56811(36.77)	23346 (18.99)
Agricultural labourers	691 (0.45)	9069(7.38)
Mining, Quarrying, Livestock, Fishing Hunting, Plantations, Orchards etc.	71555(46.32)	67568(54.98)
Manufacturing including Household Industry	4925(3.19)	3838(3.12)
Construction	3729(2.41)	550(0.45)
Trade and Commerce	7033(4.55)	6781(5.52)
Transport, Storage and Communications	2627(1.70)	2423(1.97)
Other Services	7118(4.61)	9329(7.59)

9. Medical and public health service

Among the hill people intestinal worms, producing symptoms of diarrhoea, were extraordinarily common; in 1905 no less than 3470 such cases were treated at the Darjeeling dispensary. Diarrhoea was one of the commonest diseases among the Europeans in the hills, especially among those who have just arrived from the plains.

Phthisis was also not uncommon among the natives, owing to their thin clothing, their constant exposure to cold, damp and heat. The frequency of goiter and deaf-mutism, diphtheria and enteric diseases were sporadic at that time while influenza visited the district only occasionally. Rheumatism was common during the rains but plague was very rare.

Regular medical institutions started functioning in the district towards the end of the 19th century through the assistance of govt. and of private individuals. In the town of Darjeeling there were 3 medical institutions—the Eden Sanitarium for Europeans, the Lowis Jubilee Sanitatium for natives and the Victoria Memorial Dispensary for natives and Europeans.

In the interior of the district there were charitable dispensaries at Kurseong, Kalimpong, Pankhabari and at Pedong.[24]

9.1. Vital Statistics

In the sub-Himalayan tract the average mortality was nearly 60 per 1000 in the 10 years ending in 1900. On the other hand the average birth rate in the same decade was only 19.4 per annum. In 1905, the death rate was 57.70 per thousand and the average over the previous 5 years was 60 per thousand.[25]

While total demographic mobility in a given area is governed both by internal and external factors, birth and death rates can be more preciously attributed to internal factors alone. The following table gives the figures of births and deaths as also their rates per thousand for the district for the year 1941.

Source : Banerji, Amiya Kumar, et. al. : *West Bengal District Gazetteers—Darjeeling,* 1980.

Table : 14

Table of Birth Rate and Death Rate in Darjeeling District: 1941

Year	*Births*	*Birth rate per 1000*	*Deaths*	*Death rate per 1000*
1941	11329	30.0	10717	28.4

Source : Banerji, Amiya Kumar, et. al. : *West Bengal District Gazetteers—Darjeeling,* 1980.

From the above table it will be seen that birth and death rates in 1941 moved close together.

10. Conclusion

The analysis of the various aspects of the economy of the Darjeeling hills during the colonial period, like the plantation of tea and cinchona, tourism, agriculture, construction of railways, trade etc. reveals that the establishment of Darjeeling as a popular hill station owe much to the population growth, which in turn was facilitated by the economic growth. The demography and the economic aspects flourished hand in hand. The distribution of population was made according to the plan of the colonial rulers. At the same time the male-female ratio was not too unfavourable probably because there was the absence of discrimination against female child. The development attitude behind the establishment of Darjeeling needed and at the same time invited the population growth.

NOTES AND REFERENCES

1. A J Dash : *Bengal District Gazetteers—Darjeeling,* Bengal Government Press, 1947, p. 1.
2. A. Mitra : Census 1951, *West Bengal, District Census Handbook, Darjeeling,* Bengal Government Press, 1954, p. i.
3. D. Mordecai and B P Agarwala (ed.) : *Darjeeling : Queen of the Himalayas,* July, 1960.
4. Chiranjib K Kar : *Sub-regional Movement in India—A Case Study, Political History of the Gorkhas in Darjeeling District,* pp. 5-6.
5. www.wikiepedia.com.
6. Amiya Kumar Banerji, et. al.: *West Bengal District Gazetteers—Darjeeling,* 1980, p. 98.

A. Mitra : Census 1951, *West Bengal, District Census Handbook, Darjeeling*, Bengal Government Press, 1954, p. xxx.

7. Amiya Kumar Banerji, et. al. : *West Bengal District Gazetteers—Darjeeling*, 1980, pp. 101-102.
8. Swatahsiddha Sarkar, 'Formation of a British Hinterland : Darjeeling in Colonial Days', National Seminar on Urbanisation in Eastern Himalayas—Emergence and Issues.
9. Amal Kumar Das : *The Lepchas of West Bengal*, Calcutta Edition, Indian, 1978.
10. Lopita Nath : "Migrants in Flight : Conflict-Induced Internal Displacement of Nepalis in North East India." *Peace and Democracy in South Asia, Vol. 1*, No. 1, January 2005, p. 63.
11. A. Mitra : *Census 1951, West Bengal, District Census Handbook, Darjeeling*, Bengal Government Press, 1954, p. lxii.
12. *ibid*, p. 1xiii.
13. Tusher Kanti Ghosh : *Tea gardens of West Bengal*, B. R. Publishing corporation, 1987.
14. Khemraj Sharma : *Tea industry in India : An introduction*, N.L. Publishers, 1999.
15. L S S O'Malley : *Bengal District Gazeteer, Darjeeling*, 1907 (first published), Basumati Corporation Limited, 2001 (reprinted), p. 44.
16. A. Mitra : Census 1951, *West Bengal, District Census Handbook, Darjeeling*, Bengal Government Press, 1954, p. 1xxxiii.
17. Moloy Shankar Bhattacharya : *Darjeeling Rupantarer Itibritto* (in Bengali).
18. A J Dash : *Bengal District Gazetteers—Darjeeling*, Bengal Government Press, 1947, p. 194.
19. A. Mitra : *Census 1951, West Bengal, District Census Handbook, Darjeeling*, Bengal Government Press, 1954, p. xxxvi.
20. L S S O'Malley : *Bengal District Gazeteer, Darjeeling*, 1907 (first published), Basumati Corporation Limited, 2001 (reprinted), p. 219.
21. A. Mitra : Census 1951, *West Bengal, District Census Handbook, Darjeeling*, Bengal Government Press, 1954, p. xciv.
22. A. J. Dash : *Bengal District Gazetteers—Darjeeling*, Bengal Government Press, 1947, p. 176.
23. Amiya Kumar Banerji, et. al. : *West Bengal District Gazetteers—Darjeeling*, 1980, p. 544.
24. *ibid.*, p. 546.

3

Plantation of Small Tea Gardens and the Tribals of North Dinajpur

Partha Sen

North Bengal is famous for tea industry. Almost all the tea gardens of North Bengal were established in the pre-independence day. These tea gardens are called set tea gardens. Because all these gardens have own factories alongwith their tea gardens. But from the 80s a large number of small tea gardens began to appear in the Terai-Duars area. Owners of these tea gardens in these cases have not taken any prior permission from the proper authority. All these planters have illegally converted agricultural lands into tea plantation. But according to the WBLRO act of 1955 any change or conversion of the character of land without proper permission is a punishable offence. Not a single tea planters has been punished for establishing tea gardens without proper permission, special officer of the Backward class has clearly mentioned in his letter forwarded to the District Magistrates and Sabhadhipaties of the various districts of North Bengal "I would like to inform you that the committee on pitition, West Bengal legislative Assembly is currently examining a petition on the subject of illegal conversion of land into tea garden in the North Bengal region. It appears to the committee that vast areas of land owned by S.C. and S.T. communities, *patta*-holders and vested lands have been encroached upon by the tea gardens in violation in existing rules regarding transfer of such land."[1] At present there are about ten thousand tea planters in North Bengal and neighbouring areas. About 45,000 hectors of land are at the possession of the small tea planters. About 5 lacs of people directly or indirectly are attached to these gardens.[2]

The reason for rapid growth of such illegal tea gardens in North Bengal in the 80s are more than one. In the 80s and 90s tea was most profitable business. The price of one kilogram green tea leaf was Rs. 16/- to Rs. 18/-. Indian tea has a florshing market both internally and externally. So the existing set tea gardens of North Bengal were in search of more and more green tea leaves. But they were unwillling to extend their existing plantation area by establishing new divisions. Because it was too much expensive for them. These tea gardens have to follow certain rules and regulations framed by the government and tea board. So a new class of people who have earned huge money from contractory, came forward to invest their money in tea plantation. These people have no previous experience in the tea plantation. They have no liability to the soil, labour and environment. Their only motto is to pluck early green leaves as much as possible. In order to get early leaf they began to rape the vergin soil. They began to use insectisides and pesticides at random in order to get early leaf. As a result of which the water full of pesticides of the cannals of these newly established tea gardens began to pollute the waters of the neighbouring rivers and tanks. Even polluted water is affecting the neighbouring agricultural lands.[3] It has been found that the tribals of Sonakhari area under Chopra police station were compelled to sell their land to the Mitraka Tea Estate due to the flow of pesticide water into their cultivable land.[4] Islampur Mahakuma chas -abad Gram Bachao Sangram Committee submitted memorandum to the Chief minister regarding this anti-cultivator activities of the tea planters but no action was taken by the local administration against the tea garden owners.[5]

In the North Dinajpur District about five thousand acres of agricultural, patta and vested land had been occupied by the small tea planters within the year 1998. There are at present 367 small and big tea gardens in Islampur Subdivision (324 in Chopra Block, 37 in Islampur Block, and 16 in Goalpokhor). Nearly 2116.67 acres of vested land, 718.62 acres patta land

and 568.57 acres of tribal and SC land are illegally occupied by the planters.6 As a result of which a large number of patta holders, marginal cultivators and large number of schedule caste and tribe people have been evicted from their own land. A official report of the K.G.O. of SC, ST welfare department is sufficient to prove how the New Chamta Tea Estate of Bhadrakali Mouza of Ramgang had forcefully evicted a group of tribal people from their 40 acres of land. The letter mentioned that "the Tea Estate started planting tea plant in the said Mouza around and about 1989-90. Then the tribals protested against grabbing there land for tea garden purpose. One group of tribals were trapped and polarised by the pradhan in favour of the tea planters and as a result that group of tribals were utilised as weapon to compel the other tribals protesting against giving land to the tea planters. ...Even their houses were looted and men and women were beaten. Due to such atrocities they were compelled to take shelter in the Islampur Police Station."[7] But the police and the district administration did not lodge any complain against the tea planters. The tea planters often utilise the local criminals to evict the cultivators from their land. It was reported by Nakul Biswas of Kalanagin Mouza under Islampur Police Station that he was forced to sell his five acres of land to Joysree tea garden owner due to the fear of robbery.[8] It is interesting to note that upto 1998 out of 367 tea planters in North Dinajpur District only 17 tea gardens have obtained no objection certificate from the district authority.[9] On the other hand in Jalpaiguri District upto 1999 only 31 tea planters received 'no objection certificate' from DLRO on 272.61 acres of land.[10] But the actual number of small tea planters is much more. How did so many tea gardens grow without proper permission?

In the North Dinajpur District the integrated tribal development project area was not spared by there tea planters. It is known from the government enquiry report that about 200 acres of land in the Jiropani Mouza under Chopra Police Station have been illegally occupied by the tea planters. Jiropani Mouza is an ITDP area. According to the government enquiry report "It is a fact that about 200 acres of land have been vested to the state in Mouza Jiropani JL No. 14 under Chopra. It is also there vast areas out these vested lands which were covered with jungles made *arable* by the tribals. These vested lands were gone under the possession in favour of the pineapple planters on a nominal moneytory benefit offered by these planters. Among these planters one has already started tea plantation in R.S plot No. 771 which has been vested in the state with an area of 27.62 acres. The tribals of this Mouza have also been forced for alienation of their land by black mailing them and there are a good number of *benami* transfer of tribals in this mouza.[11]

The names of the evicted tribals are Jirku Kujur, Suklal Manjhi, Mangu Tirkey, Kandra Ekka, Nansu Kujur, Matla Hemram, Bodha Murmu, Loghu Besra, Khara Soren, Suklal Hansda, Mantrin Hansda etc. The said planter named some Choudhury has purchased these lands in the name of Shyam Mahata and Bipin Mahato of Islampur thana colony. But in the voterlist of thana colony there were no persons named Shyam Mahato and Bipin Mahato.[12] Not only the tribal land even the government forest land have been illegally occupied by the Subal Vita tea estate. The owner of this new garden has acquired 2.88 acres of forest land (JL No. 66, Dag No. 55, 57, 59) and 6.16 acres of land in the Dag No. 1 and 2. BLRO of Kharibari did not dare to recover these lands even after receiving complain.[13]

Bhojpurani gachch Mouza of Chopra is another glaring example of how the small tea planters have occupied tribal lands by Benami transactions. In this Mouza 30/40 tribal families were cultivating about 40 acres of land for a long time. From the ninety's decade a person named Gopal Paramanik began to procure these lands in the name of Alima Kisku for his tea garden. Now Alima Kisku is the manager of Gopal Paramanik's tea garden. On receiving complain of illegal occupation of tribal land the T.W Department enquired the matter. After enquiry it was found by the Tribal Welfare Department that Alima Kisku was not so financially strong to purchase 40 acres of land. It was reported that land was purched by the tea planters in the name of Alima Kisku to evade the WBLR act. i.e. all lands have been purchased by Benami transactions.[14] In the Bhagabati Mouza under Chopra police station Champalal Agarwalla has occupied for his tea gardens 30/40 acres of tribal land. According to the Tribal Welfare Department the said garden has occupied these lands without the permission of the proper authority.[15]

In the Mouza Bhatra-Dahari Chopra P.S. Jului Kisku, Chain Kisku, Vapi Hasda and other 14 tribal people were in possession of few acres of vested land. From the year 1997-98 Saha Tea Estate acquired all these lands. It is reported that some tribals were forced to surrender their land and some other has sold their land for want of money. But all these transactions were without proper permission. On 21.2.2000 Jogen Tudu, Lupsa Hasda and other people of that locality complained to SDO against this illegal land occupation by the tea planter. From their petition it appears that these people were cultivating these vest land for a long time but Chopra BLRO office had not issued any patta to these tribals.16 Will it be wrong to presume that BLRO office and panchayat samity had indirectly helped the Saha Tea Estate to grab these tribal lands.[16] Almost in the same manner Mitraka Tea Estate in Bhagabati Mouza has acquired 48.12 acres of tribal land.[17]

Here is another example of eviction of tribal people by the *Jotedar* and Islampur BLRO office in favour of tea planters. Let us have a look at the Kachchu Gachch Mouza under Islampur Police Station. This Mouza is situated in Ramgang gram panchayat. Here in the year 1964-65 Local *Jotedar* Mazharul Haque had allowed Sahu Kisku, Khera Kisku, Somi Murmu some Mardi, Kandi Kusku and twenty other tribals to cultivate his 27 acres of land. After ten years i.e. in 1974-75 when the land became arable the Jotedar attempted to evict these twenty five tribal people But due to the intervention of the local administration tribals were that time. Although they were not evicted but their names were not recorded in R.S. operation. The reason for new inclusion of these tribals is best known to the Islampur BLRO office. Taking advantage of this Mazhrul Haque in the year 1990-91 has sold that lands to the tea planter. With the help of local criminals and panchayats the tea planter forcefully evicted these tribal people.[18] In the Ariagaon Mouza in Mazhiali Gram Panchayat about 25 tribals have been evicted by the Nandi Tea Estate and Jalal Mia.[19] Here all the twenty five tribals were patta holders.

Not only the panchayats and local administration indirectly or directly had helped to grab such huge area of land by the tea planters, but all most all the political parties were in favour of establishing tea garden even at the cost of all rules and regulations. According to the political parties, establishment of tea garden will help to develop North Bengal economically and will generate employment. Even the CPM Party were in favour of tea gardens. They have taken resolution in favour of the tea gardens.[20] But unfortunately the political parties failed to realise the real character of these tea planters. Like South Indian tea planters these new planters were only to pluck green tea leaf and to sell to the set tea gardens.[21] So they can avoid the implementation of the labour act in their garden. No tea garden at present pay minimum labour wage to their worker. No work no pay is the general rule of these gardens. Recent fall in the price of the green tea leaf has aggravated the situation. As a result of which most of the tea gardens are on the verge of ruin. Tea workers who have sold their land to the tea gardens are loosing their job regularly due to the recent crisis in the tea industry. To save the workers the government should come forward and restore all the lands from the planters who have occupied illegally and again distribute these among actual land holders. We know tribal land which has been illegally transferred to the non tribals can be restored even after thirty years. Will it be possible for the Left Front Government?

NOTES AND REFERENCES

1. Memo No. 262/BCW (UD), (CON) Dated 27.01.1998.
2. *Sampadakiya Pratibedan*, United Forum of Small Tea Growrs Association 1st Annual General Meeting, held at Islampur (Dinajpur) on 15.6.03.
3. *Bipannya Paribesh*, 2000, *Nagarik Mancha*, Calcutta, p. 302-3.
4. *Bhumi Sanskar Karma Suchi Rupayane Byarthota-Janma-Dichch-cha-Beganer* Partha Sen, *Aneek* January 2000, ed., Dipankar Chakrabarty, Murshidabad.
5. Memorandum Submitted to the Chief Minister on 12.6.96 by the *Islampur Mahakuma Chas-Abad-O-Gram Bachchao Sangram Committee.*

6. *Uttar Dinajpurer Cha Bagan APDR Raigang Sakha Pratibedan* in Ganatantrick Adhikar Raksha Samity. *Uttar Bangya Samanyay Committir Mukhopatro, May, 2000.*
7. KGO's (Islampur Subdivisional tribal office) letter to the SDO Islampur dated 16.05.1994. An enquiry was conducted on the basis of a complain letter of Ramgang II Pradhan (Memo No. 59/ RG II dated 03.05.1994).
8. *Aneek*, Ibid.
9. *Uttar Dinajpurer Cha Shilpa-Barta-Man O Bhabishat*, Binayak Dey, in *Krishi-O-Shilpamela, Souveunir* 1998, Raigang, Uttar Dinajpur.
10. *Bipannya Paribesh*, Ibid, p. 232-233.
11. Enquiry Report of KGO (TW) Islampur on the petitionof Ringta Tudo, Dhena Hemram etc. Dated 20.05.1987. Plot on of said land are 708, 695, 696, 697, 698, 699, 632, 702, 691, 701, 692, 688, 687, 686, 919, 718, 719, 717, 713, 715, 711 etc.
12. *Aneek*, August 1988, p. 16-22.
13. *Aneek*, January, 2000 issue.
14. *Suryapur Barta*, 15th Feb. issue, 1998, edi Partha Sen and Uttathya Bandopadhya Islampur, Uttar Dinajpur.
15. *Suryapur Barta*, 1st June, 1998 issue.
16. Petition of Jogen Tudu and Lupsa Hasda to SDO Islampur on 21.2.2000 sechedule of these lands. *Mouza* 442, 440, 439, 438, 437, 436, 424, 422, 421, 420, 419, 418, 417, 532, 531, 547, 528, 503, 522, 461, 463, 464, 466, 467, 525, 524, 526, 523, 519, 516, 412, 411, 416, 444, 435, 434, 433, 432, 431, 1183, 1182, 1179, 1181, 1189, 1190, 1157 etc. Each and every tribal were given *patta* on most that 2 acres of land. As for example Louis Oraon received pattern in 2.50 acres, Bhaku Oraon on 2.52 acres, Lusa Oraon on 2.44 acres.
17. *Aneek* January issue, 200.
18. *Bartika* ed. by Mahesweta Debi, Oct.-Dec. (1989) issue, Murshidabad, pp. 67-69; also see, Enquiry Report of K.G..O (TW) Islampur, Dated 25.05.89.
19. Personal interview with Peter Kujur, an inhabitant of Ariagaon Mouza.
20. Personal interview with some District C.P.I (M) leaders.
21. Partha Sen, *Uttar Dinajpur Jelar Cha Shilpa Sambhabana O Samasya—Ekti Samiksha in the Souvenir, Uttar Dinajpur Jelar Samtam Barsha Purti Utsab*, 1999.

4

Labour Movements in the Tea Gardens of Darjeeling

Tirthankar Ghosh

Writing on the emergence and movements of the labourers of tea plantations of Darjeeling district is more difficult as the issue is not just a history of the movements in the conventional sense. The working force (i.e. the labourers) in the plantations of Darjeeling district, elsewhere alike, emerged as parallel upshot of the capitalist structure of production but in course of time the growth of the movements among the plantation labourers with its economic and political potency has manifested itself as the reaction to the same very capitalist order. The plantation labourers' movement began to take place in a period of India's absolute servility under the foreign domination. But these type of movements from the very inception had its own problems and peculiarities which are distinctive than the working class movements of the metropolis. Moreover, these movements had hardly any connection with the mainstream national movement due to its causal nature as an offshoot of the byproduct of 'enclave economy', far distance than the mainstream society and more concerned with their own situation that was marked by inhuman suffering and extreme deprivation.[1] This study thus sets out to present the social and economic circumstances providing the background of the birth of political awakening among the plantation labourers of Darjeeling districts.

Before going into the details of trade union movements it is very much important to present here the socio-economic background of the participants of those movements i.e. the plantation workers of Darjeeling. Earlier Darjeeling ".... [F]ormed part of the dominions of the Raja of Sikkim.... who had long been engaged in a .... struggle against the Gurkhas [of Nepal] [who] ....marched into east Sikkim in 1780 [and] ...overrun Sikkim as far eastward as the Tista river, and had conquered and annexed the Tarai, i.e. the belt of country lying along the lower hills between that river and the Mechi,..."[2] English East India Company occupied and annexed this region after a victory against the Nepalese in 1814.[3] Darjeeling now began to be considered as a part of East India Company's territory. In 1834 Lord William Bentinck, the then Governor General of India had appointed a committee "for the purpose of submitting a plan for the introduction of tea culture into India" and to investigate the suitable conditions for the same.[4] From 1839 onwards the Assam Tea Company of Assam first started tea plantation for commercial purpose. Campbell, the newly appointed Commissioner of Darjeeling had started tea plantation in this region by the Assamese (Assam bush) and Chinese (China bush) species on a mere experimental basis. The experiment proved successful and by 1856 tea factories began to establish in this region on an extensive scale. By the end of 1866 there were almost 39 tea gardens "with 10,000 acres under cultivation and an outturn of over 433, 000 lbs. of tea."[5]

Table: 1

Year	*Number of gardens*	*Area under cultivation in acres*	*Outturn of tea in lbs.*
1874	113	18888	3927911
1885	175	88499	9090298
1895	186	48692	11714551
1905	148	50618	12447471

The above table[6] shows that from the year 1874 to 1905 there were increase in the number of tea gardens in the acquired land that came under the cultivation and a great outturn in the production with the exception of the last ten years because of the fact that there was no reserved land for tea that remained to be cultivated and "the number of gardens has been reduced in the consequence of the amalgamation of several estates."[7] There is no doubt that the establishment of railways in this region during the 1880s provided an impetus for the growth of this industry.[8]

This spectacular growth in production was possible at the cost of cheap labour which was brought from the East Nepal to the hills of Darjeeling.[8] In the East Nepal due to the *'raykar'* land revenue settlement the peasants were dispossessed from their land because of the non-payment of revenue.[9] They were recruited as 'coolie' by the British in the tea plantation of the Darjeeling hills.[10] Moreover, there was another reason for the British to import labour from the outside. The British had the experience of labour disturbances in the factories of Assam that caused due to the recruitment of the labourers from the local population.[11]The tribes of east Nepal namely - Rai, Limbu, Tamang, Dhami, Kami etc. were brought to the tea gardens of Darjeeling as labourers.[12] Among them Rai formed the majority of labour population in the hills of Darjeeling. In the Terai region of Darjeeling though there were few numbers of labourers came "from the adjoining districts of Purnea and Jalpaiguri" but the bulk of the majorities of labourers were recruited "from Chhotanagpur and Santal Pargana"area.[13]

Table:2

Tribes	*1891*	*1901*	*1911*	*1921*	*1931*	*1941*
Santals	NA	1859	2246	3607	4299	4045
Oraons	4632	8042	7543	10952	12412	12433
Mundas	255	3980	3365	5322	5062	4993

Among the tribes of these regions Santals, Munda and Oraons were mainly drawn to this region for the plantations and as the table shows their number had increased considerably throughout the colonial period.[14] The poor and illiterate labourers were enslaved by the planters by the enactment of their slavery through various laws passed by the British colonial administration. Workmen's Breach of Contract Act (Act of XVII) was brought forth in 1859 so that the workers could not escape from the plantations.[15] In addition to that Inland Emigration Act was passed in 1863 as a supplementary to the former.[16]

This huge influx of the imported labourers resulted in the phenomenal growth of population in the district. According to an account, "The first regular census of the district [1871-72]....gave a total population of 94, 712" whereas "in 1881, the population had increased to 1, 55, 179 or by more than 63 per cent."[17] In the census of 1891the number of total population was 2, 23, 314 with "an increase of 43.4 per cent" and census of 1901 recorded 2,49,117 as the total number of population.[18] During this thirty years (1871-1901) "the number of inhabitants" was increased more than two and half "as great as it was 30 years ago."[19]The census of 1901 informed that "the tea garden coolies and their children accounted for more than two-thirds of the total population."[20]The increase in total number of population along with their percentage during the subsequent years of colonial rule i.e. from 1911 to 1941 was as follows:[21]

Table: 3

Year	*Total number of population*	*Increase (in per cent)*
1911	265550	7
1921	282748	6
1931	319635	13
1941	376369	18

In this population "the majority of the people in the hills [were] of Mongolian origin, belonging chiefly to various Nepalese castes", that also comprised "a large number of Lepchas, Bhotias, and Tibetans."[22]Thus the censuses shows that the population of Darjeeling district that included in it a huge number of tribal labour population was 'exceedingly heterogeneous' and perhaps for this reason Darjeeling has been called as a "Babel of tribes and nations."[23]

In Darjeeling most of the gardens were directed by the British 'Managing Agency.' During the colonial period Darjeeling Planters Association and Terai Planters Association of Indian Tea Association were the two most powerful regional organizations of the planters in this region. Indian ownership of tea garden in the district was limited to a very few estates.[24]Though the planters made huge profit from the export of tea but the labourers had to face severe torture and coercion from the planters. On the other hand, the Terai areas were affected by Malaria and Black Fever while the labourers of hills had to face the threat of Tuberculosis along with the shortage of food. Women had to suffer the worst.[25] In the plantation it was not only the male labourers but the "whole families came under contract."[26] The process of recruitment of these labourers from very beginning was followed by the method of extreme "coercion, violence and various other abuses"[27] that compelled "the destitute rural masses fell into the clutches of the unscrupulous recruiting agents"[28] i.e. the *arkathis*. Apart from the *arkathis* there were other recruiting agents viz., *sardars* (belonged from the local tea garden labourers[29]) and the local recruiting agents of the concerned district. Though *sardari* system was mostly used for the purpose of recruiting labourers but in some cases where *sardars* were not allowed to go outside the garden the recruitment was done through the *arkathis* and local agents.[30] In this recruitment "the entire family – males, females and children – worked on the plantation at wages determined by the planters."[31] Though there is hardly any scientific reality but it is said to believe that women are more efficient in plucking of tea leaves while men are fit for other types of work associated with the maintenances of the garden. But the main reason for "widespread employment of women" was to keep "wages depressed."[32] The wage policy carried out by the colonial administration was such that the wage rates in the tea gardens were considerably lower than in the other industries viz., jute, textile etc.[33]During the cultivation or winter operations the labourers were paid "for on a *bigha* or piece rate (*thika*) system"[34]and the wage that was paid for this was called '*haziri*.'[35]Though the planters made huge profits from the export of tea but the rate of wages did not have improved in course of time. In fact there was no increase in the 'real wage' of the labourers till 1939.[36] During 1940s for the *haziri* system the basic rates were as follows:[37]

Table: 4

Area	*Men* *Annas*	*Women* *Annas*	*Children* *Annas*
Hills	5	4	3
Terai	4	3	1½

The increase of wage in the years between 1939-45 did not help the labourers in any way since the price of crops were increased to 200 per cent.[38] Labour Investigation Committee (1944) had recommended for the partial development of conditions of the labourers in respect to the medical treatment, facilities for the pregnant women, mid-day meal for the non-labour children, housing facilities etc.[39] But in the post -war period there was no sign of further improvement in wages. In the post- independent phase in March 1950 the State Government of West Bengal appointed the Minimum Wages Advisory Committee for Tea Plantations in order to secure a minimum wage that "must not merely be a subsistence wage."[40] In December 1960 the Central Wage Board for Tea Plantation Industry recommended further enhancement of wages though hardly in any considerable way.[41]During the year of 1969-70 "in....Darjeeling district...the rate is midway at Rs. 2.07 for men, Rs. 1.96 for women and Rs. 1.11 for children."[42] In fact, these statistics could hardly reveal the "actual methods of exploitation but they do reveal the objective facts of increase productivity of labour."[43]

During the colonial period the low level of wages was justified by the colonial authority as wages above the subsistent level could cause 'indolence' for the 'coolies,' and "a higher wage is no remedy [for scarcity of labour]; for it only means less work and more leisure."![44] In the tea gardens the 'labour rules' and 'wage agreements' were made separately where labourers had "continued to live and work in a state of various forms of unfreedom, servitude and brutal treatment."[45] Moreover, "disease, epidemics and the unhealthy condition"[46] in the estates also caused even death to the labourers. On the other hand colonial government pursued the policy of settling the labourers on the garden rice land since "many garden....[had] no land which can be given out to the labourers" and in Darjeeling 97.4 per cent of the families possessed garden land with an "average holding per family being 0.64 acres."[47] As the plantation industry is labour-intensive, in order to maintain cheap labour the planters sought to hold an enslaved labour force which was bound to serve on any rate of wage.[48] The plantation system has a distinctive form of production which eventually leads to the certain social and political tensions in the areas concerned.

Emergence and development of political consciousness and organization among the tea garden labourers "was a completely delayed phenomenon."[49] There were certain factors for this delayed response, as Nirban Basu, an expert in this field of studies, argues-firstly, the protest movements of the tea garden labourers were started comparatively later than the jute or engineering industries because the tea gardens were isolated from each other as well as far distance from the localities. Secondly, these garden areas had lacked the excitement as well as response to the call of the nationalist movement due to the very nature of being aloof from the center of the movement that was gaining momentum in the other districts of North Bengal.[50] Moreover, he opines that Congress had no organization in this region worthy of mention till the 1930s. In fact, the Darjeeling District Committee of Indian National Congress was established in 1938. This coupled with the other factors like, internal strife among the leaders, conflict between the Nepali-Bengali leadership and above all, the lack of sense among the Congress leaders to understand the class character of the labourers were the major impediments to form any revolutionary nationalist ideology among the tea garden labourers.[51] Though there were sign of protests from the labourers during the days of Non-cooperation in 1920-21 but the earlier agitations by the tea garden labourers were only concerned with their immediate grievances, sometimes followed by acts of violence, and were suppressed easily by the planters.[52] There were some irregular demonstrations by the labourers in the Terai region of Darjeeling in pre-1940's which were in the form of breaking of clock, attack on the tea factory and even sometime killing of tea garden 'manager', although the last item was very rare.[53] Despite these sporadic outbursts the tea garden labourers of this region could not initiate any organized protest movement. On the other hand during the 1930s, the entire hill region was least concerned about the prevailing inequalities than the Terai and the probable cause may be the small numbers of gardens and obviously the labourers there as well.

The Communists (particularly the Communist Party of India) had played the pioneering role towards the establishment of labour organizations in Darjeeling district. Sushil Chatterjee, a communist leader, was sent to Darjeeling in 1944 to set up the district committee of Communist Party of India and in 1945 Darjeeling District Committee was established.[54] In the same year Darjeeling Zilla Chia Kamni Worker's Union was formed by the communists.[55] They had, however, to face numerous problems to organize the labourers of tea garden that some time even brought life-risk for them. They used to conduct meeting very secretly at night. The Legislative Assembly Election of 1946 provided a great opportunity for the Communists to communicate and spread their ideology and organization in the nook and corner of the tea estates. Ratanlal Brahman who had considerable hold over the tea garden labourers was the candidate for the CPI. Along with Brahman there were other party comrades in hill namely, Bhadra Bahadur Hamal, Ganeshlal Subba, Madan Chhetri, Bhim Bahadur, Paganlal Chhetri etc. who had played active role in organizing labourers.[56]On the other hand Congress had started to build their organization in the hills. Congress leader Saryu Prasad Poddar made valuable contributions in this direction. But this effort on the part of Congress did not successfully last for long. Planters of the gardens did not remain silent. They also reacted strongly by fighting back with these two organizations. So Ratanlal Brahman had to contest with the Congress candidate named Gaga Tshering and another candidate named M.K. Tshering who was backed by the planters.[57] Ratanlal Brahman had won the election by a thumping majority. Thenceforth, labour consciousness began to take a concrete shape centering the election issue that introduced for them to understand the necessity of being organized and proper ventilation of their demands and grievances.

On the other hand another party named Gorkha League began to germinate its roots among the tea garden labourers. Gorkha League was mostly concerned with the interest of the Gorkhas.[58]This difference played into the hands of the British as well as the tea planters. In order to divert the attention of the labourers from the agitations it had been put forward by the British and the tea planters that it was not possible to ensure the demands of the Gorkhas in the present administrative system of Bengal; so Darjeeling Hill should come under a separate administration.59Needless to say that Gorkha League had a positive response in this regard and a labour union of Gorkha League came into existence named Darjeeling Chia Kaman Shramik Sangh.[60] The Gorkha League trade union had a close contact with the tea planters and this resulted in the frequent clashes between the Communists and the Gorkha League union.[61]

Partition of India (1947) and other related issues shifted the attention of the Government from the hills. This provided a great chance for the planters to increase their torture machinations upon the Communists. Dhwaj Tea Estate was one of the strong bases of the Communists.[62] A number of labourers of this garden had to face the hapta-bahar (dismissal from the garden). As a result of this constant labour agitations were organized and at last in July 1947 the owners of the garden had to declare lock-out. This lock-out was lasted for nearly 9 months.[63] The Sum Tea Estate had also witnessed regular labour unrests during these days.

Terai did not go through any movement during these days. Though there were sincere attempts on the part of the Communist leaders like, Souren Basu, Biren Basu, Atin Basu, Sushil Chatterjee, Satyendra Narayan Mazumdar, Shanti Bose but until 1952 there was no organization for the labourers. In 1952 Communist trade union was established in Sonachandi and Merry View Tea Estate. Khokan Mazumdar, one of the leading Communist activists of tea gardens of the Terai area has recorded the impenetrable condition for the communists to organize meetings and demonstrations (sometime even prohibited to enter) in the tea gardens even in late 1954.[64]It is important to mention here that labourers' agitation campaign in the Terai region was extensively supported by the adivasi and Rajbanshi peasants of the region concerned.[65] In fact, the peasants provided links between the party comrades and the labourers since the labourers were bound by the very nature of 'enclave economy.' Kanu Sanyal, Charu Mazumdar, Jangal Santal, Kanti Kalita, Panchanan Sarkar had started to organize the workers under the 'Lal Party Union.' Bhupen Bhowmik had also played an efficient role in this direction. Not only the leaders, among the workers Lalghai Kheroyad, Howrah Oraon, Bandhu Oraon, Silvinia played important role among the labourers of tea gardens of the Terai region.[66]In 1954-55 Communist organizations were set up in Khoribari, Fulbari, Belgachhi, Kamala and Thanjhora tea estates.[67] Kamala and Gangaram tea estates had witnessed direct clashes with the authorities.[68] For their outstanding contribution in the field of workers movement Biren Basu became the President and Satyendra Narayan Mazumdar became the Secretary of All India Trade Union Congress (A.I.T.U.C).[69] From 1952 onwards the Communist-led movements in Terai displayed certain specific issues of the labourers like, abolition of *hapta-bahar* system, increase in wage and ration, reducing the duration of work etc. which gained much support from the labourers. While the labour movements of Terai had the peasant support but the movements in the hill had lacked this due to absence of any sizeable peasant population in the hill.

The members of the Communist Party of India and those of the Indian National Congress were involved in clashes with each other to establish their domain of influence among the labourers. During the latter half of the 1940 few Congress trade unions (I.N.T.U.C) had emerged in the different tea estates of Terai. In 1956 the Martibar, Bijlimani, Syedabad and Sahabad areas of Purnea district of Bihar were adjoined with Darjeeling district. I.N.T.U.C leaders like T. Paramanand, Govind Das had started to organize trade union activities in these areas.[70] Kiran Chandra Bhattacharya, despite of being an owner of a tea estate, participated in the trade union movements of Congress. Iswar Tirkey was another prominent figure of I.N.T.U.C who was successful in organizing the Christian workers along this line.[71]Apart from them Yogendra Singh,

Kalidhar, Mukund Roy, Sulekha Roy, Bireswar Mazumdar were prominent Congress trade union leaders of the Terai region.

In 22nd June, 1955 the labourers of tea gardens of Duars, Terai and Hill went for a massive strike that centered round mainly on the question of bonus along with other issues like, increase in wages, reducing the duration of work etc.[72] Both Communist Party of India and Gorkha League had supported the strike and as a result of this the strike took a form of an all-round protest against the planters. Though in Terai the strike was over-all peaceful and non-violent but in Hill it took a violent turn. In 25th June on a police firing 6 tea garden workers of Margaret Hope's Tea Estate died which included two female workers named – Moni Shobha Raini and Amrit Maya Raini, one 14 years old Kale Limbu, and three male workers named –Jitman Tamang, Kanchha Sunuar and Bahadur Kami.[73] The death of the workers generated strong sensation among the tea garden workers of the Hill. There was a huge procession of around 20000 workers at the Hill town of Darjeeling.[74] After achieving of Rs. 100-130 bonus per-head the strike was finally withdrawn.[75]This strike was a manifestation of first organized protest on a large scale in the arena of Indian trade union movement of the tea garden labourers.[76]

But the role of the Communists in this agitation was marked by controversies and disparagement. Communists had a secret compromise with Congress leader Kiran Chandra Bhattacharya who had guaranteed the authorization for the Communists to enter into the Congress influenced tea gardens in exchange of keeping out his tea estate from the strikes.[77] This sort of collaboration inevitably brought about serious criticism for the Communists.

The Indo-China war of 1962 brought about significant changes in the Communist leadership. Indian Communists' support to China led to the arrests of several leaders of this party and consequently for the time being there was ebb in their hold over the tea gardens. Moreover, in 1964 when Communist Party of India was divided into two sections most of the trade union leaders of this region went to the new organization of the Communists i.e. Communist Party of India

(Marxist). Very few remained in the erstwhile CPI (Bhadra Bahadur Hamal was one of them). But the Communists soon recovered their position and efficiently took up the organizational activities.

Congress had also faced certain changes in its labour organization. Ranjit Ghosh appeared as the new leader of I.N.T.U.C in the Darjeeling plains (Terai) who renamed his organization as Rastriya Chia Majdur Congress (R.C.M.C) while K.T. Chaku was brought to undertake the leadership among the labourers of Christian majority tea gardens which subsequently reduced Iswar Tirkey's influence over these areas.[78]This internal strife and dissension in the Congress leadership had failed to generate any uniform ideological spirit that could enable the labourers to assimilate and display their protests against the injustice deliberately imposed upon them by the planters. This conflict within the Congress leadership was efficiently capitalized by the Communists of this region who tried hard to spread their organization in the grass-root level. But this process was interrupted in Terai by the Naxalite movement of 1967 which shook the very nature of agrarian protest India has ever witnessed. Though it did not have any immediate repercussion in the hills where Communist activities among the labourers were same as before. Labourers' consciousness took a major leap forward in a massive strike in 1969 that surpassed all the successes of the earlier movements.

1970s exhibited the weakening of CPI (M) organization that was partially substituted by the Revolutionary Socialist Party (R. S. P), though only in the Terai and Duars region of North Bengal. Gorkha Land movement in the 1980s declared the retreat of the Communist organizations in the hills. The plight of the tea garden labourers in the hills of Darjeeling were censored out by the most pressing issue of 'identity' politics. Thus the formation of Gorkha National Liberation Front (GNLF) by Subhash Ghising in 1980 marked the beginning of a new political chapter in Darjeeling that would bring, as anticipated by a labour-poet, blessings of happiness for the hill people:

"Pakhera bhir, pahar tir
Suman phule ko
Ispandan her, mutuko hamro
Umangale nache ko."[79]

(Consciousness is rising in the corners of hills, my expectations are also dancing in the beats of my heart)

But it is a matter of further analysis that to what extent the expectations of the labourers as well as the people were fulfilled.

Tea labourers' agitation against all sorts of injustices and exploitation had found their way through the strikes, rallies, and even through violent protest against the planters. The tea workers movement in Darjeeling has been characterized as a combination of vertical and horizontal protest.[80] From above it was an attempt to organize the labourers under the banner of ideology (particularly under the influence of political party) and on the other hand, from below it was a spontaneous response on the part of the wretched labourers.[81] In fact these two forces were culminated and directed towards the same direction that consequently evolved into an all-round protest against the planters. The tea gardens of Darjeeling which were possessed by the European planters during the colonial period went to the Indian hands after the independence. But still the sufferings of the labourers of these gardens did not end. More interestingly the scale of protest and agitation of the laboures became more intense during the post-independence period that manifested through the massive strikes and demonstrations against the Indian planters. Political parties were very much instrumental to bring about the workers under the fold of political activities. Capitalist domination and bourgeois exploitation had hardly changed its nature in course of time, only the authoritative power passed from the colonial hands to the 'nationalist' hands. Though there was growing consciousness among the labourers in post-colonial period "but remaining far away from modern industrial centres, they were very slow to imbibe the outlook and attitude of the modern proletariat and the degree of their class consciousness in most cases, remained comparatively low."[82]Even the leadership for these movements had come from outside, not within. The isolation from the mainstream society did not help to create any leadership from within. Moreover, on the one hand labourers were homogenous in offering their services or works and also in terms of wages, but on the other hand these labourers belonged from the heterogeneous social and geographical settings viz. the labourers of the hills had come from east-Nepal and the labourers of Terai were *adivasis* (tribes) such as Oraon, Munda, Santal, and Mech who were migrated from Chhotanagpur. Though this incoherence between the "homogenous economic activity" of the labourers and their "heterogeneous social life" contributed to the "class formation" among them but their "consciousness" towards it, as argues by Andre Beteille, "has grown in an uneven manner for it has had to contend not only with the traditional distinctions of tribe, caste and clan, but also with divisions within the trade union movement and rivalries between political parties."[83] This sort of assertion leads us to a very pertinent question that how far the trade union leaders (irrespective of any political party) were successful in moulding the workers about the reality of 'class' inequality or to what extent the labourers were equipped to understand their existence as a 'class'. But there is not the slightest doubt that the activities of different political parties helped to break down the isolation of the labourers and brought out the opportunities of organized political action which virtually added to the growth of perception of their rights and privileges. The demand for increase in wage rate etc. has subsequently provided the platform for 'joint action' under the leadership of trade unions. But that does not, in any way, include the sense of necessity of fundamental over through of the entire system of exploitation or the torture machinations despite of knowing their future distress and misery which would not come to an end through the sporadic protests or agitations. The labourers' endeavor was aimed to ensure their moderate basic needs remaining within the framework of existing mode of production that prevailed in the plantation system. The piecemeal achievements (i.e. increased wage rate, bonus, housing and medical facility etc.) were the results of the efforts of these 'notoriously oppressed classes' who despite of being wretched and illiterate had fought, according to Eric Hobsbawm, for "the desire for the ordinary life, behind which, waiting to emerge, is the dream of the really good life; the sense of all gates closing against [them], but at the same time the sense of the possibility of bursting them open....."[84]

NOTES AND REFERENCES

1. Manas Dasgupta, Darjeeling Jelar Arthanaitik Parichay in Ajitesh Bhattacharya (ed.), *Madhuparni* (Bishes Darjeeling Jela Sankhya), November, 1996, Kolkata, p.205.
2. L S S O'Malley, *Bengal District Gazetters – Darjeeling,* Logos Press, New Delhi, (First published in 1907 by the Bengal Secretariat Book Depot.), Second reprint, 1999, p.19.
3. *Ibid.*
4. *Ibid.*, p. 72.
5. *Ibid.*, p. 74.
6. *Ibid.*
7. *Ibid.*, p. 75.
8. Asok Gangopadhyay, Darjeeling Jelar Cha-Bagichay Shramik Andolon in Ajitesh Bhattacharya (ed.), *Madhuparni* (Bishes Darjeeling Jela Sankhya), November, 1996, Kolkata, p.146.
9. Manas Dasgupta, Cha Baganer Shramik Samasya in Kamalesh Goswami (ed.), *Bidroho O Andolane Uttarbanga,* Kolkata, 1420 B. S.; p. 258.
10. *Ibid.*
11. Ashesh Kumar Das, Darjeeling Cah-Bagichake Ghire Rajnaitik Tatparata: *Sekal Ekal in Sharad Uttardhwani* (Uttarbanger Bhasha – Sahitya – Samaj-Sanskritimulak Bishesh Sankhya), Siliguri, 1405 B. S., p. 69.
12. *Ibid.*
13. LSS O'Malley, *op.cit.*, p. 39.
14. Arthur Jules Dash, *Bengal District Gazetters – Darjeeling,* Bengal Government Press, Bengal, 1947, pp. 68-69.
15. Soumen Nag, "Swadinata-Purba Darjeelinger Rajnaitik Patabhumikay Cha BagicharBhumika", in Ajitesh Bhattacharya (ed.), *Madhuparni* (Bishes Darjeeling Jela Sankhya), November, 1996, Kolkata, p. 187.
16. *Ibid.*
17. LSS O'Malley, *op.cit.*, p. 35.

18. *Ibid.*
19. *Ibid.*, p. 36.
20. *Ibid.*
21. Arthur Jules Dash, *op. cit.*, p. 49.
22. LSS O'Malley, *op. cit.*, p. 40.
23. *Ibid.*, p. 41.
24. Nirban Basu, Darjeeling Cha-Bagichay Shramik Andolon, *Aitihasik*, Year 3, no. 3-4, Kolkata, 1981, p. 106.
25. Asok Gangopadhyay, Uttarbanger Shramik Andolon, *Dainik Basumati*, Siliguri, 1st May, 1994.
26. Manorama Savur, Labour and Productivity in the Tea Industry, *Economic and Political Weekly*, vol.8, no.11(Mar. 17, 1973), p. 552.
27. Ranajit Das Gupta, *Labour and Working Class in Eastern India–Studies in Colonial History*, Calcutta, 1994, p. 145.
28. Sukomal Sen, *Working Class of India: History of Emergence and Movement, 1830-1990 (with an overview upto 1995)*, Calcutta, 1997, p. 55.
29. Sharit Bhowmik, *Class Formation in the Plantation System*, New Delhi, 1981, p. 55.
30. P. Griffiths, *History of Indian Tea Industry*, London, 1972, p. 286, cited in Sharit Bhowmik, *op. cit.*, p. 56.
31. Kanchan Sarkar and Sharit Bhowmik, Trade Unions and Women Workers in the Tea Plantations, *Economic and Political Weekly*, vol. 33, no. 52 (Dec. 26, 1998- Jan. 1, 1999), p.50.
32. *Ibid.*
33. Sharit Bhowmik, Wages of Tea Garden Workers in West Bengal, *Economic and Political Weekly*, vol. 17, no. 40 (Oct. 2, 1982), p. 1600 and also see Ranajit Das Gupta, *op. cit.*, p. 144.
34. Arthur Jules Dash, *op. cit.*, p. 119.
35. *Ibid.*, and also see Sharit Bhowmik, *Class Formation in the Plantation System*, p. 67.
36. Nirban Basu, *op.cit.*, p. 107.
37. Arthur Jules Dash, *op.cit.*, p. 119.
38. Nirban Basu, *op.cit.*, p. 107.
39. *Ibid.*
40. Sharit Bhowmik, *Wages of Tea Garden Workers in West Bengal*, p. 1600.
41. *Ibid.*

42. Manorama Savur, *op. cit.*, p. 554.
43. *Ibid.*, p. 553.
44. Ranajit Das Gupta, *op. cit.*, p. 153.
45. *Ibid.*, p. 150.
46. *Ibid.*
47. *Ibid.*, pp. 158-9.
48. Kanchan Sarkar and Sharit Bhowmik, *op. cit.*, p.50.
49. Sukomal Sen, *op. cit.*, p. 60.
50. Nirban Basu, *op.cit.*, p. 108.
51. *Ibid.*
52. *Ibid.*, 109.
53. Asok Gangopadhyay, *Darjeeling Jelar Cha-Bagichay Shramik Andolon*, p. 147.
54. Nirban Basu, *op. cit.*, pp. 109-110.
55. Asok Gangopadhyay, *Darjeeling Jelar Cha-Bagichay Shramik Andolon*, p. 148.
56. Asok Gangopadhyay, *Uttarbanger Shramik Andolon*.
57. Souren Basu, Darjeeling Jelar Gana O Rajnaitik Andolon in Ajitesh Bhattacharya (ed.), *Madhuparni* (Bishes Darjeeling Jela Sankhya), November, 1996, Kolkata, p. 174.
58. This is for take into account that to consider all Nepalese as Gorkha or all hill people as Gorkha will be an over simplification of the matter. Gorkhas were chiefly the inhabitants of a district of Nepal. Soumen Nag, *op. cit.*, p. 191.
59. Though the British and the tea planters had sought for several times (in 1934, 1939 and 1943) to separate the Darjeeling Hills but there was no conscious attempt in this respect from them in the line of 'racial identity.' Their main motive was to divert the movements as well as to weaken the bonds of unity among the labourers. *Ibid.* p. 189.
60. Nirban Basu, *op. cit.*, p. 113.
61. *Ibid.*
62. Asok Gangopadhyay, *Darjeeling Jelar Cha-Bagichay Shramik Andolon*, p.149.
63. *Ibid.*
64. Khokan Mazumdar, *Nakshalbari – Bharater Buke Basanter Bajranirghosh*, Siliguri, 2004. For details see ch. 1.
65. *Ibid.*, p. 1.

66. Asok Gangopadhyay, *Darjeeling Jelar Cha-Bagichay Shramik Andolon,* p. 151.
67. Manoranjan Roy, *Samrajyabad Birodhi Sangram O Shramik Andolon,* Calcutta, 1987, p. 130.
68. Khokan Mazumdar, *op. cit.*, p. 2.
69. Asok Gangopadhyay, *Uttarbanger Shramik Andolon.*
70. Asok Gangopadhyay, *Darjeeling Jelar Cha-Bagichay Shramik Andolon,* p. 151.
71. *Ibid.*
72. Souren Basu, *op. cit.*, p. 177.
73. *Ibid.*
74. *Ibid.*
75. *Ibid.*
76. Manoranjan Roy, *op. cit.*, p. 91.
77. Asoke Gangopadhyay, *Darjeeling Jelar Cha-Bagichay Shramik Andolon,* p. 152.
78. *Ibid.*, p. 155.
79. Souren Basu, *op.cit.*, p. 179.
80. Nirban Basu, *op. cit.*, p. 115.
81. *Ibid.*
82. Sukomal Sen, *op.cit.*, p. 62.
83. For details see the Foreword written by Andre Beteille in Sharit Bhowmik, Class Formation in the Plantation System.
84. Eric Hobsbowm, *Revolutionaries,* London, 2007, p. 324

5

A Comparative Study of the Tea Garden Labour Movement in Darjeeling and Dooars in Colonial and Post Colonial Period

Nirban Basu

The tea plantation labourers formed an important segment of the newly emerging industrial labour force in Colonial Bengal. In Bengal, the gardens producing tea, the principal plantation crop of India, are located mainly in the hill areas and the plains of Terai in the Darjeeling district and the Dooars in the Jalpaiguri district.

Tea production was experimentally started in the hills of Darjeeling in 1840 and in the plains of the district in 1862. The industry, mostly under European control, rapidly grew since the 1860's. By 1947, the number of gardens rose to more than 60 in the hills and 17 in the plains.[1] The tea growing area of the Jalpaiguri district known as the Dooars in the planting parlance, is situated in Bengal–Bhutan border area. After the Dooars had been annexed by the British from Bhutan in 1864-65, the tea planters of Darjeeling explored the possibilities of growing tea there. Soon, the Dooars became the largest tea producing area in the province. British planters started the first tea garden in the Dooars in 1873. Within two years, the number of the gardens rose to 13. The growth of tea industry in the Dooars in the 1880's was so rapid that the acreage under tea in 1892 was over six times that in 1881. During the period between 1901 and 1951, the area under tea nearly doubled and the labour force nearly trebled. By 1951, the number of gardens in the Dooars was 158 with a total labour force of nearly two lakhs (1,76,195).[2] The Dooars plantation however, did not remain an exclusively British enterprise. A few Bengali lawyers and clerks from Jalpaiguri formed the first Indian tea company in 1871. Since then many more gardens were opened in the district. However until the 1960's, the British companies owned the majority of gardens here.[3]

As the background of the working class movement in the plantation two things are notable: *a)* the organization of the industry and *b)* the composition of the labour force.

In order to look after their common interests, the tea planters formed the Indian Tea Association (1881). The I.T.A, with its headquarters in Calcutta, had its branches in the tea districts such as Dooars Planter's Association in the Dooars and the Darjeeling Planter's Association in Darjeeling hills and Terai Planter's Association in the Terai. As the I.T.A and its local branches represented mainly the interests of the British planters, the small Indian tea planters subsequently formed another organization, the Indian Tea Planter's Association (I.T.P.A) the Colonial government always backed the management, ostensibly in the name of industrial peace. The real reasons for the special concern of the government were mainly two folds: first, the all –powerful monopolistic body was one of the major pillars of British capitalism in India. Second, tea, as the principal plantation industry in India, had a crucial importance in the export trade. An unlimited sway of the management was established over the labourers, bordering almost the tyranny.

The nature of composition of the tea labour force helped the management in this. In the Darjeeling hills, the immigrants or descendants from immigrants from the neighbouring country of Nepal constituted nearly the whole of labour force. They might be regarded as a permanently settled population engaged in a occupation. The composition of the labour force in the Terai and in the Dooars was almost similar. These gardens initially employed only the local Nepalese. But with the rapid increase of the industry they proved insufficient and the planters had to turn to Chotaa Nagpur and the Santhal Parganas for labour party. Migration of Santhals, Oraos and Mundas to Jalpaiguri increased rapidly during the decades 1891 to 1911. But since then the new migration diminished[4] partly because of the gradual development of the recruiting districts and partly because of the availability of local labour from amongst the descendants of the settlers in the tea districts. Thus since the 1920s, we find in the Dooars and Terai a heterogeneous but more or less fixed population of plantation labourers.

A Comparative Study of the Tea Garden

As tea plantation is a semi-agricultural and semi-industrial process generally everywhere the "family system" of production prevailed; men, women and even children worked in the gardens through granting of plots, both residential and agricultural, the workers tended to be tied down to a particular garden. Whatever may be technically the exact form of recruitment, the garden workers were reduced to a semi-servile status which prevailed till the 1940's.[5] The Sardars encouraged by the management played an important role in the day to day life of workers and kept an eye upon individual workers.

II

In spite of discontent of the tea labourers, there was no outward manifestation of organized labour agitation till the Non co-operation Movement. The industrial disputes were almost unknown. Even if there was ever an occasional strike, it was almost confined to a single estate resulting from purely local and temporary issues and was generally very quickly settled. The same was the case both in Darjeeling and Dooars.

During the Non-Cooperation days (1920-21) "Swaraj" was in the air though few understood what it meant. In Darjeeling, Dal Bahadur Giri, a dismissed government servant and a local fireband Congress leader of Kalimpong fomented agitation among the Gurkhas in the name of Gandhi. He popularized the slogan : Uproot the tea plants and grow maize or paddy instead. Tea garden labour came to believe that British rule was soon to end and the hated tea-garden managers would also go.[6] The tea planters alleged[7] that in 1921, paid agitators were sent by Non Cooperation organization in Bengal with the specific object of stirring up the tea workers against the managers and proprietors. The government reports, however, showed8 that only sporadic unrest, instigated by the Non-Co-operators, continued for sometime and although there were several strikes in July 1921, they were spontaneous and unorganized.

Similarly in the Dooars the Non Cooperators had been discontent of the "Coolies". They urged the labour to take over the land and management themselves. Several strikes broke out. A wide spread rumour to the effect that on a certain date, which was conveniently moved forward from time to time, a terrible storm would destroy all those who had not yet declared for Gandhi was in part, responsible for these stoppages.[9] Such prophesies were consistent with the cosmological belief system of the aboriginal tribes from which the Dooars plantation labour was drawn. The Intelligence Branch10 reported that labour unrest spread from the Darjeeling hill gardens further downhill in the Dooars in July 1921 and later on in the month of February 1922, this unrest manifested itself in attempts to boycott tea garden hats(markets) in Jalpaiguri.

The movements, however, proved to be sporadic in nature in both Darjeeling and Dooars. A great deal was done to restore the confidence of the workers through some material concessions and propaganda undertaken by the garden managers. On the other hand, the government relied on strong measures to contain the movement. In any case due to lack of any organizational infrastructure no trade union movement worth the name, grew out of this agitation.

Nothing happened for two decades or more. The Civil Disobedience movement of 1930-32, the political upheavals of 1937-39 which agitated the labourers in other parts of Bengal as well in the Assam gardens and the Quit India movement of 1942 could scarcely "break the peace" of the gardens. Neither was there any local initiative nor any serious outside attempt to mobilize the tea garden workers.

III

As a result of a steep rise in the prices of essential commodities, during the Word War II, the discontent of tea workers naturally intensified as elsewhere. The I.T.A's declared policy of supplying the labor with foodstuffs and cloth at concessional rates was not always properly implemented.[11] But in spite of such economic hardships, the agitation of the tea workers remained sporadic due to lack of any organization. From the very beginning, the tea labour movement was closely connected with the advent of the Communists The Communist organization in the Darjeeling district started around 1943 and a District Committee was formed in 1945. But the most important development was that, in the meantime, Ratanlal Brahman, who had already become widely known among the poor tea garden labourers of Darjeeling as an unfailing friend and courageous fighter and to his enemies as a notorious 'dacoit Sardar' gradually but firmly came over to the Communist Party through the campaign for cheap grain shops and rationing while the famine was raging (1943 -44) and became the party's leading light.[12]

Radical ideas started to infiltrate the Jalpaiguri district some time during 1938-39 when a small District Committee of the then illegal C.P.I working under the banner of the Congress Socialist party was formed. But compared to the work among the peasants, trade union work was not considerable. Even during the World War II, after the CPI had been legalized, the Communists could not penetrate the tea gardens to any appreciable extent. At this stage, their attention was concentrated mainly on the railway labour.[13] The D.P.A reported to the Labour Investigation Committee(1946) that there were only two small strikes in the last five years.[14]

The proposed election to the Provincial Assembly in March 1946 offered an ideal opportunity to the Communists to extend their base throughout the tea gardens of the Darjeeling district. According to the provision of the Provincial Legislative Assemblies Election Order, the garden constituencies were of a shifting nature. In the first election of 1937, the garden labour seat was constituted by the Bengal Dooars (Western) constituency. Due to absence of any kind of organization, neither the National Congress nor the Trade Union Congress could sponsor any candidate for this seat. Sardar Babu Litta Munda Orao (Independent) backed by the white bosses was elected unopposed. He cut a poor figure in the Assembly, hardly spoke never raised the issue of the oppressed tea garden labour and generally sided with the Europeans.

In 1946 election, labour seat was constituted by the Darjeeling (Sadar) constituency. In the area of about 100 gardens, only 12 of the smallest gardens were grouped together to make the labour constituency. There were only 2500 voters in the constituency which had an adult population of nearly 18,000. But in inspite of all limitations, the Communists took the election as an opportunity for a wider movement and started work in right earnest.

The Communists began with the formation of a Central Trade Union, the Darjeeling district Chiza Kaman Worker's Union which appeared sometime in 1945. The individual garden units of the union were formed. The reports relating to the composition of the Central Workers' Union in the second year (1946-47) show that most of the office bearers were the whole timers of the C.P.I while only two Vice Presidents were actual tea garden workers.[15] Nevertheless, for the first time in the long history of the tyrannical rule of the white planters over the workers, the Communists had begun to awaken the garden labour to a sense of their elementary human rights.

The announcement of Ratanlal Brahman's candidature unnerved the planters, the government and the Congress. The planters brought both the anti-Communist candidates, one from the Congress and the other independent, right inside their gardens, arranged election meetings and ordered their workers to vote for either of them, but never for the Communists and created all sorts of obstacles in the way of campaign of the Communists.[16] The Congress came to an understanding also with the Gorkha League to the effect that the Congress would support the Gorkha League nominee for the Darjeeling General seat who would join the Congress Parliamentary party inside the Assembly, and that in return the Gorkha League would support the Congress candidate in the Labour seat.

Although the Communists were banned from entering the gardens, they clandestinely contacted the labourers, distributed various leaflets among then endeavoured to call the coolies away from their work and delivered political speeches. The electioneering soon created signs of tensions in different areas. But in spite of all obstacles created by the white bosses and the Congress leadership, Ratanlal won the election while both of his rivals lost their deposits. This landslide victory of the Communist candidate in the face of strong anti-Communist wave which swept almost all other labour constituencies deserves an explanation. This victory has been attributed partly to the organizational skill of the Communists and to a greater extent to the personal popularity of Ratanlal. It has been admitted by the Communists themselves[17] that it was wrong to attribute the election victory solely to the strength of the Communist organization among the workers.

The election victory encouraged the Communists to think of channelizing the spontaneous enthusiasm of the tea workers through formation of branches of Central Union in every garden. In months following the election, Darjeeling witnessed an intense labour agitation by the Communists. But in the face of the repression launched by the management and the police, the sporadic resistance and agitation of the tea workers in most of the cases had little chance of success which adversely affected the newly founded Central Union. Under these circumstances the only way to get out of the impasse was to take the strategy of an all-out offensive.[18]

On June 3, 1946, a representation on behalf of the CPI met the Bengal Labour Commissioner at Calcutta. But as no follow up action was taken, on June 15 the Union served a strike notice on the management of 17 Tea Estates and also submitted a representation to Minister of Labour, Bengal. The 12 point demand charter included[19] demands for increase in wage rates; Dearness Allowance of 25 per cent; fixation of a minimum pay, leave facilities, improvement in the working conditions, and recognition of the Chiya Kaman Workers Union. At a meeting of the tea garden labourers held in Darjeeling on June 19, the Union publicly announced its decision to go on a general strike if the demands were not fulfilled within the stipulated period. At this time, the C.P.I sought the support of the Congress and the Gorkha League. The G.L leadership, after great hesitation agreed to protest against the repression by the police and the management, although not jointly with the Communists.[20]

At this stage, the government seriously attempted to prevent the workers from going on strike from July 1. After meeting the Labour Minister and the Commissioner, the Union initially agreed to postpone the strike notice for two months and finally to withdraw the strike notice altogether . The only concession which the union gained was the promise of the management to recognize the trade union rights to a limited extent. All other demands including such important ones as wage increase were summarily rejected. The Communists however, claimed[21] that whatever might be the material results of the negotiations their political significance was notable. This was the first organized united struggle of the tea workers in the hills whose impact was far reaching. After the withdrawal of the strike, a significant development was that the Communists for the first time turned their attention to the Terai plains of Darjeeling district where the composition of the labour force was completely different from that in the hills.[22]

But it can not be denied that the withdrawal of the strike notice was in a great extent a setback for the Communists. Still they were down but not out. Soon they had to face stiff challenges from the opposition forces, particularly the Gorkha League. From the beginning, the Gorkha League was unsympathetic towards the Communist–led Union mainly for two reasons.[23] First, to them the movement seemed to be a challenge to their influence. They branded the C.P.I as an agent of the Bengalis as the two main organizers of the Union were Bengalis. Secondly, much more important was the fact that the clerks and Sardars of various gardens, who acted as intermediaries between the planters and the managers on one hand and the workers on the other and often had to face the spontaneous wrath of the workers, were, in general, the main support-base of the Gorkha League and were becoming increasingly anti-Communist. The increasing tension between the C.P.I and G.L. supporters were almost regular features in different gardens.

IV

White in Darjeeling, the Communists did the initial ground work in the trade union organization among the tea workers during the later years of the World War II, in the Dooars the process began after the end of the World War II. Only by the middle of 1946 there were first visible signs of movement among the Dooars workers. In the immediate post-war period, the economic conditions of the tea workers worsened considerably due to price-rise, scarcity of essential commodities and large scale retrenchment in other sectors. In such an economic background the political agitations taking place in the district, began to affect the tea garden labour. The ground work of trade union organization was done by the trade union organizers of the Bengal-Assam Railroad Worker's Union (B.A.R.R.W.U). It was a non-political union but most of its whole-time organizers were Communists. Their work was facilitated by the fact that the railway lines passed by or even through the gardens and that the lowest-ranking railway workers- the unionized gangmen and pointsmen many of whom themselves were tribals came into frequent contacts with the tribal garden labourer.[24] Furthermore, the election campaign on behalf of the two Communist candidates in the neighbouring Darjeeling tea labour and Jalpaiguri rural reserved constituency for the first time carried the message of the Red Flag to the garden-labour in the sprawling tea belt of the Dooars.

By the middle of 1946, Communists trade unionists were able to stir up unrest in several gardens. Sometime in the latter part of 1946, the first Central trade union of the tea workers of Jalpaiguri– the Jalpaiguri Zilla Cha Bagan Mazdur Union, was formed with headquarters at Mal with Ratanlal Brahmin as chairman and Debaprasad (alias Patal) Ghosh as Secretary. Both of them were prominent Communists. The mood of labourers at the time was one of revolt. This found expressions in spontaneous and sporadic fashions in the form of gheraos, sudden work stoppages, violent incidents, occasional beatings of babus notorious for corruption and espionage of the 'Sahibs'.[25] Thus while Darjeeling, a traditional Communist base for the last few years, witnessed a decline in the Communist activities in the second half of 1946, at least compared to the first half, the Dooars where the tea workers movement had a late start became a hot bed of agitation in the closing months of 1946.The planters as well as the government overlooked the fact that these might be genuine reasons for labour discontent and stressed only the role of the Communist organizers in the unrest.[26]

The continuous labour unrest in tea gardens in different parts of India became so alarming that it forced the Central Government to convene in January 1946, a Tripartite Conference in Delhi representing the employees, the employers and the Government. At the Tripartite Conference certain long standing demands were recognized. The CPI naturally regarded the Tripartite Conference as the high water mark of its success. But the Communists were soon to be disappointed because of the non-fulfilment of the promises they claimed to have been made at the Tripartite Conference. The labour unrest went on increasing both in Darjeeling and the Dooars. The Dooars tea labour agitation took a serious turn in the context of the Tebhaga movement, the movement of the share croppers initiated by the C.P.I demanding an increase in their share of harvest, which rocked almost the whole of Bengal during the autumn and winter of 1946–47 spread also to the Dooars, though somewhat later between February and April, 1947. It provided an ideal opportunity for united action by workers and peasants, both mostly tribal, in and around the gardens. Here again, thee unionized railway workers took the initiative, publicized the Tebhaga movement among the tea workers through leaflets and clandestine meetings. Volunteer groups were formed among the tea workers who would strike work in order to participate in the movement.[27] Since the end of January 1947 the unrest at the Dooars gardens was heightening. Khagen Dasgupta, the local Congress MLA from Jalpaiguri described in the Assembly that there had been labour "risings" in the tea gardens.[28] Dasgupta's speech clearly suggests that the local Congress not only disapproved of the militant agitation of the garden coolies but also felt much alarmed about the safety and security of the Indian supervisory staff. The government, however, disagreed with the assessment and described it only as unrest.[29]

After the failure of the initial attempts to control the labour force by the alternate methods of concession ad repression, the only alternative remained was to crush the movement with all the might of the administration. Finally, the government intervened. Order u/s 144 CrPC PS was promulgated, sufficient police was posted, meetings and processions were prohibited and carrying of dangerous weapons in public were banned. Finally, the Tebhaga movement in the Dooars was called off in the beginning of May 1947 as it was felt that since most share-croppers had two-thirds of the harvest, there was no need to prolong it. The government of the Dooars tea garden labourers also came to an end without any significant gains for them.

The apparent failure of the Communists to fulfil the expectations they roused after the Tripartite Conference encouraged the non-communists to try to extend their bases among tea workers. In Darjeeling, the Gorkha League was going increasingly powerful. In the Dooars, the Congress Socialist Party (C.S.P) and also the Revolutionary Socialist Party (R.S.P) sought to make important inroads. But the most serious challenge came from the Congress who actively backed by the planters wanted to form unions in the gardens.

V

The trends, noticeable in the colonial period, were further strengthened in the post-colonial period.

In the Darjeeling hill areas the ruling Congress party in tacit understanding with the management, developed quickly a base among the tea garden labour as against the Communist dominated Tea Worker's Union. The role of the All India Gorkha League is very important in this connection. The Gorkha League had always a strong support base among the middle class Gurkhas against both the Congress and the Communists. The Gurkha subnationalism which was always there became gradually solidified . The demand for a separate province or at least autonomy became gradually strengthened. The economic class demands of tea garden workers steadily lost importance to the overarching aspirations of Gurkha subnationalism.

But as Gorkha League failed to deliver the goods, a new ultra outfit GNLF (Gurkha National Liberation Front) led by Subhash Ghishing became a strong force and after protracted agitation, often violent, the demand for a separate Gurkha Hill Council was formed in 1988 by a tripartite agreement between Central Government, State Government and the FNLF supremo for the Gorkha Territorial Area (GTA). But the highhandedness, inefficiency and corruption of the GNLF functionaries made them increasingly unpopular. Another ultra-radical group called the Gorkha Janamukti Morcha (GJM) came into being under the leadership of Bimal Gurung, one time associate of Ghising. The continuous agitations and disruptions ultimately forced Ghising to resign. The GJM came into power in Gorkha Hill Council as nominated members by the state government without any election. Though these Gurkha organizations tried to secure the support of the tea-labourers and form unions, but instead of fighting for the causes of labour, they mainly tried to enlist their support even by intimidation, forcible collection of subscriptions both from ordinary labour and the garden management. Normal trade union activities were almost stopped. Production sharply fell in the gardens. Both the Red Trade unions and the Congress Labour Unions became almost non-existent.[30]

In case of the Dooars, the situation is more complex. The Gorkha political outlets have considerable influence over Nepalese tea-labour concentrated mainly in the gardens bordering Bhutan. But as the overwhelming majority of the Dooars garden labour are tribals in origin, the organizations like Adivasi Vikas Mancha gradually entered the scene dislodging the traditional parties working in the Labour Front– The Congress, the Communists, the R.S.P and the Socialist Party. Here also, the gardens are in dying stage because of the rapidly dwindling demand of Indian tea in international market and the increase of production cost. A large number of gardens are closed, thousands of tea labourers have lost their jobs. What is lacking is the united struggle of the workers. The ethnic demands for autonomy are getting more importance than the economic demands of the tea labourers.[31]

VI

Taken as a whole compared to other organized industries, the development of labour movement in the tea industry was a much belated process. This late start can be attributed to three factors. First, the restrictions imposed by the planters made it extreme.ly difficult for outsiders to contact the garden labour. The social factor was the inability of the nationalists to organize the tea workers partly due to the "communication gap" between the local leaders, mostly educated middle class "Bhadraloks" and the tea labourers mostly Nepalese or immigrant tribals. The third and the most important factor was the unwillingness of the nationalist leaders to take up the cause of labour. For these reasons it was not the nationalists, but the left radicals, more precisely the Communists who started the trade union organization in Bengal tea gardens and set up a tiered structure of well knit organisation. Still there were differences between the nature of movement in Darjeeling, and Dooars. In Darjeeling, the party had a firmer control over the labour organizations and directly guided them. In the Dooars, the element of spontaneity in the labour movement was much more pronounced. But although the pioneering worth in the trade union organization was done by the Communists, soon they had to face challenges from other political groups, some of which were actively encouraged by planters themselves. So, neither in Darjeeling nor in the Dooars, the Communists for long remained the unchallenged force. In spite of some glorious historic moments of militant struggle, the Communists failed to sustain the political awareness of the tea workers and to raise it to a higher level so that the tea workers could play the vanguard's role in the struggle of the industrial proletariat. The trend was not reversed in the post-colonial years, rather it became more complex and complicated.

NOTES AND REFERENCES

1. Indian Tea Association (I.T.A) – *Annual Report,* 1947.
2. A Mitra – *Census of India, 1951,* Vol VI, Pt IA (West Bengal) Report (Calcutta, 1953) p.253.
3. Sharit Bhowmik – *Class Formation in the Plantation System* (New Delhi, 1981).

4. A Mitra – *op.cit.*, p.264, statement 1.91.
5. Ranajit Dasgupta – 'Structure of the Labour Market in Colonial India' in *Economic and Political Weekly*, Special Number Nov, 1981 and also, the Report of the Labour Investigation Committee on the Tea garden Workers (henceforth as LIC) 1946.
6. Satyendra Narayan Majumdar - *Patabhumi Kanchanjungha* (Calcutta, 1983), p.16.
7. *Report of the Royal Commission on Labour in India (1929)* – Vol VI, PtI, p.49 (R.C.LI)
8. Intelligence Branch, 1921 – Fornightly Report of the Government of Bengal on the Political Situation, 1921-22, quoted in R.K Ray– 'Masses in Politics: The Non Co-operation Movement in Bengal' (*Indian Economic and Social History Review*, Dec. 1974).
9. Government of Bengal, Political Department, Confidential/ 1924, F.No. –S.C 395 /1924 – *History of the Non-Cooperation Movement and the Khilafat agitation in Bengal* (Printed Report).
10. Intelligence Branch, 1921 – *Fortnightly Reports of the Government of Bengal on the Political Situation, 1921-22.*
11. Report of the L.I.C –p.76.
12. *People's Age* – 3.12.1945.
13. Ranajit Dasgupta – 'Peasant's Workers and Freedom Struggle: Jalpaiguri, 1945 -47' in Amit.K.Gupta (ed) – *Myth and Reality: The Struggle for Freedom in India (1945 – 47).*
14. Report of the L.I.C – p.96.
15. Intelligence Branch, Weekly Confidential Report, Darjeeling dt 6.7.46 (henceforth as W.C.R).
16. *People's Age* – 2.12.45.
17. S.N Majumdar – *op.cit*, p.31.
18. *Ibid.*, p.38.
19. *Amrita Bazar Patrika*-20.6.46.
20. IB, Bengal Police Abstract – 29.6.46.
21. S.N Majumdar – *op.cit.*, p.43.
22. IB, B.P.A – 2.11.46.
23. S.N Majumdar– *op.cit.*, pp.39-40.
24. Dasgupta Ranjit – *op. cit.*, as in Ref No. 13 also Sharit Bhowmik– Origins of Trade Unions Among Tea Plantation Workers of Bengal (Marxist Miscellany, No. 4, June, 1976).
25. Ranajit Dasgupta – *op. cit.*, as in ref no. 13.

26. Sharit Bhowmik - *op. cit.*, as in ref no. 24.
27. *The Statesman* -26.4.47.
28. *Ibid*.
29. Annual Report of the Dooars Planters Association 1947
30. Jaharlal Sen–Darjeeling Jelay Palabadaler Pala (*Yuger Dak*, Autumn No, 1420 Bangabda).
31. Ananda Gopal Ghosh– Uttar Swadhinata Parber Jalpaiguri Jilar Rajnaitik Andoloner Chala Chitra, Jalpaiguri Jila Sankalan Pt II (Jalpaiguri, non dated).

6

Jangal Santal and the Peasant Movement of Naxalbari: A Glance over a Forgotten Chapter of Indian History

I. Sarkar

The historical literature of peasant history of India is fairly rich and it is under this trend of historiography we hear about the peasant movement of Naxalbari – which by its course and action was a shock to the age old feudal society. Leaders like comrade Charu Mazumder, Kanu Sanyal, Keshab Sarkar, Khokan Mazumder, Sauren Basu, Santosh Rana, Azizul Haque, Sushital Roy Chaudhury, Jangal Santal and few others are some of the names who got involved in this movement and the peasants of North Bengal specially that of Naxalbari region vis a vis of India at least for the first time found some people to be identified with their rights and aspirations. But it is a surprise that when a good number of scholars have noted down the history of movement from different angles, they are conspicuously silent about comrade Jangal Santal who was not only the son of the soil but also a leader worth the name to lead the peasants for such a multidimensional movement. For example, we have in our disposal a well-documented book titled Left Extremist Movement in West Bengal: An Experiment in Armed Agrarian Struggle by Amiya K Samanta which is a well-researched work but surprisingly this peasant leader has been mentioned here in some insignificant occasions along with the key leaders of the movement.[1] It is a fact that comrade Jangal was an 'adivasi', a member of a downtrodden community but his plan of action sparked the fire of the Naxalites to unite against the jotedars of the region who had been exploiting the peasants and the poor people by various means and excuses. In this light it is no less a curious matter that the author of such an acclaimed work could analyze this peasant movement by some stray references to comrade Jangal Santal just as a nominated CPI (M) candidate from Phansidewa Assembly constituency(Siliguri Sub-division) for the general election in 1967.[2] A good number of other known titles both in Bengali and English are there to enrich our knowledge about Naxalite movement but most of them have assessed the contributions of comrade Jangal with one or two sentences.[3] Even in Bangladesh there are serious studies about Naxalite movement but there too one may hardly come across the reference to this adivasi peasant leader.[4] The list of such works may be multiplied but a question arises why this comrade Jangal Santal who initiated the Naxalite movement could not or did not draw the attention of the historians and only some memories of his contemporary leaders have come down to us as sources to study the leader as a person or his ideology and background that prompted him to protest against the injustice and exploitation of the peasants and workers down the ages. This may be a background of investigation of the present article to find out the silence of the scholars about this personality and whether the so-called established norm and methodology of writing Indian history where the subaltern people are hardly referred to or ignored, and if at all discussed, it is under mere obligation. Keeping in mind such a trend of historical research in Bengal nay India the present study is an attempt to focus some of the unexplored issues of the life and activities rather achievements of comrade Jangal Santal who has never been brought to public notice side by side with the comrades who came forward to organize popular movements in the region concerned. The main source of the information are some of the leaflets, pamphlets and rare interviews published in book form or memoirs which provide us some hints about Jangal Santal and his mechanism to mobilize the people of the region.

It may be noted that comrade Jangal Santal started his humble political life in Nepal sometime during 1949.[5] The name of his Kanna Kisku and from this it seems that his family title was Kisku. Kanna Kisku was a tea garden labourer of Kamalpur Tea Estate, Bagdogra, in the district of Darjeeling.[6] However, comrade Jangal was associated with direct politics for about thirty years and it was an eventful carrier when he became known all over India as an active peasant leader. According to comrade Kanu Sanyal, after the death of his (Jangal's) father his mother brought him to Naxalbari along with his other two brothers and one sister.[7] Comrade Kanu Sanyal also informs that comrade Jangal settled at Naxalbari as a *bargadar* (share-cropper) under a *jotedar* named Durlabh Mohammad.[8] After few years he again went to Nepal (1949) and started a family life with his first wife Gangu Hansda. It was sometime in 1949, the Nepali Congress and the Communist Party of Nepal jointly organized a jail-breaking movement against the Ranashahi. Incidentally, this was a movement of Nepal named 'Chandragadi Jail Breaking Movement'[9] in order to force the Government for the release of the detainees. A born rebel like comrade Jangal could not sit idle and naturally got involved in it. But as the movement failed, arrest and inhuman torture on the agitators started. At this juncture comrade Jangal had no alternative but to come back to Naxalbari sometime in 1950.[10]

As we have been reported, comrade Jangal had started a full-fledged political life in 1952 and first of all he took basic knowledge of politics as a member of Kishak Sabha.[11] He then enrolled himself as a member of the Communist Party of India (1953) and comrade Kanu Sanyal seems to have been the monitor behind this lift.[12] In spite of any proper ideological training or association with any Marxist leader comrade Jangal soon earned reputation as a leader and gradually turned into a leading figure in the party due to his extra-ordinary commitment and unparallel sympathy for the poverty-stricken people of his locality. In no time he became a symbol of 'class struggle.'

Comrade Jangal Santal was ever a leader of masses and his confidence on this account gave him an honoured position among the suffering people. This may be the reason why he could counter the dictation of the superiors. Example may be sought in his strong voice against the principles and decision of distribution of the illegal landed property of the jotedars/ zamindars within the existing rules. This was a decision of the Krishak Sabha. In the conference of the Krishak Sabha held in 1959, he protested against it even if he was a President of the Krishak Sabha of Naxalbari-Hatighisha region. According to a report Jangal could not welcome and appreciate the land issue or its distribution among the landless as a means to capture power.[13] According to comrade Kanu Sanyal this was the background or origin of the outburst known as Naxalbari Movement and comrade Jangal was brought to the lime light as a peasant leader.[14] Incidentally, comrade Biswanath Mukherjee, the then leading communist leader was present in the said conference but curiously he remain silent while hearing the comments from Jangal.[15] In fact comrade Jangal was very much adamant on this issue and it seems that he might have experienced the matter in view of his fight against the *jotedars* and he realized that it was not at all possible for the peasants to enjoy land right, whatever in its form, so easily and on the question there might be unnecessary bloodshed, laws of lives of the unarmed poor people of India.

So far as the leadership of comrade Jangal is concerned it appears that he was a born-leader and was identified with the term *ladai* (struggle).[16] It was not only concerned with peasant issues but was also linked up with working class people. It is said that being in constant touch with the tea garden labourers he was deeply associated with their day to day problems and if anybody looks at the reporting of comrade Kanu Sanyal, Jangal Santal played a historic role in the strike of the tea garden workers of Darjeeling in 1955 who stood up with protest for legal bonus.[17] This was followed by the programme of the capture of illegal lands. Thus the time was not far when he took up a leading role to form a wing of Communist Party of India in strictest sense of the term. This may be the probable background which prompted him and his followers to organize and form CPI (ML) in 2nd April, 1969.[18]

The testing points of comrade Jangal's leadership for the cause of the peasants had, in fact, started in 1952 when he came into an open conflict with a *jotedar* named Serket Sing of Hatighisa on the question of tebhaga issue.[19]But as it is said his organization at that time was so weak that he and his followers were brutally beaten by Serket Sing and his associates. In fact comrade Kanu Sanyal was also a victim of this *jotedar*'s gundas who did not spare him from physical torture. According to comrade Kanu Sanyal, the issue of bonus of the tea garden workers (1955) and his stand for *tebhaga* movement of 1952 made comrade Jangal a popular figure as a leader. Because comrade Jangal had the capability to bridge the toiling classes and stood beside them in time of crisis. In fact this was a favourable trend of politics and there was no difficulty to mobilize people on 24th May, 1967 when comrade Jangal Santal and other leaders could call for the historic peasant movement of Naxalbari.[20]

The rise of comrade Jangal Santal as a popular peasant leader was spontaneous like leaders named Titumir, Birsa Munda, Sidhu and Kanhu and so on. According to comrade Asim Chattopadhyay, comrade Jangal Santal had no opportunity of any traditional education, political background or training to become a mass leader.[21] He was not a theorist but a leader from within. Incidentally, we come to know from a source that at first he came to know about Karl Marx and peasants from one milkman named Chunilal.[22] It is interesting that once comrade Souren Basu asked him how comrade Jangal Santal had come to politics. To quote comrade Souren Basu the reply was "One Chunilal Goala (milkman) talked about Marxism and agrarian movements to me for the first time and it impressed me very much. In fact it was the first step of my coming to politics. This had taken place sometime in 1951."[23] Comrade Souren Basu, one of the prominent figures of Naxalbari movement says about the originality of comrade Jangal Santal as a peasant leader. In his opinion "Any man may acquire knowledge and wisdom through study and interaction with the academic intellectuals. But in no circumstances are we able to distinguish these two wings of our human quality. But the uniqueness of comrade Jangal's leadership is that his course of action always showed what knowledge and wisdom stand for.[24]It is said that the measures, steps and principles he used to take up for any party-programme or action were based on reality and not on any theory. This may be possible because comrade Jangal had no hazards of the so-called middle class identity or obligation which helped him to remain unnerved or could explain easily many crucial problems of politics of his time.

Comrade Jangal Santal had come from a very big family in terms of its member consisting of his two wives and children. His whole family was a victim of his political activities and wives and children were not spared. Comrade Souren Basu informs about a moment when the Naxalite movement was at its peak hours, the police had given a warning not to offer any job to his wives in any tea garden so that they (wives) along with their children would starve and die in the long run. Even then comrade Jangal is said to have remained unmoved rather took the challenge as a genuine communist. Over and above when in 1969 he was released from the jail he was offered Rs. 190 as relief from the *jotedar* in order to repair his broken cottage. As the matter may be he sought the permission from the party whether he would accept the money. Comrade Basu says, the party leaders at that point of time directed him to refuse the relief offer and he followed and his house remained unrepaired. Comrade Souren Basu again notes that, comrade Jangal Santal was never found to repent on such a situation.[25]

A unique quality of comrade Jangal's leadership was that he never supported the line of political 'action' through killing, murder and bloodshed which was known as *khatam* line (murder) of the Naxalites propounded by comrade Charu Mazumdar.[26] Another interesting side of his leadership was his device of class struggle but not by bloodshed.[27] There was also a common trend among the leaders to malign and slandering of the fellow comrades. This was overtly followed in order to belittle the activities of comrade Charu Mazumdar and also to disown his achievements, if any, at all level.[28]In such a situation comrade Jangal Santal is said to have been turned furious and had a warning to all comrades that, "I do not believe for all the disaster that has fallen on the party is due to Charubabu."[29] This particular feeling and stand of comrade Jangal Santal has fairly been reported by another comrade Azizul Haque who by referring a letter of comrade

Santal writes about the quality of leadership of that leader and that how he could achieve the same through faith and confidence by showing due honour to the fellow comrades in addition to the ideology of self-sacrifice. In this respect we may quote the reference of the letter of comrade Santal which is not only self evident but sufficient to assess the attitude of comrade Santal towards his fellow comrades. It is said that when the dilemma of faith and no-confidence on the leadership of comrade Charu Mazumdar became an issue of discussion comrade Jangal requested all comrades to consider the matter in a straight way. To quote comrade Azizul Haque "*Sangrame anek rakter badale katakgula namer upar manusher bishwas janmay, sei namgulake hathat nasyat karle manusher sangramer opar astha bhenge jay. Se astha ar sahaje gare othe na.*"[30] (i.e. people develop confidence on some names (of great men) who shed blood in the struggle. If there is an attempt to wash out those names suddenly, people are supposed to lose confidence on any struggle and that lost confidence does never develop again easily). Comrade Haque has not produced the original letter but he admits that it is the exact version of the letter.

It is interesting that dilemma of faith and question of no-confidence are nothing new in the political culture of India. But this statement of comrade Santal is said to have reminded him the same political ideology of Russian scholar Plekhanov who is said to have categorically condemned such attitude of the political leaders and the disaster that may come over the prospect of party organization. According to comrade Haque it is no less a wonder how comrade Santal being an illiterate person could perceive the truth of political organization and the ideology propounded by the Russian scholar long before the Naxalite movement. Because it is sure and no less a reality that comrade Jangal had no opportunity to hear about Plekhanov nor did he get any chance to read the literature of the Russian Revolution.[31]

Comrade Jangal's course of action and the spirit of people's war is an excellent example of 'class struggle' in Indian history. There was a situation at Terai region when the outsiders had no right or capacity to mobilize the tea garden workers or to unite the peasants and *bargadars* of this region against the *jotedars* and *zamindars*. Infact, these *jotedars* and *zamindars* had established a monopoly right to exploit the people on various excuses. Union of the tea garden workers or any peasant association had no place there and the tea garden managers or the jotedars had never been ready to appreciate voice of protest from any quarter. In spite of this awkward situation some secret societies and organizations came into being in course of time and this became much more prominent just during the middle of the 1950s and a few but spontaneous workers' movement on the question of wage began to take place. Side by side, the share-croppers of the area made united effort for three-fourth part of dues from the jotedars. Infact it was a moment when the workers and peasants together came forward in a common platform and leaders like comrade Kanu Sanyal, Jangal Santal, Kadam Mallick, and Souren Basu came out as recognized communist leaders.[32] In 1962 comrade Jangal Santal contested in the General Election as a candidate of the undivided Communist Party, but he was defeated by the Congress candidate by a small margin.[33]

In course of time there started a conflict within the Communist Party of India and the division came much prominently with the emergence of CPI (M) and CPI. But right from 1966 workers, peasants were very much adamant for their rights and the defeat of the Congress in 1967 and formation of the United Front Government of West Bengal gave another leap to the toiling masses of the Terai region. As per programmes, comrade Jangal and his associates took up the cause of the tea garden workers and also to search out the illegal lands of the *jotedars* of the Terai. But unfortunately the torture of the police and the arrests of the leader gain pace on this issue. A good number of CPI (M) leaders were expelled from the party and thus the stage was prepared for the emergence of CPI (ML) on 22nd April, 1969.[34] But as comrade Jangal Santal, comrade Kanu Sanyal, comrade Charu Mazumdar took up the cause of the peasants and raised revolutionary voices against the *jotedars* and *zamindars,* a large scale arrest of the leaders started with a consequences of awe and tension in the region. In the long run the above mention leaders became famous and historical figures so far as the peasant history of India is concerned.

One of the interesting aspects of this development was that the volume of such movement at least convinced the Government as well as the *jotedars* regarding land reforms and one of the issues and programmes of the then West Bengal Government was to look after the interest of the peasants and workers in general and that of the tea gardens in particular.

In concluding the paper, there is a need to look at the origin and popularity of the Naxalite movement for the cause of the peasantry and how it brought comrade Jangal Santal to the lime light of history. His leadership was no doubt an exceptional example being a fore front leader of a downtrodden community of India named Santal. His emergence no doubt broke the traditional belief and so-called historical truth that a political leader might come also from a lower class and caste origin. In a caste-ridden society like India the rise of comrade Jangal Santal may thus be an uncommon incident in the historiography of India in which a clear bias is often experienced in the writings of the historians. He was given a membership in the Provincial Committee of the CPI (ML) and this is also another recognition of comrade Jangal as a mass leader. The most interesting side of his personality and leadership was that he was identified with the interest of the peasants and the toiling people and his voice was the last one to mobilize the people at large for a movement. We know how the so-called extremist line of 'action' (*khatam* line) had damaged the movement and in this respect comrade Jangal was an exceptional because he could not and did not appreciate this principle in the name of people's right vis-a-vis people's movement.

But in spite of the contradictions put forward by many quarters, fact remains that his rise was not an accidental but a reality. This has become clear when there is an opinion to assess the whole incident of Naxalbari in a way that "Sanyal (i.e. Kanu Sanyal), Jangal Santal and others who had every reason to feel disgusted with the plant machinations of the Mazumder (Charu Mazumdar) clique for taking all credit of the Naxalbari struggle..."[35] So a clear picture emerges while studying comrade Jangal Santal, his recognition as a mass leader has not received unanimously rather has been seen from a parochial standpoint. The literature that has developed on the Naxalite movement has also hardly made justice to him. Because if someone looks at the statement of comrade Kanu Sanyal, it may be clear the quality leadership of comrade Jangal Santal. In his language "Jangal had not become a Jangal Santal in a day. Its history is very cruel and at the same time very much pleasant. Indomitable courage, uncommon sincerity, unlimited loyalty, unbelievable diligence and above all genuine sympathy for the toiling masses and also human sense were the elements of his character and in totality these had raised him to a higher level of leadership."[36] Comrade Kanu Sanyal seems to have been touched with the so-called rumour against comrade Jangal Santal who was very often identified with a Tarzan and, as if, being a hero of many adventures. In this way, he (comrade Sanyal) wandered, how a man like comrade Jangal Santal was supposed to be a symbol of terror, bloodshed or murder.[37] But comrade Kanu Sanyal has emphatically stressed that the truth is something opposite of such comments and remarks against comrade Jangal Santal. Here it may be relevant to refer a poem composed by one modern poet Jayanta Choudhury by name with the title 'Jangal Santal' and a few lines of the same are –

Aguner gabhirata ei nashta upanibesher
Hingsra dant, nakh aar tar samasta garal
Ki rakam dhelechhilo Banglay Bihare, Andhre./
....
Ja chilo tomar samne, charpashe
Ja halo tomar samne, chaturdike
Ekhano Jangal tar mukhomukhi
Ekhano Bihar Bangla Andhra ar patakar rang
Saradesh aroyal tar mukhomukhi
Tumi mrita. Jangaler samuha binashe
Jantrana, ghrinay aaj asahay
Dhanuker moto benke jaoya ei desh
Tumi rekhe gele.........[38]

(i.e. The gravity of fire /and how the harmful teeth, nails of the spoiled colonialism had poured its poison/

In Bengal, Bihar and in Andhra./

Whatever was in front of you, all around/
Whatever was at your front- step in all directions/
Jangal still stands face to face/
You are now dead, and due to the complete disappearance of Jangal /
(We are) at present helpless, there are pains and hatred/
You have left a country with the shape of a bent-bow).

The poet has portrayed here the feeling of a revolutionary that might have occurred in the mind of the departed leader and also the condition of our nation symbolized with a bent bow (i.e. backboneless) he left to the coming generation with his death. At the long last let us conclude with the famous statement of comrade Kanu Sanyal who could not but paid his homage by saying – "*Samaj jekhane sreni bibhakta muktikami manusher ladai sekhane abyahata. Ar ei abyahata ladaier gatipathe barbar uchcharita habe Jangal Santaler nam.*"[39] (i.e. ...where the society is stratified, the fight of the emancipationists would remain unending. And in this fighting-march the name of Jangal would be uttered all the time to come). If the after generation considers comrade Jangal Santal in this light and Indian history is written accordingly, it would be a great justice to this man and be a tribute to this son of India.

NOTES AND REFERENCES

1. Amiya K Samanta, *Left Extremist Movement in West Bengal: An Experiment in Armed Agrarian Struggle,* Firma KLM Private Limited, Calcutta, 1984.
2. Amiya K. Samanta has mentioned the name only but no detailed account has been given about Jangal Santal.
3. Marius Damas, Approaching Naxalbari, Calcutta, 1991; *Spring Thunder Over India* (Anthology of Articles on Naxalbari) published by Arun Kumar Hnesh, Calcutta, 1985; C. R. Irani, *Bengal: The Communist Challenge,* New Delhi, 1968; Samar Sen et el (ed.), *Naxalbari and After: A Frontier Anthology,* vols. I and II, Calcutta, 1978; Sumanta Banerjee, *In the Wake of Naxalbari,* Kolkata, 2009 (second edition); Sankar Ghosh, *The Disinherited State (A Study of West Bengal), 1967-70,* New Delhi, 1971; Asoke Kumar Mukhopadhyay (ed.), *The Naxalites* through

the Eyes of the Police: Select notifications from the Calcutta Police Gazette, 1967-1975, Kolkata, 2006; Srila Roy, *Remembering Revolution: Gender, Violence, and Subjectivity in India's Naxalbari Movement*, New Delhi, 2012; Parimal Dasgupta, *Nakshalbarir Krishak Sangram Sutre Abartita Rajniti Ebang Tar Punaruththan O Punhapratishthar Samasya*, Calcutta, 1984; Azizul Haque, *Nakshalbari: Bikshobh-Bidraha-Biplab Ebang Rassia....*, Calcutta, 1991; Arun Prasad Mukherjee, *Maoist 'Spring Thunder': The Naxalite Movement (1967-1972)*, Kolkata, 2007; Swapan Kanti Ghosh (ed), *Rashtriya Santras (Nakshalbari Theke Netaigram)*, Kolkata, 2011; Amar Bhattacharya, *Lal Tamsuk (Nakshalbari Andolaner Pramanya Tathya- Sankalan)*, Kolkata, 2013 and so on.

4. Mention may be made a book edited by M. R. Akhtar Mukul titled *Nakshalder Shes Surya*, Dhaka, 1989.
5. Ashis Maitra et al (ed.), *Jangal Santal*, Calcutta, 1989, p.2. This book has recently been reprinted with the same title in 2007 from **Radical,** Kolkata. We have, however, utilized and followed the first edition of this book.
6. Sudirgha Sangramer Ekti Utkrishta Phasal – Jangal, a lecture by Kanu Sanyal delivered on 24.12.1988 at Tripura Hitasadhani Hall, Calcutta, incorporated in the book *Jangal Santal* edited by Ashis Maita et el, Calcutta, 1989,(henceforth Kanu Sanyal), p.1.
7. *Ibid.*
8. *Ibid.*, p.2.
9. *Ibid.*
10. *Ibid.*
11. *Ibid.*
12. *Ibid.*
13. *Ibid.*, p.3.
14. *Ibid.*
15. *Ibid.*
16. *Ibid.*, p.4.
17. *Ibid.*
18. *Ibid.*
19. *Ibid.*, p.3.
20. *Ibid.*, p.4.
21. *Ibid.*, p.15.

22. This information has been given by Souren Basu in Ashis Maitra et al (ed.), *op.cit.*, p.8.
23. *Ibid.*, p.8.
24. A Bengali article by Sauren Basu, Chhinnabandhan Pramithues in Ashis Maitra et al (ed.), *op.cit.*, p.9.
25. *Ibid.*
26. *Ibid.*, p.10; and also the article titled Jangal Santal: Ek Sangrami Anuprerana by Asim Chattopadhyay in Ashis Maitra et el (ed.), op.cit. p.15. Comrade Asim Chattopadhyay has nicely stated the uselessness of this politics of terrorism vis a vis murder and bloodshed. From his experience he has noted that some comrades of the movement along with himself had wanted to materialize this course of action in some border areas of Bengal, Bihar and Orissa. But he admits that everywhere he experienced the irrelevance of such a line of action.
27. *Ibid.*, p.16.
28. For details see Jangalda Ekta Siksha, Ekta Pratik by Azizul Haque in Ashis Maitra et al (ed.), *op.cit.*, p.20.
29. Sauren Basu, Chhinnabandhan Pramithues in Ashis Maitra, et el (ed.), *op.cit.*, p.10.
30. Azizul Haque op.cit. in Ashis Maitra et al (ed.), *op.cit.*, p.20.
31. *Ibid.*
32. Pradip Banerjee, Kingbadantir Nayak: Jangal Santal in Ashis Maitra et al (ed.), *op.cit.*, p.31.
33. *Ibid.*
34. Kanu Sanyal, p.4.
35. Sajal Basu, *Politics of Violence- A Case Study of West Bengal*, Calcutta, 1982, p.105.
36. Kanu Sanyal, *op.cit.*, p.3.
37. *Ibid.*
38. Jayanta Choudhury, Jangal Santal (a Bengali poem), *Aneek,* edited by Dipankar Chakraborty, Khagra (Murshidabad), February, 1989, p.8.
39. Kanu Sanyal, *op.cit.*, p.7.

7

Was the British Hill Station an Isolated Retreat? A Case Study of Kurseong

Nupur Das

What were the implications of the integration of the hill stations into the social fabric of the British India? The first generation of social historians to study the British Colonial community tended to potray it as socially cohesive, composed mainly of upper middle class officials intersected with scattered pockets of planters and merchants.[1] The culminating approach of this study was its emphasis on the homogeneity and high social standing of the colonizers.

Today a huge number of scholars have totally demolished previous interpretations. Many generations of modern historians has shown that the British Indian population in the hill stations was far less homogenous then previously supposed and was fractured into many occupational, ethnic groups with disparate interests and concerns.[2] The main argument of this study is that hill stations were at the heart of the British effort to define and defend their boundaries that set them apart from Indians and that it sustained their identity as agents of a superior culture.[3] The construction of those qualities that distinguish 'us' from 'them'. This act happened when the British turned their attention to the Indian mountains. The decision to establish health sanitariums was a significant step in the forms of differentiation they created in the medico climatic terms that most British expatriate could appreciate at a visceral level. The hills were cool, the plains hot; the hills were healthy, the plains were disease ridden; the hills therefore were safe the plains dangerous. The contrat became all the more evident when nature took a front seat in the highlands. They privileged the sites and the hill stations culminated into places of beauty and splendour; places that resembled a home away from home—they made their resemblance compelling by adding artificiality in the form of colonial cottages, malls, clubs, churches introducing various aesthetic preferences in the physical environment. The hill stations were thus settings where they could renew their sense of themselves as members of a common community.[4]

Like the moment when Hillary and Tenzing first set foot a top the Everest the British too were faced with the task of defining and delimiting the boundaries of the community. In nearly all the hill stations the British created environments that reminded them of their homeland and heritage that bound them together. Comments John Abraham Francis Hawkins in his Second Report from the Select Committee on Colonization and Settlement [India] in 1858 session. The geopolitical isolation of the colonized population, creating an illusionary escape from rebellions, disease heat and degeneration. The social structure created British patterns of behaviour like get-togethers, parties, picnics lunches and other forms of entertainment that set the wheels of social interaction in movement. The demographic disequilibrium was further equated by drawing large number of women to the hill stations where emphasis was laid on love matrimony children and family. The ideological commitment and sense of duty was transferred from one generation to the next through the various educational institutions modeled on the English public schools. Birth, education, courtship, marriage, retirement, death most of the major transition in the lifecycle of the colonizers occurred with far greater frequency in the hill stations than anywhere else in the India. These were the places where the British in India went to cultivate a shared identity as a ruling race and to perpetuate its properties over time.[5]

In its final analysis a contradiction occurs, and this very contradiction can be seen in the history of the hill stations in India. These very remote and exclusive enclaves were not immune to the forces that overturned the Raj. On the contrary they were an example of many of the contradictions of the British endeavour. They were created to provide a heaven from contact with the Indian masses, but they depended on these very Indian masses for their construction and maintenance. They meant to provide a setting in which the government could exercise its authority, but they isolated the very government from the public interest. They were meant to be centers where they could define themselves according to an exclusive standard of cultural values, but instead they attracted a westernized Indian elite whose adoption of some values created dents on the British claims on exclusivity. So the hill stations must be considered not only in terms of the social history of the British but of the Indians as well. The testimony to the fact that they have not just survived but thrived since independence. It is in this background a case study of Kurseong situated at present in the district of Darjeeling in the state of West Bengal has been under taken. The *Imperial Gazetteer of 1901* mentions Kuseong town as a subdivision of Darjeeling District Bengal situated in 26^{0}53 N and 88^{0}17 E on the Lower Himalayas 4860 feet above the sea about 20 miles south of Darjeeling. Population (1901) 4469. The town is situated on the "Darjeeling HImalayan Railway" and is a centre of the tea trade. It was constituted a municipality in 1879.[6] By the turn of the century Kurseong lost its maze of aloofness like most of the hill stations in India an instead of being an exclusive European enclave was in turn surrounded by Indians in every sphere. From the beginning developments in Kurseong generated demands for native labour. Roads, Railways, Municipal reservoir, public offices, sub jail with an accommodation for 24 prisoners and a dispensary with 16 beds. The principal educational institutions namely the Victora Boy's School founded in 1879 started with 15 pupils as a co-educational in 1879 at Constantia on the Parkha Bari Road. and the Dow Hill Girl's School founded in 1898 and and at the opening in the 1898, the school had 80 children and only one staff of a Head Mistress, 5 junior mistress and a matron each relied upon the Indians for its basic developments.[7] McGrath's Census of 1872 shows that in Kurseong out of a total population of 4469—3231 were Indians[8] —suggesting the fact that at least ten Indians were necessary to support each European. Most of the initial labour force came from the surrounding hills. The *Imperial Gazetteer of 1902* mentions the local trade of Kurseong is practically confined to supplying the wants of the tea plantations. A considerable trade is carried out by the hill men. The British found the intrusion of these people highly problematic. They came in such large numbers from such varied origins that it was almost impossible to 'know' and manage them.[9] They stayed together in crude crowded quarters along narrow lanes that were impenetrable to municipal authoroties. Municipal records of 1905[10] of Kurseong mentions that coarse cotton cloth is woven by all the aboriginal tribes, especially by the Lepcha. There are breweries at Sonada and S.T. Mary's Kurseong and the out turn of beer in 1903-4 was 70000 gallons. The railway works at Tindharia employ a daily average of 110 natives. The British were therefore presented with an ongoing dilemma, how to maintain the labour that made their life in the hill stations so pleasant without eroding their psychic and social walls that set them apart from the rest of India and that helped them sustain a common identity and purpose.

Nearly every European who went to the hill stations in the early years relied on local people for porterage services. It was not uncommon for a visitor to employ fifty or more men, the clothing, crockery and other effects needed for a season's stay in the hills. Apart from porterage—the opening of the stations to regular traffic depended on the construction of roads through rugged mountain terrain, and most of the muscle for this huge intensive enterprise came from neighbouring villages. In 1839 some twelve hundred local men were set to work on the Cart Road by Captain G.S. Lloyd.[10] The service economy too saw a seasonal influx of visitors in the form of domestic servants including *kitmatgars* (butlers), *khansamahs* (cooks), *malis* (gardeners), *dhobis* (washermen), *mehtars* (sweepers), *chokidars* (gaurds) and others. A dearth of Census data makes it difficult to determine the hill stations in the first half of the 19th century. Kurseong's population mushroomed from about 4469 in 1901 to 7451 in 1931 and the entire district (including Darjeeling and Kalimpong) experienced the most rapid rate of growth on record for 19th century Bengal expanding from 10000 in 1850 to nearly 250000 in 1901.[11]

The overwhelming majority of the Indians in the hill stations were adult males engaged in seasonal migrant labour. Where did this labour come from? Each hill station drew its migrant population from many sources. Although Darjeeling has been described as a 'Babel of tribes and nations'[12] suggesting ethnic diversity—this phrase is misleading. The tribe that dominated both Darjeeling and Kurseong were the immigrants from Nepal who formed 34% of the population of which 9% was concentrated in Kurseong.[13] Nepalis also came to this area to enlist in the army. It was the founding of the tea industry in the mid 1850s however that brought the inflow of Nepalis to full flow. According to the *District Gazetteer* compiled by A.J.Dash (chairman of the Public Commission Bengal) in 1947 in the chart below shows the percentage increase in population of Kurseong town.

Year	*Population*	*Increase percent*
1881	4033	
1891	3522	
1901	4469	27
1911	5574	25
1921	6445	16
1931	7451	16
1941	8497	14

The expansion due to the development of tea will be appreciated when it is explained that in 1857 there was one tea garden around Kurseong started by Mr. Smith called Hope Town. In 1859 the Dhutaria garden was started by Dr. Brougham and between 1860 and 1864 many tea gardens around the surrounding areas in Kurseong grew up at a rapid speed—Ging, Ambutia, Badamtam, Makaibari, Pandam and Singell tea gardens were laid out in Kurseon. By 1902 the number of tea gardens around Kurseong increased to 25. While the labour force in the industry was 8000 in 1870, and 44279 in 1921, the distribution of Kurseong Thana was practically half. Nearly all of these tea workers—96% according to 1941 Census were Nepalis. In the hill subdivision of Kurseong as well as Kali pong the Nepalis constituted 86% the population. This race had come to dominate the district.[14] However in the townships of Darjeeling, Kurseong and Kalimpong the population was more heterogeneous. The coolies mostly comprised the Lepchas and Bhutias. Tibetans dominated hilly trade. Most of the merchants professionals and other middle class Indians in Kurseong were Marwaris, Biharis and Bengalis. Butchers were generally Muslim immigrants. Still two thirds of the station's population were Nepalis.[15]

The case study shows that like most of the other hill stations Kurseong acquired a totally different demographic and ethnic shape than the British had originally planned. Instead of remaining small and isolated from the influence of b British and Britishers—Kurseong became a bustling centre of administration, education, commerce and service.

Apart from the massive influx of labourers, the first Indians to establish some sort of presence in the hill stations were the princes. Drawn by the prestige and political might associated with these stations, a number of wealthy princes began to take up seasonal residence in the early 20th century. By 1902 many princes had already purchased the finest houses in Kurseong. The Burdwan Maharaja had sconsiderable property in Kurseong. Kakina House was purchased in 1920. Kakina was a native state in Rangpur now Bangladesh. Chachal Maharaja of Malda, West Bengal along with Shantabir Lama the prince of Elam now modern Nepal too purchased properties in and around Kurseong.[16] The princes however, were not the only Indians to enter the hill stations, a growing number of elites were entering the hill stations in the late 19th and early 20th centuries. With the extension of railways there numbers doubled. India's prominent nationalists the Boses, namely the brothers Sarat and Subhas Chandra Bose purchased a summer retreat in Kurseong in 1923. By 1924 Gol Kuthi on the Dow Hill Road was purchased by Junimal Goenka where resided Abinandranath Tagore and the poet Atul Prasad Sen. In 1933 Head of the Department of Pali occupied Udayan where resided Sistern Nivedita. Haq Manzil came into existence in 1931 under the properietorship of Fazlul Haq Chief Minister Undivided Bengal. Similarly Apoorva Villa was purchased by Barrister

B.B.Das in 1928, Romola Villa by B.C.Sen I.C.S. in 1920. Bunglows were also purchased by Biswas & co. gun dealers in 1921, Civil Surgeon Mr. Bal in 1928. Nalini Sarkar—finance Minister of undivided Bengal under Fazlul Haq too purchased a bunglow in the early 20th century at Kurseong.[17]

Soon Kurseong too like the rest of the hill stations in India started loosing its reputation as an exclusive retreat only for the Britishers. The presence of upper and middle class Indians sought to inhabit the same social space that the Britishers themselves occupied. Unlike the common laborers whose places in the hills were clearly demarcated, this could not be done with the members of the Indians elite.

The Indianization of Kurseong began long before India obtained independence in 1947. Its origin can be traced, as the case study shows to the late 19th century when labourers, middle class and westernised Indians began to reach Kurseong in large numbers. These people posed the greatest threat to the insular world that the British had established for themselves in the hills like Kipling's snide remark about the "Babus-stealing to Darjeeling" in his poem 'A Tale of Two Cities' evidenced the growing popularity. But none of these advances were liked by the British. They viewed their sharers with distrust and aversion. Far more than porters, servants and labourers, the Indian upper and middle class penetrated into the heart of the hill stations. They purchased land, occupied houses, imvolved themselves in the principal affairs and shattered the British illusion that the hill station was a realm apart from the rest of India. Once this illusion evaporated, it was only a matter of time before the Britishers began to pack their bags and leave as proves the numerous sale deeds in Kurseong.

NOTES AND REFERENCES

1. Philip Woodruff, *The Men who Ruled in India,* Vol 1, reprint (New York, 1964).
2. Francis G Hutchins, *The Illusion of Permanence British Imperialism in India* (Princeton 1967).
3. Ann Laura Stolen, *Rethinking Colonial Categories European Communities and the Boundaries of Rule,* 1987, p. 152-154.

4. Dane Kennedy, *The Magic Mountains—Hill Stations and the British Raj* (Delhi, 1996), pp. 175-179.
5. Dane Kennedy, *The Magic Mountains—Hill Stations and the British Raj* (Delhi, 1996), p. 180-187.
6. *The Imperial Gazetteer of India,* Oxford Clarendon Press, 1908.
7. Dick B. Dewan, *Education in the Darjeeling Hills—An Historical Survey : 1885-1955,* New Delhi, 1991, p. 129.
8. Mr. C.T. Magrath's, District Census Compilation.
9. Emily Eden, *Up the Country, Letters From India,* 1930, reprint, London, 1984, p. 162.
10. H. Hosten, *The Centenary of Darjeeling, Bengal Past and Present,* London, 1930.
11. L.S.S. O'Malley, *Bengal District Gazetters, Darjeeling,* Logos Press, New Delhi, 1907 (reprint 1977).
12. L.S.S. O'Malley, *op.cit.,* p. 41.
13. Dr. Lathami's, *Ethnology of India,* London, 1859.
14. W.W.Hunter, *A Statistical Account of Bengal,* Vol. 10, London, 1876, p. 53.
15. Tanka B. Subba, *Dynamics of Hill Society,* Delhi, 1989.
16. Municipal Records, Kurseong Municipality, 1930.
17. *Settlement Records,* Depar.

8

Changing Economic Status of the Rajbanshis from Domination to Alienation: A Case Study of Northern Part of West Bengal

Madhab Chandra Adhikary

I

The Rajbanshis are considered the most important indigenous group inhabiting at the northern part of West Bengal, comprising the districts of Cooch Behar, Jalpaiguri, Darjeeling North and South Dinajpur and Malda. According to Census Report 1981, the Rajbanshis constitute 19% of total of Scheduled Caste population of West Bengal. Out of the total Rajbanshis of North Bengal, about 74% lives in Cooch Behar, 32% in Jalpaiguri, 13% in North and South Dinajpur and 8% in Darjeeling and Malda districts. Therefore, the major concentration of the Rajbanshis is in the districts of Cooch Behar and Jalpaiguri. The sex ratio of the Rajbanshis of North Bengal is 952 females per 1000 males (1971 Census). The Rajbanshis is one of the major Scheduled Castes in West Bengal.[1] Out of total 2258760 Rajbanshis in West Bengal, 77.19 percent of them are found to live in the northern part of the state known as North Bengal. Some scholars believe that North Bengal is the homeland of the Rajbanshis and since long as a local community, have been dominating the ethnic situation of this climate.[2]

II

Economically the Rajbanshis are more dependent on primary sector, i.e. agriculture. The agricultural structures prevailing in different parts of Bengal varied widely. The Mughal land revenue system, the British land revenue reforms, the customary practices of different areas, and the ecological conditions largely determined the patterns of agrarian relations in different parts of Bengal. We may distinguish the Bengal agrarian structures into three categories-

i) peasant small holding system in Eastern Bengal, *ii)* the prevalence in Bengal and Central Bengal of vast personal demesne of lands cultivated by landless labourers, and *iii)* rich farmer-share-cropper system of Northern Bengal. Sugato Bose also frames the same structure of agrarian system of Bengal.[54] In the present section of our study the agrarian structure of North Bengal will be focused in which the Rajbanshis as a cultivating community are to be situated.

The *Jotedari-adhiari* system was dominant pattern of the agrarian relations in North-Eastern part of India. However, there are different parts of the region like –Dinajpur, Rangpur, parts of Jalpaiguri, which were permanently settled areas, and where zamindari system existed. There was no zamindari system in the Western Duars of Jalpaiguri and in Cooch Behar. The land was given to *jotedars* or rich farmers by the government in exchange of some undertaking to pay annual rent in these regions.[55] There were also variations of position and privileges enjoyed by the jotedars and other under tenants in different part of northern part of present West Bnegal.[56]

In pre-British time, there were vast stretches of uncultivated lands which were given to rich men at very low rents in order to motivate them to bring waste land under cultivation .This rich men gave the lands to poor cultivators, initially for no or minimum return. However, once cultivation started regularly the cultivators paid, generally in kind, 1/2% of produce to the original titleholder. Thus, the cultivators who reclaimed the wasteland become the sharecroppers and the rich men by virtue of their economic supremacy became the landlords.[57] During the British rule, this system of agricultural structure became much more popular among the substantial landholders.

The sharecropping system became popular in this region due to the scarcity of labour compared to the availability of land. It results that land is being less precious than labour.[58] Under this circumstance, the wastelands are attributed to a want of farmers, and common workers or porters cannot be procured without the utmost difficulty.[59] There were also other causes like rise in prices, purchase of land by money lenders, and merchants, effects of the war, and the depression- all contributed to the expansion of the share- cropping system. Landlords, particularly those who had no link with land, like traders, and moneylenders or upper caste gentry, preferred share-cropping because it ensured good returns without any direct involvement in the agricultural process. Thus, because of this gradual extension of the sharecropping system a highly stratified and complex agrarian structure developed in North Bengal.[60]

If we follow the agrarian structure of this region, we will find that the *Zamindar* was the top of the hierarchy. He got land from the government, subject to the payment of a fixed amount of revenue. Next to the *Zamindar*, there was the *jotedar* who got land from the *Zamindar*, subject to the payment of rent at prevailing rates. The rent paid by the *jotedar* was subject to enhancements.[61] Though the *jotedars* formed an exclusive group of landlords, there were differences among them in terms of amounts of land hold. There were very big *jotedars* as well as a good number of small *jotedars*. A. Beteille has observed that *jotedars* were not an economically homogenous group and there were both rich and poor *jotedars* owing or cultivating large as well as small lands.[62] There were enormous sizes of *jotes* in different parts of northern part of present West Bengal.[63]

III

There were different categories of land holders in northern part of present West Bengal.[64] However, the classes which were eventually recognized in law and by sufferance were four i.e; *jotedar,Chukanidar, Dar-chukanidar* and *Adhiar.*

Jotedar

A jotedar is a person who holds land directly of Government.

He is a tenant with a heritable and transferable title in his holding vested in him by the fact of possession with power to transmit this title to those to whom he sublets. He has the right to resettle of the land included in his *jote* on the expiry of the term of the settlement, but subject to an increase of rent.[65] His title to possession of the land included in his *jote* is, however, always subject to the superior right of government as proprietor to resume any portion required for public or other purpose or proportional abatement being made in the rental and compensation allowed for any payment improvement. A *jote* may be acquired by direct settlement, by purchase and by inheritance.

Chukanidar

The tenant immediately below the *jotedars* is the *chukanidar* or *mulandar*. The rent payable by him is fixed. His title to his holding is heritable and transferable. He is not allowed under the provisions of the *jotedar*'s lease to sublet the whole or any portion of the tenure under pain of immediate forfeiture of such tenure. But he is permitted to employ *adhiars*.[66] *Chukanidars* can not be ousted from his holding, except by order of a competent court, notwithstanding the fact that he may not have been twelve years on a jote. There is an unwritten land between him and his jotedar that he cannot be ousted from his land as long as he pays his rent.[67]

Dar-Chukanidar

This class of tenants hold direct from the *Chukanidars*. The tenure rights of this class of tenants were neither found relevant by the Bengal Government nor approved by it. In a letter sent by the Revenue Department to Mr. Sunder, the settlement officer, it was stated, "The Lt. Governor approves your proposal that the newly created under-tenure of *Dar-chukanidar* in the Duars estate should be absolutely ignored, as much as these tenures have been made contrary to the express order of the government".[68] The *dar-chukanidar* was the under tenant of *chukanidars*. All these under tenants had occupancy rights in Cooch Behar, but not elsewhere.[69]

Adhiar

Adhiars or *Prajas* are holders on the *metayer* system. They cultivate land immediately under the *jotedars, chukanidars* or a derivative *chukanidar*, but whatever the designation or status of the *adhiars* immediate superior be, he is known as the *adhiars giri,* half the produce of the land. The *giri* usually makes an advance of seeds and cash to the *adhiar,* which is adjusted when the produce is divided. The cattle and plough sometimes belong to the giri, sometimes to the *adhiars.* The legal status of various classes of *adhiars* unfortunately remained uncertain.[70] As the adhiars had to pay half of his produce, he was in a chronic state of debt and had very little means to improve his position. He had to take advance from his landlord to survive, and this the landlord realized with heavy interests during harvest time.[71] There were no doubt variations in the position of adhiars in different areas of North Bengal. However, it was in this section of the local peasantry who had to bear the major burden of exploitation by the state and the landlord.[72]

From the above discussion, it is cleared that the jotedars constituted the most dominant group in local agrarian social structure. An important to add in this context is the absence of non-cultivating upper caste gentry in this region under study. Some parts of Bengal there was a class of upper caste gentry who owned substantial amounts of land. They did not cultivate themselves, as manual labour was a matter of disrespect in society. They, however, enjoyed maximum power in society by virtue of their social and economic position. There was another situation in northern part of India. Till the advent of the ninetieth century most of the land in North Bengal was in the possession of the local people i.e.; the Koches, the Rajbanshis, the Mechs etc. Unlike the upper caste gentry, these local peoples did not face the problem of status inconsistency if they themselves cultivated the land. However, the situation began to change from the late ninetieth century with the migration of people in this region. They not only consolidated their position as non-cultivating gentry, but also came to form a middle class at the village level, as it was form the group that the majority of the Zamindari agents and the staff of the local cutchery were recruited. Taking advantages of the backwardness of the local cultivators or poor rayots, they began to exploits them. In this respect we may refer from the Rangpur settlement report as follows[73]

> "These men, of whom one or two are to be found in almost every village, are the leaders of the local factions who by a smattering of legal knowledge and ready wit have gained the confidence of their co-villagers. Often they are retained by the Zamindar's staff and in return for land at favourable rates of rent or even rent free they watch their interest".

IV

Thus, the non-cultivating *jotedars* increased day by day in this region and secured a dominant position in the local agrarian structure. Based on the settlement reports, Amit Mitra has shown the ethnic composition of the *jotedars* of the Falakata tahsil in Jalpaiguri district between the year 1894 and 1905 where the Rajbanshis held 40% of the total jotes in 1894 and around 34% in 1905.[74] There, were however, subsequent changes in the pattern of land control in North Bengal with the result that the Rajbanshis were gradually pushed out by the non-Rajbanshi land holders from their position of eminence. In 1911, only 1.2% of the Rajbanshis who had any occupation derived their income from rent. In Rajshahi division, which contained the major concentration of this caste population, they constituted only 10.68% of the rent-receivers, while, the representation of the Brahmins in this category amounted to 25.26 %.[75] Another example may be given here; one fairly big jotes (618 bighas) in the paragana Mekhliganj where Chunder Kishore Nandy was the proprietor of this jote. He leased out the entire jote to one Chutiram Doss, who after retaining 335 bighas and his direct management (Nij Chukanidars) sublet the rest to 10 Darchukanidars. By title (or family names), these were 7 Dosses, 1 Nasya, 1 Doss Mali and 1 Singh Doss. Thus a caste from Bengal obtained this *jote* and sublet the whole to nature inhabitants of Koch Behar, namely, a Rajbanshis (7 Dosses, 1 Doss Malli and 1 Singh Doss) and a native convert to Muslim (Nasya).[76]

The changes that were taking place in the economic share because of war, depression, and famine in Bengal also severely affected the existing pattern of land ownership in the North Bengal districts. The rise in prices of food grains, and other necessities, following the World War II, also seriously affected the middle and poor peasants and this culminated in the great Bengal famine. The beneficiary's from this crisis were the merchants, moneylenders, and speculators- those who also invested their capital in land. The result of this development was the transfer of land from small *jotedars* and middle peasants to rich farmers, moneylenders, and speculators.[77] In the North Bengal, large-scale transfer of land from the Rajbanshis to this non-Rajbanshis, which had started, from the late nineteenth century was only accelerated further by these later developments.

Another important reason for land transfer to the non-Rajbanshis was the migration of a large number of outsiders to different districts of North Bengal. At the earlier stage, the attraction of this region were the abundance of land, possibility of good business, job opportunities in Government offices as the local people were not in a position to compete with them, opening of tea gardens which provide job facilities for both the 'Babus' as well as labourers.[78]

Regular settlement work was undertaken and the Duars had been brought under regular administration providing security to the inhabitants. This administrative stability had particularly induced migration. However, most important factors that had encouraged the migration of the landed gentry were the land price of land and low rent compared to the situation in other parts of Bengal. Therefore, in the third settlement a large number of people who were not born to the soil could obtain lease could obtain lease from the Government as jotedars in the settled area.[79] Some ones acquired jotes through purchase. Escalation of land price caused by migration furthered transfer of jotes through sale to outside. In fact, the migrants were controlling many of the jotes paying revenue from Rs. 20 to 2000 per annum after the 1895 settlement in Western Duars.[80] Comparing the population statistics of the 1881 Census with that of 1891 one finds an increase of

114277 in the population of the Western Duars. The break up of the increased population, who were migrants, can be studied based on the following table.[81]

Table 1: Number, and place of migration

Place of Origin	*Number*
Darjeeling	1588
Dinajpur	505
Rangpur	10101
Kuch Behar	32224
From other Districts of Bengal Proper	11364
Bihar districts	8491
Orissa	292
Chhotnagpur	20341
Other Province	29371
Total	114277

Source: Sunder's Report; Gruning, Jalpaiguri District Gazetteers; Census Statistics, 1881and 1891.

This process continued as the 1901 Census shows that nearly one third of the inhabitants of Western Duars were foreign born and the figure of the migrants rose to 188223. All the migrants i.e; 73946 persons after 1818 have settled in different thanas of Western Duars.[82] Most of the migrants from Darjeeling, Bihar and Chhotonagpur have been employed by the tea gardens as workers. People from Dinajpur, Cooch Behar have taken up land as Jotedars. The census figure on migration for the period between 1891 and 1921(table No. 2) in Cooch Behar, Jalpaiguri and Darjeeling districts give us an idea of the volume of migration that was taking place in north eastern part of India.[83]

Table 2: Migration to Cooch Behar, Jalpaiguri and Dinajpur from contiguous and other District between 1891-1921

Year	*From contiguous District*		*From other districts to*	
	Male	*Female*	*Male*	*Female*
	Migration to Cooch Behar			
1891	12997	15191	3262	1201
1901	9161	12531	12668	2255

1911	11000	13000	5000	2000
1921	9000	12000	10000	6000
		Migration to Jalpaiguri		
1891	30920	27835	12431	7641
1901	24354	23856	65272	48636
1911	18000	15000	15000	10000
1921	21000	19000	5000	4000
		Migration to Dinajpur		
1891	22670	18819	9308	5894
1901	13901	13319	60143	34871
1911	19000	16000	12000	6000
1921	12000	13000	10000	7000

Source: A Mitra ,*West Bengal District Hand Book*, Calcutta 1951, Cooch Behar, P.XXXVi, Jalpaiguri,P.Lii, West Dinajpur, p. Xii.

This large influx of people not only led to a growing demand for land but also led to a rise in land prices. Local people, tempted by the spiraling prices soon began to sell their lands leading to the transformation of the local small and middle jotedars into under tenants, subservient to a new class of immigrant landed gentry. In Rangpur and Dinajpur, the big jotedars and non-agriculturists brought the maximum number of jotes.[84] In Jalpaiguri, the number of jotes held by the Rajbanshis are decreased, while the jotes held by the Marwaris, the upper caste Bengali, middle–class people, others are increased sharply[85] By 1872, in Cooch Behar 54% of the revenue paying land had passed into the hand of the outsiders.[86] Indeed all over North Bengal the phenomenon of transfer of land from the hands of the Rajbanshis to those of the non-Rajbanshis became a standard pattern and in course of time it generated a sense of grievance among the disposed Rajbanshi gentry.

V

Migration of population created demographic changes in an issue of concern while figures quoted by authorities are suspect it is pertinent to note that in the 20th century under British rule, immigration and migration, particularly into Assam ,North Bengal and Tripura,was probably to the extent of about 30% of the population of which about 2/3 was from East Bengal (Bangladesh).[87] Unfortunately, after independence this trend was allowed to continue, with the majority of the migrants, being from East Pakistan (present Bangladesh). In 1971 again was a major refugee exodus from East Pakistan (present Bangladesh), the majority of who never returned owing to the situation, which leads to the Indo- Pak war. The population growth of North Bengal may show in Table No. 3 during 1951-2001.

The table 3 shows that the decadal growth of the population of North Bengal in every district is higher than the growth rate of West Bengal. Darjeeling and West Dinajpur is most high rate. However, there are certain causes of growth rate of population in North Bengal. It is situated at national and international boundary and the media for communication with Eastern India. This geographical situation helps to induce the migration problem. Besides, in 1960 the Tibetan refugees settled in the Duars of North Bengal, the Bengalese from Assam came to North Bengal due 'Bangal Kheda Andolan' in 1960-61, Nepalese from Meghalaya and Bhutan were driven away who took shelter in India and the extensive pressure of migrants for Indo-Pak war in 1965. This influx of immigrants' people created an extensive pressure and crisis in socio-economic structure in North Bengal.[88] Marcus Dam says, "Indian authorities continue to thwart attempt by Bhutanese refugees back to their homeland. The problem of these displaced people is expected to snowball into a major geographical crisis in North Bengal specially Darjeeling and Jalpaiguri because they are sandwiched between Nepal and Bhutan".[89]

VI

In addition to the demographic changes, the policy of the West Bengal Government, particularly the land reforms programme had directly contributed to the growth of ethno-cultural regionalism in North Bengal. After the introduction of land Acquisition Act (1953), a large number of Jotedars of North Bengal lost their lands in excess to the limit of seventy-five bighas. *Khas* (vested) land had been distributed to the landless cultivators. Although the victim *zotedars* were mostly of the Rajbanshi community, but their caste fellows were not sole beneficiaries. Hence, there was a strong voice for the

Table 3

The Growth of Population from 1951-2001 (Population in Lakhs).

District	Area sq km	1951	1961	1971	1981	1991	2001	% of decadal growth (1971-81)	% of decadal growth (2001-2011)
Darjeeling	3,386	459.6	624.6	781.8	1,024.2	1299.9	1609.1	28.74	14.47
Cooch Behar	3,075	668.1	1,319.8	1,414.2	11,771.8	2171.1	2479.1	25.27	13.86
Jalpaiguri	6,224	916.7	1,369.3	1,750.1	2,214.8	2800.5	3401.1	26.11	13.77
West Dinajpur	5,206	976.9	1,323.8	1,857.9	2,404.9	*1897.0 **1230.6	*2441.7 **1503.1	29.19	*22.90 **11.16
Malda	3,313	937.6	1,221.9	1,612.7	2,031.8	2637.0	3290.4	26.19	21.50
West Bengal	21,625	3,959.7	5,549.4	7,418.7	9,447.6	68077.9	80176.1	22.96	13.93

Source: Census Reports

distribution of the vested land to the Rajbanshis only. Naturally, land alienation to the non-Rajbanshis began with the first phase of land reforms in West Bengal germinated the seeds of deprivation among the pre-settled communities of North Bengal.[90]

Second phase of land reform was undertaken in West Bengal with the coming the United Front (UF) Government in 1967. The UF Government during 1967-70 vested one million acre of land, which broken the backbone of social dominance of the landed aristocracy (zotedars) of West Bengal.[91] The zotedars of North Bengal could not escape from it. However, third phase of land reforms called "Operation Barga" under the Left Front Government was successful in vesting family land and recording 1.2 million of sharecroppers with in three years (1978 -81).[92] According to the official sources, 428179.95 hector vested land has been distributed among 2605432 beneficiaries. In North Bengal 170081.80 hectares vested land was distributed among 671841 beneficiaries out of whom 301498 are SCs and 144181 are STs.[93]

Land reforms and distribution of vested lands to the landless agricultural labourers by the UF and LF Governments had direct impact on the socio-economic pattern of the indigenous elites in North Bengal. Although SC/ST people were benefited by the land distribution process of the Government, the anti foreigner feelings and feelings of deprivation of the indigenous people were capitalized. Under this situation, the Rajbanshis were forced to migrate into the nearby urban areas and to the other province only to be absorbed into the marginalize section workers, domestic servants whose survival depended upon the selling of labour power. Alienation from their ancestral land and the transformation of Rajbanshi from land owing peasants to wage labour proletariats had various social connotations too and tension has been grown in North Bengal from time to time in respect of separate state and autonomous power in North Bengal. The self–sustain village community[94], however, began to change with the beginning of the commercialization of agriculture[95] particularly tea production, Jute, Tobacco production and the introduction of railways in North Bengal. The gradual penetration of moneylenders, merchants and middle-class service groups as appendages of the market economy, brought significant change in the existing agrarian social structure as well. However, the Rajbanshi who constitute the bulk of the adhiars in this region did not benefit from this transformation and they did not able to compete with the Caste Hindus.[96] There was also a tendency among the Rajbanshi adhiars to work under the jotedars of their own community and this is one of the causes of Rajbanshis economic depression. Another important causes of miserable economic condition among the Rajbanshis that they did not invest money in other economic fields than cultivation though the latter was not fit for modern cultivation system. As a result, it is to be mentioned here that after the abolition of Zamindari system in West Bengal (1953), the upper caste gentry would managed their economic crisis but the Rajbanshis could not.

The miserable condition of the Rajbanshis in the occupational field had been shown in census reports. From the table No.4 we may get a general impression about the occupational patterns of the Rajbanshis. There are, however, ambiguities in categorization and classification of different occupations in the census reports. The table shows that a small section of Rajbanshis was rent receivers and their representation in other subsidiary occupations was insignificant. An over whelming majority of them were various kinds of cultivators, including a vast section of adhiars and field labours. This makes one point adequately clear, that whatever be the magnitude, there was a vertical division within the Rajbanshi community along the economic lines.[97]

The Table No.5 also shows that the Rajbanshis of North Bengal mostly dependent on primary section.

The Table No.5 depicts that in 1981, 57.76 percent of Rajbanshi workers were cultivators, and 33.27 percent were agricultural labourers. Therefore, about 91 percent of the Rajbanshis workers were principally engaged in agriculture and allied activities. Among the Rajbanshi workers, although the cultivators outnumbered the agricultural labourers in all the districts, the ratio of latter to former was high in the districts of Darjeeling and West Dinajpur.

Table No.4: Occupational pattern of the Rajbanshis .[98*]

General Field

Income from labourers Rent of Land cutters		Cultivators off of all Kinds		Agent & Managers of landed Estates, Planters, Rent Collectors		Field workers	
Male	Female	Male	Female	Male	Female	Male	Female
3767	537	414812	9110	482	1	23230	385

Public Administration

Traders		Gazetted Officer		Others		Lawyers, Doctors Teachers		Religious persons	
Male	Female	Male	Female	Male	Female	Male	Female	Male	Female
3009	1863	18	(Not found)	116	2	497	2	610	39

Source: Census of India, 1911, Vol. V, pt II, Bengal ,Table XVI,PP.374-7.
Note: *Rajbanshis of Darjeeling, Cooch Behar, Faridpur and North Bengal are included.

Table 5: Percentage distribution of Rajbanshi workers into different occupational categories.

District	Census	I	II	III	IV	V	VI	VII	VIII	IX
Darjeeling	a	87.77	6.42	0.23	0.85	0.23	0.07	1.17	0.16	3.10
	b	55.13	23.75	12.83	0.40	0.51	0.20	2.24	0.88	4.06
	c	47.30	39.03	0.67	0.30	1.89	1.13	2.16	1.58	5.88
Jalpaiguri	a	89.40	4.09	0.98	0.86	0.39	0.15	1.03	0.43	2.61
	b	68.85	13.05	9.97	0.86	0.81	0.20	0.08	0.90	5.28
	c	57.06	32.77	0.84	0.41	1.37	0.29	1.35	1.93	3.98
Cooch Behar	a	89.89	5. 81	0.06	1.09	0.23	0.02.	0.57	0.12	2.21
	b	78.58	16.77	0.17	0.53	0.44	0.03	0.56	0.27	2.65
	c	59.89	32.21	0.25	0.74	1.50	0.14	1.13	0.88	3.26
W.Dinajpur	a	73.64	19.63	0.84	1.71	0.39	0.11	1.05	0.14	2.49
	b	64.50	29.64	0.86	0.37	0.74	0.06	0.83	0.32	2.68
	c	56.27	36.17	0.84	0.83	1.45	0.11	1.44	0.58	2.31
Malda	a	69.88	13.78	1.16	6.62	0.96	0.05	0.67	0.47	6.41
	b	39.45	30.19	6.68	5.85	3.93	0.58	6.63	1.26	8.43
	c	59.13	27.96	1.58	2.18	4.68	0.16	1.25	0.92	2.18
N.Bengal	a	87.03	7.04	0.53	1.29	0.34	0.08	0.82	0.25	2.62
	b	70.73	18.57	4.01	0.85	0.78	0.12	0.65	0.53	3.76
	c	57.76	33.27	0.63	0.71	1.61	0.22	1.31	1.16	3.33

Note: a=1961, b=1971, c=1981Censu;Occupational, category:I=Cultivators, II=Agricultural laboureres, III=Mining, quarrying, livestock, fishing, plantation etc;IV=Household Industry;V-Manufacturing other than household industry, VI=Construction;;VII=Trade and Commerce;VIII=Transport, storage and Communication;IX= Other Services.

Only about 9% of the Rajbanshi workers were engaged in various non-agricultural pursuits. However, excepting in manufacturing, trade and commerce, transportation, and other services, the proportion of Rajbanshi workers in remaining categories of occupation was less than 1 %. In 1981, about 2% of Rajbanshi workers were manufacturing industries and only 3.33 percent were in other services. Thus, it appears that up to 1981, the economic activities of the Rajbanshis of North Bengal were less diversified and they were dependent an agriculture.

In urban areas, about 59% of the Rajbanshi workers were dependent an agricultural activities. Little changes in the means of livelihood of the Rajbanshi who were otherwise urban by their residential background. The participation of the urban Rajbanshis in service was less 19%. The corresponding percentages were 32, 28 and 38 for the non-scheduled people, the other SC and the ST respectively.99 In the manufacturing field the participation of the Rajbanshis of this region is insignificant than the other section of the people. Overall, it appears that urbanization among the Rajbanshis was not accompanied by any significant change in their employment pattern.

Tapas Kumar Raychoudhry observes that the Rajbanshis were always prone to static. As all primitive communities, they were tied to family profession (agriculture) and were normally disinclined to changes professions.[100] He also says, when the tea gardens were opened the Rajbanshis never opted out to work as tea garden workers; this factor had compelled the planters to import labour from the tribal of Bihar and Chhotonagpur. The Railways too failed to induce the local people to work in railway construction programmes, though the wages were high. All the labourers used to come from the United Province and Bihar. Even during season time when a labour could have earned as much as Rs. 1.00 a day in jute Godwans, Rajbanshis labourers were not available.[101] Total abstentions from the non-family professions was the basic norms of the Rajbanshis milieu until the externals caused some important changes to be introduced in their attitude towards new professions. As they contact with the new forces of the society, a sense of exclusives gradually developed among the Rajbanshi elites, which created status differentiation with in the community.[102] Ultimately this Rajbanshi elite class played an important role to whip up this community consciousness in latter period in order to mobilize social and political movement.

VII

From the above discussion, it is to be mentioned here that in the late nineteenth and until the end of the twentieth century, some important changes had been taken place in the socio-economic structure of the region under review. One of the most significance changes was that the Rajbanshis who once dominated the local society and economy were gradually subordinated and alienated from land by the newly settled dominant upper caste Hindus (elites). This domination of an essentially immigrant gentry as well as the cultural differences between them and the Rajbanshis created a sense of community solidarity among the latter. The most articulate section of the Rajbanshi people, the elites took an important part to whip up the community consciousness in order to formulate socio-political organizations in the late nineteenth and early twentieth century Bengal. They raised a new identity based on social, political and linguistic problem and articulated movement in the form of autonomous and separate state movement after independence in North Bengal.

NOTES AND REFERENCES

1. As per the article of Constitution of India and the List of Scheduled Caste in Bengal under 1936,1950,1956 Orders.
2. Biman Dasgupta, A Note on the Rajbanshi of Eastern India with special reference to Social Movement in *Bulletin of Anthropological Survey of India* 18(I), p. 1; Accoding to the Census of 1921 out of total Rajbanshis 89% were found in North Bengal, Part I, Bengal Report, p. 357.
3. R.S.Mukhopadhyaya, Socio-economic Transformation of the Rajbanshis and Kamatapuri Movement in North Bengal, *Journal of Indian Anthropology, and Sociology*, 1995, Vol.30, p. 223. 4. Census of India 1951,1961,1971,1981,1991; Surajit Kumar

Chakraborty (ed):*The Scheduled Castes in India,* Vol. 3, pp1159 1160, N.Delhi, Gyan Publishing House.

5. Census Report of India, 1872, 1891, 1901, 1911, 1921 ,1931, 1941, 1951, 1961, 1971, 1981,1991, Government of India.
6. B. Mukherjee, Socio-economic and Religious Organization of the Rajbanshi, *Bulletin of the Anthropological Survey of India,* Vol. XII, Nos.1 and 2, 1963, p. 65: Charu Chandra Sannyal, *The Rajbansis of North Bengal,* Calcutta, 1965, p,124; Swaraj Basu, *Dynamics of a Caste Movement:The Rajbansis of North Bengal (1910-1947);* New Delhi, 2003, p.41.
7. Being as a Rajbanshi ,the author has much experience about the matter.
8. Charu Chandra Sannyal, *op.cit.,* p. 125.
9. W.V. Schendal, *Peasant Mobility : The Odds of life in Rural Bangladesh,* Delhi, 1982, p.69.
10. H.H.Risley, *The Tribes and Castes of Bengal,* Vol. I, rpt. Calcutta, 1981, p. 494.
11. Swaraj Basu, *op.cit.,* p.41.
12. Charu Chandra Sannyal, *op.cit.,* p.20.
13. *Ibid.,* p.21.
14. Khakrabhat- cooked rice kept over night without addition of water to it. Pantabhat- cooked rice kept over night with addition of water to it.
15. Charu Chandra Sannyal, *op. cit.,* p.29.
16. It is only in the transplanting of paddy season that the mid day meal is carried to the field when the cultivators have hardly any time to come back. It is done in July- August for about twenty days.
17. Bhuti is a thick and long rape made of paddy straw, which is kept slowly burning all day and night, used for lighting a *biri* or prepared tobacco in a *chillim.*
18. Charu Chandra Sannyal, *op.cit.,* pp. 29-30.
19. Sekh Rahim Mandal, Rokaiya Begum, Status of Rajbanshi Women in West Bengal :Problem and Prospects; *Bulletin of the Cultural Research Institute,* Vol. XIX, No. 3, 1997, pp.49-52.
20. D.H.E. Sunder, Report on the Survey and Settlemnet in the Western Duars in the Jalpaiguri District, 1889-1895, Calcutta, 1895, p 48; J.Ray, Economic and Social Customs of the Rajbanshis, *Modern Review,* August 1954, p.133.

21. Sekh Rahim and Rokeya Begum, *op. cit.*, p. 52.
22. *Ibid.*, p. 54; Charu Chandra Sannyal, *op. cit.*, p.173.
23. J.F.Grunning, *Eastern Bengal and Assam District Gazetteers: Jalpaiguri,* Allahabad, 1911, pp. 32-33; F.W. Strong, *Bengal District Gazetteers: Dinajpur,* Allahabad, 1912, pp. 34-43; Risley, *op.cit.*, pp. 494-7.
24. Charu Chandra Sannyal, *op. cit.*, p. 91; W.W. Hunter, *Statistical Account of Bengal,* Vol. X, 1876, rpt.1984, p. 374.
25. Charu Chandra Sannyal, *op. cit.*, p. 88; Swaraj Basu, *op.cit.*, Says in ghor-dzia- biha an Orphan or a poor boy who could not pay the bride-price was kept in ,the house of a girl and after sometime, it the girl's father was satisfied with the nature and behaviour of the boy, he was married to his daughter in a regular form of marriage.
26. Charu Chandra Sannyal, *op.cit.*, p.95.
27. *Ibid,* p. 96; Swaraj Basu, *op.cit.*, p.43.
28. B. Mukherjee, Socio- Economic and Religious Organization of the Rajbanshi, pp.68- 9; M. Ray, Economic and Social Custom of the Rajbanshiis, pp.131-2; Charu Chandra Sannyal, *op.cit.* pp.95-8; S.Basu, *op. cit.*, pp. 42-3.
29. Charu Chandra Sannyal, *op.cit.*, p.99.
30. B. Mukherjee, *op.cit.*, p.63; B.Dasgupta, *op.cit.*, pp.11-12.
31. Charu Chandra Sannyal, *op.cit.*, pp.92-94; The author himself married with the daughter of a Kayastha family at Cooch Behar town and proves that there is no social barrier and also family affairs in his personal life.
32. Charu Chandra Sannyal, *op.cit.*,p.99; Basu, *op.cit.*, p.43; S.R. Mandal and R. Begum, *op.cit*, p.52.
33. J.A.Vas, *Eastern Bengal and Assam District Gazatteers: Rangpur,* Calcutta, 1911, p.44.
34. Risley, *op.cit.*,p.498; Girijasnakar Roy, *Uttarbanger Rajbanshi Kshatriya Jatir Puja Parban,* First Edn. 1970, rpt.1991, pp.12-91; *Encyclopaedic Ethnography of the Himalayan Tribes,* pp. 1344-1345; *Baitanik* (Bengali) (ed), Gautam Ray, pp.247-256, Siliguri, 2004. Some of the God and goddess among the Rajbanshis society are given below.

    Tista Buri : Goddess of the River

    Madar or Satyapir : Islamic deity adopted by the Hindus

    Haribhola : Vaishnava deity

    Sannyasi: Saiva deity

Sona Rai : God of wild animal

Hudum Deo : Rain God

Madan Kam : God of Procreation; This was worshipped in every village is a place away from homes and goats and pigeons were offered as scarifices.

Kali : Female Shakti energy

Devi Chandi: Female shakti energy

Vishari : Snake deity

Bhandani : Mother goddess for good crop in the field

Masan : Malicious sprit.

35. *Encyclopaedic Ethnography of the Himalayan Tribes,* p,1344.
36. Risley, (in Microfilm), Real No.5,NAI, Delhi; *Encyclopaedic Ethnograpohy of the Himalayan Tribes,* p. 1344.
37. G.S. Ray, *op.cit.*, pp.1-2; Charu Chandra Sannyal categories the adhikari as Pad-dhari and Kantulsi, *op.cit.*, p. 134.
38. G.S.Roy, *op.cit.*, pp.2-3; Charu Chandra Sannyal, *op.cit,* p.134; S.Basu, op.cit., pp.43-44.
39. G.S.Ray, *op.cit.*, pp.4-5.
40. Charu Chandra Sannyal, *op.cit.*,p.123; Mukherjee, *op.cit.*, p.77.
41. L.S.S.O' Malley, Census of India, 1911, Pt-I, Subsidiary Table VI, p.373.
42. Census of India, 1911, Vol. V, Pt. II Bengal, Table-IX, p.84.
43. Census of India, 1921, Table-IX, Education by Selected Castes Tribes or Races concluded, Vol. 5, part- II, p.96.
44. R.S. Mukhapadhyaya, The Rajbansis of North Bengal: A Demographic Profile,1951-1981, *North Bengal University Review* (Humanities and Social Science, 1997, p. 15.
45. ___________, Socio- economic Transformation of the Rajbanshis and Kamatapuri Uttarkhanda Movement in North Bengal, *Journal of Indian Anthropology and Sociology,* Vol. 30, 1995, p.224.
46. Karyabibarani, Kshatriya Samity :4th Annual Conference, 1320 B.S., p.19.
47. Sri Panchanan Sarkar, secretary, Karyabibarani, 4th Annual Conference : Kshatriya Samity, 1320 B.S. p. 18; S.Basu, *op.cit.*, p.44; Madhab Chandra Adhikary, Artho- Samajik Prekshapate Rajbanshi Samaj (1947-79): Ekti Samiksha, (in Bengali) The Confederation of Rajbnashi Kshatriya Societies, First State Conference, Smarak Grantha, Calcutta, 2004, p.30.
48. Sunders, *op.cit.*, p.90; Vas, *op.cit.*, pp. 131-132; Grunnings, *op.cit.*, p.139; D.N. Sarkar, Rai Sahib Panchanan (Bengali), Rangpur,

1391B.S. pp.35-36.

49. Shib Shankar Mukhopadhaya, Jalpaiguri Jelar Samajik Kathamo, *Madhuparni* (Bengali) Jalpaiguri Special Number, 1987, p.153-154; M. Kabyabhusan, *Rajbanshi Kshatriya Deepak* (Bengali) Dinajpur, 1318 B.S. pp.40-41.
50. Charu Chandra Sannyal, *op.cit.*, pp.27-32.
51. The author had taken an interview with Sri Ramoni Mohan Ray (78) Member of the Rajbanshi Kshatriya Society, Head teacher of Kashaldanga Primary School, Falimari Gram Panchayet, Cooch Behar (26.12.2003)
52. Shib Shankar Mukhopadhyaya, Cooch Beharer Samajik Kathamo: *Madhuparni* (Bengali), Cooch Behar Special Number, 1990, p.110.
53. Kabyabhusan, *op.cit.*, pp. 48-49 complied on Swaraj Basu, *op.cit.*, p. 47.
54. Sugata Bose, *Agrarian Bengal, Economy, Social Structure and Politics 1919- 47*, Cambridge, 1986, p.33.
55. R.Ray, *Change in Bengal Society; 1760-1850*, Delhi, 1979, p. 203.
56. J.A. Miligan, *Final Report of the Survey and Settlement Operations in the Jalpaiguri District; 1906-1916*, Calcutta, 1920, Appendix, pp. xxi, xxvi; A.C.Hartly, *Final Report on the Rangpur Survey and Settlement Operation, 1931-38*, Calcutta, 1940, pp.54-55; H.N. Choudhury, *The Cooch Behar State and Its Land Revenue Settlement*, Cooch Behar, 1903, pp.511-514.
57. Sugata Bose, *op.cit.*, pp,11-12; A .Cooper, *Sharecropping and Share Croppers Struggles in Bengal, 1930-1950*, pp.26-28.
58. S. Taniguchi, Structure of Agrarian Society in Northern Bengal, 1765-1800, Unpublished Thesis, Calcutta University, 1977, pp. 205-206.
59. F.B. An Account of the District of Dinajpur, 1808-09 cited in A. Mitra, *District Hand Book West Dinajpur, 1951*, Appendix-III, pp. ii-vii.
60. S.Basu, *op cit.*, p. 48.
61. W.W.Hunter, *A statistical Account of Bengal*, Vol.-VII, 1876, First rept. 1974, rept. 1984, p.279.
62. A.Beteille, *Studies in Agrarian Social Structure*, Delhi, 1979 1st edn, pp.135-6.
63. Beckett in his settlement Report that the average size of a jote in Mekhligange subdivision of Cooch Behar was 79 acres (Preceding of Revenue Department, July,1872 Vol. 210) whereas Sunder reported that the average size of a jote in Western

Duars was 38.6 acres. W.A.O Backett *Completion Settlement Report of Pergunnah Mecklingange,* Cooch Behar, 1874, p,v; D.H.E. Sunder, *op.,cit.,* p.118.

64. Tweedie, First Deputy Commissioner of Jalpaiguri District in his report, Land Tenure of Western Duars he has mentioned three categories of tenures- *jotedars, chukanidars,*and farm labourers; Revenue Department Proccedings,1866; Mr. Nalon, the commissioner of the Rajshahi Division recognized that only two categories of tenants –viz, *jotedars* and *adhiars,* the other classes namely *chukanidars* or *Dar-chukanidars* were introduced at later phase or might have emerged on account of the amulgamation of *prajas* and *rayats* mentioned by Tweedie; Nalon, Note written in the Settlement Report on D.H.E. Sunder, 1895.
65. Sunder, *op.cit.,* p.118
66. *Ibid,* p.118.
67. T.K. Ray Choudhury, Land Control: Class Structure and Class Relations in Western Duars (1811-1905); *Journal of Asiatic Society of Bangladesh,* Vol.XXXII, No.1, June 1987, p.27; Basu, *op. cit.,* p.49.
68. Sunder, *op.cit.,* p.118.
69. W.W. Hunter, *op.cit.,* Vol.X, p.389; Sunder, *op.cit.,* p.119.
70. J.F. Grunning, *Jalpaiguri District Gazetteer,* Allahabad, 1911; F.O.Bell, Final Report on Survey and Settlement Operation in the District of Dinajpur, 1930-40, Calcutta, 1941, p.22.
71. Hartly, Rangpur Settlement Report, pp. M-15.
72. Special Report from the Jalpaiguri Deputy Commissioner, dt. 2nd August 1872 Extensively cited in Hunter's *A Statistical Account of Bengal,* Vol.X, pp, 286-92; Basu, *op.cit.,* p.49.
73. Hartly, *Rangpur Settlement Report, op. cit.,* pp. 14-15.
74. A. Mitra, Emergence of a Land Market in Jalpaiguri (North Bengal)in the early Twentienth Century, Occasional Paper IV, Centre for Social Studies, Surat, 1986, p.12, cited in Basu's *Dynamic of a Caste Movement,* p.51; Ray Choudhury, *op.cit.,* p.35.
75. Census Report of India 1911, Vol. V, pt.I, p.574;Vol.V, pt. II, Appendix to Table XVI, p. 379.
76. Proceeding of the Revenue Department, June 1873, No.8o cited in (ed) P.K.Bhattacharjee, *The Kingdom of Kamta Koch Bihar in Historical Perspective,*article written by Shinkichi Taniguchi, A Perspective into the Changing Agrarian Structure in the

Koch Behar Princely State During the 13th Century, pp.182-183.

77. Sugata Bose, *op.cit.*, pp.58-69, 87-97, 134-140; Cooper, *op.cit.*, pp.37-62.
78. Charu Chandra Sannyal, Chatrader Prati(Bengali) ,Phamplet Published from Jalpiguri, N,D, pp.1- 3 ; R. Dasgupta, *Economy, Society and Politics in Bengal, Jalpaiguri 1869-1947*, Calcutta, 1992, pp. 31-32.
79. T.K. Roy Choudhury, *op.cit.*, p.35.
80. *Ibid.*, p.36.
81. Sunder, op.cit.; Grunning, *Jalpaiguri District Gazetteers;* Census Report 1881 and 1891.
82. Gruning, *op.cit.*, p,32.
83. A. Mitra, *West Bengal District Hand Books*, Calcutta,1951, Cooch Behar, p,xxxvi, Jalpaiguri, p. iii, West Dinajpur, p.xii.
84. Bell, *op.cit.*, p.26; Hartley, *op.cit.*, p.22.
85. V. Xara, Evolution of Agrarian Stucture and Relations in Jalpaiguri District (W.B), *Sociological Bulletin*, Vol. 29, No.I, 1980, p.77; Roy Choudhury,*op.cit.*,pp.13-17; Mitra, *Emergence of a Land Market in Jalpaiguri (North Bengal) in the Early Twentieth Century*, pp.10-13.
86. Sekhar Sarkar, Land Settlement and Revenue Administration and Taxation under the Maharajas of Cooch Behar, Unpublished Ph.D.Thesis, NBU, 1990, pp.vii-32; Ray, *Change in Bengal Agrarian Society*, pp.203-4.
87. *The Statesman*, 29.1.2005.
88. Sixth Central Conference Proceeding, UTJAS, Dinhata, 1991,p.10; Itihas Anusandhan-19, Pashimbanga Itihas Samsad,2005, pp.339-40.
89. Marcus Dam, Bhutanese Refugees and Indian Game Politics, *The Statesman*, 02 .02.1996.
90. Rupkumar Barman, *Contested Regionalism*, Abhijeet Publications, N. Delhi, 2007, p. 128.
91. D.Banerjee, Land Reforms in West Bengal, Remembering Harekrishna Kongar and Benoy Choudhury, *EPW*, Vol. XXXVI, No.21 and 22, p.1797.
92. *Ibid.*, p.1797.
93. Department of SC and ST Welfare Government of West Bengal; Hataman jara Tulechhe Shir (Bengali), Calcutta, 1987, p. 7; Dinesh Chandra Dakua, *Kamtapuri Andolon Ekti Jana Bichhinna*

Andolan, Calcutta, National Book Agency, Pvt. Lt. 2003, pp.30-31.

94. Roy Choudhury, *op.cit.*, p. 2; U.N.Barman, *Uttar Banger Sekal O Amar Jeevan Smite (Bengali)*, Jalpaiguri, 1392, B.S., pp. 1-15; Land was surplus, while cultivation was still had being conducted in a traditional way. Communication system had not been properly developed, there was no proper connection of different markets, need of production was determined largely by the need for the production of the consumption.
95. V. Xara, *op.cit.*, p.72; Ray Choudhury, *op.cit*, p.38.
96. Adhikary, op.cit., p.34; Basu, *op.cit.*, p,53; K.Bhattacharya, Rajbanshi and Dhimal: Struggle Stories Contemporary Socio-economic Survey of two Indigenous Communities of North Bengal, Calcutta, 2005, p. 23.
97. Sarkar, *op.cit.*, p.35.
98. Census of India, 1911, Vol. V,Pt. II, Bengal, Table XVI, pp.374-377.
99. R.S. Mukhopadhyaya, Socio-ecnomic Transformation of the Rajbanshis and Kamatapuri Uttarkhanda Movement in North Bengal, p.226.
100. Ray Choudhury, *op.cit.*, p.45.
101. J.F.Gruning, *op.cit.*, p.96.
102. Ray Choudhury, *op.cit.*, pp.45-46; Shib Shankar Muhkopadhyaya, *Cooch Beharer Samajik Kathamo, op. cit.*, p.110.

9

Migratory Labour in the Tea Gardens of North Bengal : A Socio-Economic Study

Md. Gholam Kibria

Objective:

The objective of the study is to find out the causes of labour migration from other parts of India to Bengal, specially in the Tea gardens of North Bengal. The socio-economic impact of this migration of huge labour force in North Bengal is of great historical importance and therefore along with that economic and social status of migratory labour is also taken into consideration with the help of different reports, books and periodicals.

Justification of the Study:

Tea is one of the important plantation industries of North Bengal. It is one of the oldest industries of Bengal next to coal. The industry flourished rapidly in this region due to climatic condition, cheap migratory labour and demand of tea in the home market and abroad. Adequate supply of migratory labour helped to develop the industry to its highest peak. Labourers used to migrate from U.P., Bihar and Nepal to this region. So it deserves discussion, why people used to migrate from those areas in one hand and the socio-economic impact of this migration on the economy of North Bengal on the other.

Migration of labour can be traced back to the slavery system. From the pre-historic ages slavery was in practice almost throughout the world. Slaves engaged in the production process and to perform some odd jobs. The well to do families used to keep some slaves for their house hold works.

A slave, said Aristotle, is "a living tool", and slavery may be defined as the ownership and use of human property stock. The master inherits, buys, sells or bequeaths his slaves as he does his pick or his spade. His treatment of him or her may be controlled, like the usage of other positions, by custom or law of the society to which he belongs; but in general slave's life and labour as much at the masters disposal as those of his horse or his ass (Coupland, 1933:7).

Slavery began in prehistoric ages and has been practiced ever since. The slavery of ancient times reached its peak in Greece and the Roman Empire. During the middle ages, slavery declined. Then, during the 1500s and 1600s, the colonization of the new world by Europeans resulted in a great expansion of slavery. The Spaniards developed sugar plantation in Cuba and other Caribbean island that became known as West Indies. The Spaniards also needed large number of labourers to mine, gold and other metals. Portuguese colonies started huge sugar plantation in Brazil. These Europeans enslaved thousand of Indians. But most of the Indians died from European diseases and harsh treatment. The Spaniards and Portuguese than began to import Blacks from West Africa as slaves (*The World Book of Encyclopedia,* 1993: 180-181).

The great wave of Arab conquest ran right along the North Coast of Africa to the Atlantic, and from 9th century it was mainly Arab traders who supplied demand of the Moslem world for slaves. Nor was it only in the markets of the Arab or, later on, the Turkish Empire—at Fez, Tunis, Cairo, Damascus, Mecca, Baghdad—that they sold their human wares. From the East African ports, especially Kilwa, a steady stream of slaves was carried across the Indian Ocean to Persian Gulf and inland to Persia or along the coast of India. As late as the 15th century there were thousand of African slaves in the Moslem Kingdom of Bengal (Coupland, 1933:13-14).

In the second half of the 17th century the slave trade became notorious as one of the most profitable branch of trade, and each European country, provided it had the opportunity, sought to snatch a profitable share of the slave trade for itself. Great Britain, Holland and France were the leading slave trading powers of that time. From the late 17th century the British North American colonies, the future United States of America, also sent slave ships to American coasts of Africa. Even Denmark and Sweden built several forts for the purpose of slave trade (Abramova, 1978 : 19).

Landowners in the American colonies originally met their need for forced labour by enslaving a limited number of natives, and hiring many more European indentured servants. In exchange for their transportation across the Atlantic, the servants committed to work for the Landowner for four to seven years. A few slaves were imported from Africa as early as 1619. With the spread of Tobacco farming in the 1670's, and the diminishing number of people willing to sign on as indentured servants in the 1680's, increasing number of slaves were brought in from Africa. Eventually 600 to 650 thousand slaves arrived in America against their will (www.religioustolerance.org/sla his.htm). Slaves or indentured servants were brought into America for agricultural production ever since the early 17th century.

Sugar became the main export of the European colonies, though the settlers also developed profitable coffee, cotton and tobacco plantation. The rising European demand for sugar helped to create fierce competition for the slaves and the sugar colonies. From 1500's to 1800's, the Europeans shipped about 12 million black slaves from Africa to the Western Hemisphere. Nearly 2 million of these slaves died on the way (*The World Book of Encyclopedia,* 1993: 481).

It has rightly been stated by Sharit Bhowmik that historically, plantations were a product of colonialism. The colonizing countries used to enslave African or Indians with the aim of plantations like sugar cane, tea, coffee, tobacco, cotton, rubber or cinchona. Rubber and cinchona were used as raw material for western industry-especially for the colonizing country. Tea, coffee and sugar had a very high demand in the markets of developed colonizing countries. The growth of tea plantations in India were a result of a rise in popularity of Indian tea in England (Bhowmik, 1981: 10). Tea plantation of North Bengal and India also started and developed to a large scale by British colonial power.

Slave transportation, and slavery in general in the U.S. was inhuman institution. During the passage from Africa mortality rate was almost 50%. Slaves who were too ill to survive the trip were sometimes thrown overboard to drown. When slaves arrived on the American soil, slaves were largely treated as property, to be freely bought and sold. Slaves were treated like beasts; they had to work from sunrise to sunset. Slavery was also brutal in Canada. For example, even in 1824 an 18 year old New Brunwick boy was hung by the neck until dead for having stolen 24 (www.religioustolerance.org/sla his.htm). There were much news of aggression and revolt also. Prolonged suppression, oppression and brutality made the slaves aggressive.

During the 1700s, noted philosophers and religious leaders in Europe and North America began to condemn slavery. They declared that slavery violated human rights and God-given laws. Many Americans turned against slavery during the American Revolution (1775-1783) (*The World Book of Encyclopedia,* 1992:481).

Later on the mass movement to abolish slavery started in England in the mid 18th century, though British ships controlled much of the slave trade at that time. Ships from Bristol and Liverpool transported tens of thousands of Africans annually to the Americas (www.religioustolerance.org/sla his.htm). At last good sense prevailed among the devils. The movement against slavery started in the big slave trading nations. Chief Justice, Lord Mansfield, ruled that slaves in England could not be forced to leave the country in 1772. William Wilberforce (1759-1833) was persuaded to lead an attack on slavery in the parliament in 1787. A committee of the Privy Council was appointed to study the question *(Ibid).* At last in the early nineteenth century, two of the biggest slave-trading powers abolished the slave trade : Great Britain in 1807 and the United States of America in 1808 (Abramova 1978 : 25).

In the course of time, the horrible condition of slaves aroused public sympathy throughout the world and there developed a growing demand to stop the system. Later on export of man power started under the system of indenture. Unemployment, illiteracy and extreme poverty compelled the people of Asian and African countries, especially the colonial countries to migrate as indentured labour to different countries. Sometimes they used to migrate from one region to another as indentured labour. Recruiters used to give them false hopes of lucrative wages, better working conditions and other amenities and facilities of life. But in most cases they were being cheated. After going abroad they had no alternative than to accept odd jobs, hard labour in exchange of very poor wages. So this labour migration was nothing but slavery in another form. The workers were paid very low wages and other benefits.

India was a British colony for about two hundred years. A large number of Indian workers went abroad to British colonies and other countries under the system of indenture. (The flow began around 1830 and continued until the system was abolished in 1922). Workers went as far as the Fiji Islands and as far west as the West-Indies. Large numbers of them went to south and East Africa, to Malaya, Burma and Ceylon. Terms and conditions under which they had to work were not far different from those of slavery, the only difference being that the contract was for a limited number of years. Though workers seldom returned home after the expiry of the contract period (Ahmed, 78: 1). This system of indentured labour began around 1830 and continued until the system was abolished in 1922. The movement against the system was organized by the eminent personalities and the civil society of India, not by the workers. The workers were unorganized, backward and too immature to think of themselves and their fellow workers in far off countries. However under the pressure of public opinion the Government prohibited recruitment in 1917 and abolished the system in 1922 (Ahmed, 1978 : 1).

Export of indentured labour had been stopped, but the system remained in India in a less onerous form. Sometimes the workers used to migrate from one region to another as indentured labour. The plantation industry of India was almost totally dependent on inter-state migration, and the Tea industry of North Bengal was no exception. In British period tea plantations were localized mainly in Assam and Bengal, specially in North Bengal. Tea producing areas of Northern Bengal are at present situated in West Bengal. So far as West Bengal is concerned, the Tea gardens are exclusively in North Bengal districts: 147 in Darjeeling and 187 in the Jalpaiguri districts (and one each in the Coochbehar and West Dinajpur districts) (Ghosh, 1987: 3).

A report on 'Industrial labour in India' conducted by International Labour Office of Geneva, presented valuable information regarding the area of Tea plantation in Bengal as follows :

"The plantations in the North are principally located in Assam and Bengal. The planting areas in Bengal comprises in Darjeeling, Terai and the Dooars in the north and Tripura in the South East. In Darjeeling the Tea gardens occupy slopes from 600 feet down words; Teria is level country at the base of and surrounded by high mountains and is only 300 feet above the sea level; the Doars is a sub-mountain country south of Bhutan and 22 miles in width, between Teesta and Sunkosh River (ILO report, 1936: 36).

Tea plantation requires huge labour, as it is labour intensive and an agro-industrial product tea was one of the largest industries of the Indian sub-continent. Its development necessitated two basic requisties, large areas of cultivable land and secondly, a huge labour force. But the areas situated for plantations were initially sparsely populated. Moreover tea gardens were generally located in jungle lands where there were wild animals, mosquitoes and other poisonous insects. So the working conditions during developing stage of the garden were very hazardous. Local people having minimum means to live were disinclined to work in the Tea gardens. In this situation all the tea producing areas had to depend on immigrant workers of Bihar, Orissa, U.P., Santals from Santal Pargana, Nepal and some local areas. Not only on the Tea plantation of India, but the plantation industry all over the world had to depend on migrant labour, like cotton plantation in North America, rubber in Malaysia and tea in India (Bhowmik, 1981 : 11). All these plantations were dependent on migrant labour.

As previously stated most of the Tea gardens were dependent on immigrant workers. In Jalpaiguri for instance, the majority of the workers were immigrants, more than half coming from Chota Nagpur (Census of India, 1911: 538). The growth of Jalpaiguri gardens is significant as it started with 13 gardens in 1876, and rose to 235 in 1901, employing some 90,000 persons. (*Bengal District Gazetteers,* Jalpaiguri, 1911: 102 -103) Whereas in the Darjeeling Tea gardens almost half of the labour was local, the bulk of the remainder coming from Nepal (Broughton, 1924: 77). It is the special characteristic of the Darjeeling Tea gardens that there were good numbers of local labourers.

Regarding the formation of working class of the planting areas of Darjeeling, Terai and Dooars the following few sentences of S.G. Panandiker is more compact. The laboureres in Darjeeling and the Terai are the descendants of immigrants from Nepal and Sikkim who have settled there permanently. Those in the Dooars are aborigines from Chota Nagpur and the Santal Parganas in the province of Bihar and Orissa, ninety percent of whom have also settled permanently on the gardens. In spite of the entire absence of any system of agreement or penal contract, there have been no labour difficulties in these areas (Panandikar, 1933: 195).

There were different types of migrations, out of which three types were applicable to industrial labour in Bengal : 1) Periodic migration arising from seasonal causes, such as harvest; 2) Semi-permanent migrations when persons reside and earn their living in one place, but retain their house and family connections in another; 3) Permanent migrations when for various causes, families are settled in permanent areas other than home districts (Saha, 1978:13).

The Tea industry was first established in Bengal as a commercial enterprise in Darjeeling in 1856. In 1870 there were only 56 gardens, employing about 8000 labourers in Darjeeling and by 1901 there were 148 Tea Gardens, employing 64,000 coolies (*Bengal District Gazetteers of Calcutta,* 1907: 44-45). The areas under Tea plucked in 1915-16 were about 151,000 areas (Statesmen Year Book, 1918: 136). The area under Tea in 1932 was 207,011 acres (including figures for the Tripura state). The quantity of Tea manufactured was 110,506,855 lbs. as against 90,096,271 lbs. in 1931. There were 392 Tea plantations employing on an average 180,879 permanent and 7173 temporary hands daily. There were 288 Tea factories under the operation of the Indian Factories Act. and the total daily average number of operatives employed was 15,722. This number excluded those employed in the gardens outside of factory premises (Report on the Administration of Bengal, 1932-33: 143). However European Companies owned the majority of the tea gardens of Assam and Bengal, but as has already been seen Indian enterprise was growing in regard to the private ventures (Census of India, 1921 : 266).

The industry was getting repid progress. The development of tea industry in North Bengal and India was also due to the growth of the western market for tea and the colonial area in the East which encouraged and in fact supported the tea plantations with foreign capital and enterprise (Ghosh, 1987: 2). Indian tea earned much superiority over Chinese tea, which was popular in England in the early nineteenth century, because of its thick brew. Moreover plantations in the colonies were fundamentally international in character (Bowmik, 1981: 10).

The average incoming workers were unskilled; they came to seek work, and had no definite idea as to what the work might be. They preferred to work in close proximity to their fellow villagers and relatives. However workers were recruited through Sardari system of recruitment. A labourer was thus recruited by a Sardar (Saha, 1978: 13). The people came from areas where there were almost no industries, low fertility and productivity of soil and the menace of feudalism, and where the wage was far below that of Bengal and Assam. In the census of 1919 more than half a million people of Bihar enumerated in Bengal proper. According to 1921 census about two million people of Indo-Gangetic plain (East) were enumerated in Bengal, out of which Bihar and Orissa comprised of 66.1 percent and people from U.P. was 17.8 percent. Thus, in the metropolitan industrial area and also in the Asansol-Raniganj (under district of Burdwan) coal field area and the North Bengal Tea area, the immigrant population varied from 100 to 150 per thousand inhabitants in Burdwan to 287 to 870 in Jalpaiguri and Darjeeling respectvely (Saha, 1978: 12-13).

Table : 1

Workers on Tea plantations in all India

Year	*No. of plantations*	*Garden labour (permanent)*	*Outside labour (permanent)*	*Outside labour (temporary)*	*Total*
1924	4300	690212	51022	70306	811540
1929	4714	778937	78514	73021	930742
1932	4848	753430	45251	61032	859713
1933	4974	763728	44135	56640	864503
1935	5134	801430	43598	54011	899039

Source : ILO Report on Industrial Report in India 1938: 35.

Table : 2

Area under Tea cultivation and work force (Bengal, 1929).

Place	*Plantations (acres)*	*Production (Lbs)*	*Labour*
Darjeeling	158	230009	65522
Jalpaiguri	288	84427	125632

Source : Saha, 1978: 9.

Table : 3

Number of Tea workers district-wise.

Place	*Permanent garden labour*	*Outside permanent labour*	*Outside temporary labour*
Darjeeling	134691	1860	5023
Jalpaiguri	70103	1916	1828

Source : Saha, 1978: 9.

The movement of people within and across geographical or political frontiers has been an enduring component of human civilization. People have been moving from one state to another or from one country to another for economic reason from the pre-historic ages in different forms. The movement of people has far reaching effects on the society and economy of both countries of origin and destination. It has been recognized that migration can help to forge economic, social and cultural bonds between people and countries (Haque, 2002: 1). Industrialization of Bengal was possible with the help of migratory labour from other states. This large scale migration of people from other states helped to develop a cosmopolitan city like Calcutta and a state like Bengal.

The economy of two North Bengal districts—Darjeeling and Jalpaiguri was highly underdeveloped in comparison to other parts of the state, while the tea gardens were seen to be the pockets of prosperity (Ghosh, 1987: 4). This prosperity was possible due to the roaring tea industry of these two districts and which was the contribution of migratory labour.

Persian, Arabic, Hindi, Urdu, English even Nepalese words have been adopted in Bengali, which enriched our Bengali language. Our food habits, dress, music, art culture have been enriched with the gradual and natural influence of different cultures. In Jalpaiguri, tea garden workers used to speak not less than 48 languages where Bengali itself was comparatively unimportant (Broughton, 1924: 77). In course of time different words of other languages had been adopted in Bengali.

The workers were paid very low wages in the most tea gardens of Bengal and Assam. For example, the Darjeeling Company Ltd. had its four companies, established between 1869-1864 in Darjeeling district, and had its head office in London. The labourers were paid by this company at the rate of about Rs. 3 per month for children, up to Rs. 5 or Rs. 5.50 as for able bodied men (Ghosh, 1987: 25). Moreover another factor which affected wages was the employment of plantation workers in gangs under the supervision of Sardars, who in addition to their fixed monthly wage received rates of commission. This commission has been found to vary from half an ana to two anas in the rupee on the earnings in Assam and in the Dooars. The commission was one piece for each hazira worked by the gangs and was paid by the planter (ILO Report, 1938: 246). Planters were dependent on Sarders for labour supply and workers were dependent on them for work, so the menace of Sardari system had to be born by both the parties without having no other alternative.

In general, local variations in wages are largely eliminated by 'wage agreements' among the planters. The tea industry in Assam, for instance, is organized by the Indian Tea Association, which promotes wage agreements among its members with a view to securing uniformity in wages. Wages are similarly controlled by the Dooars planters Association and the Indian Tea Planters' Association in the Dooars and by the Darjeeling Planters Association in the Darjeeling District...(ILO Report, 1938: 246-247).

Table : 4

Plantation wages in 1929

Centre	*Period*	*Men*			*Women*			*Children*		
		Rs.	*a*	*p*	*Rs.*	*a.*	*p*	*Rs.*	*a.*	*p.*
The Dooars[1]	Month	14	4	1	10	5	8	02	14	5
Darjeeling and the Terai[2]	Day		7	6		6	0		2	9

1Average earnings

2 Minimum earnings

Source : ILO Report, 1938: 27.

Not only wages, so called housing arrangement of plantation workers was very pathetic. Most of the workers used to reside within the garden area. They are housed in rows of huts which are called labour lines. These lines are scattered all over the tea garden...(Bhowmik, 1981: 6). In Terai, the source of water was only Kutcha wells, in some gardens Pucca wells are also found. Rivers and streams were also served their necessity of water. There was no separate arrangement for washing or taking bath (Bengal District Gazetteers, Darjeeling, 1947: 19). Scenario of all the gardens of North Bengal was almost same.

The workers of Terai and Dooars had very minimal medical facility. Medical facility was better in Darjeeling gardens. Especially the Terai workers used to suffer from different diseases like Malaria, Black water fever and cholera. But Darjeeling is a healthy place, where qualified doctors were available in good number in comparison to Terai. Moreover Terai was an unhealthy region. In Terai, most of the gardens had outdoor dispensaries and indoor accommodation was rare. These indoor accommodations were not popular as there was no nurse and servants (Bengal District Gazetteers, Darjeeling, 1947: 119). Thus, medical facilities in Terai tea gardens remained more or less static and it remained almost unaltered since 1862.

In Dooars the medical facilities was same as Terai (Bhowmik 1981: 62-63).

It was not only the case of Tea or Jute, but for other industries growing around Calcutta a large number of workers were immigrant. There were certain reasons of labour migration to Bengal. On the other hand Bengalis could not migrate to other provinces and seldom used to accept odd jobs like immigrant workers.

Bengal is a fertile state in comparison to other states of India. There was large demand of agricultural labour and the wage was also high. The peasant class is more affluent than in other parts of India. So they were reluctant and not capable of strenuous work in factories and mines. Still a certain number of agricultural workers in Bengal do however seek employment in mills and factories for long and short spells especially the less intelligent who enters as unskilled workers. Intelligent Bengalis were more interested in clerical and other skilled operations. So they started getting necessary training for technical jobs. They were for instance largely in demand in the various engineering works that were springing up in Bengal at that time and the adjacent province of Bihar (Broughton, 1924: 73-74). The Jute mills in Bengal had to recruit the bulk of their labour from other provinces. Local labour was available. This labour gradually drifted to more lucrative employment with the extensive introduction of the very profitable jute crop which was absorbed in agriculture. Where conditions were good and suitable housing was provided, Bengali labour had not been displaced. Jute mills of South Calcutta had the design and ventilation in accordance with the modern ideas. Up-to-date machinery made it possible for the workers to earn good wages in addition to the housing which was exceptionally good. In these factories Bengali workers were content to work (Ibid, 74). So the Bengali workers were less rough and tough than immigrants or migrant workers of Bihar, U.P etc. In general Bengali workers were by nature comfort loving as their life is easier than the other states of India. The immigrant labour, on the other hand, has not generally speaking as high a standard of living. They contentedly live in crowded busties just as the Irish immigrant in the early days of the industrial revolution in England was content to accept lower wages and worse conditions than English agricultural labourers. The immigrants to Bengal from outside the province the same (*Ibid,* 74).

Moderate climatic condition of Bengal was another reason for attracting immigrant workers. Uttar Pradesh and Bihar had always more aggressive weather than that of Bengal. It can also be said that Bengali people over all were very tolerant, such that they never opposed influx of huge migration of workers from other parts of the country. The migratory workers seldom used to return to their state of origin. Generally they used to settle. Jalpaiguri District Gazetteers of 1911 also indicates the same trend. Coolies used to come up for about three years and then take long leave, but now a days they do not return to their country so frequently as before and show a tendency to settle down (*Jalpaiguri District Gazetteers of 1911:* 108).

As the last reason it can be said that factory system had been introduced first in Bengal and Bombay. So Bengal required huge supply of labour and the people of comparatively backward states required jobs. However Tea industry of Bengal also required huge amount of labour as it was a labour intensive industry.

Process of migration is still in practice all over the world in any form in private level or in government level. In old days it took place in the form of slavery. When slavery had been considered as a condemned act, indentured labour came up, but in course of time the process came to an end. Later on movement of labour continued as migration of labour with their consent and labour receiving country as well. Now the popular term, export of man power in government and non -government level is much better than the previous state. There is also migration of labour in a systematic way for a contract period. Workers are willing to go for higher wage and other facilities and government encourage it as a source of foreign earnings.

At present migration has become a global problem. People moving from underdeveloped countries to the developed ones, specially in western countries or oil-rich middle-eastern countries in search of job for survival, education or political system. The United Nations estimates that by early 1985 there were nearly 106 million international migrants in the world,

45 percent of whom were in developed countries (i.e. Australia, Canada, Japan, New Zealand, the United States, the former USSR, and the whole of Europe). In 1985 the United States alone was hosting nearly 16 percent of all international migrants and had the largest migrant stock of any single country (Russell, 1997: 41).

At the regional level, only the whole of Europe, with 22 percent of all international migrants, and South Asia, with 18 percent, surpassed the United States in number of migrants. Even the region comprising western Asia and North America, which includes the oil-rich countries of the Gulf have been major importers of foreign labour, accounted for at most 13 percent of all international migrants. Sub-Saharan Africa followed, with 11 percent, a share that includes all the refugees present in the region as of 1985; Latin America and the Caribbean accounted for further 6 percent (*Ibid,* 41).

There was a time when people were trapped or induced to go abroad as slave or indentured labour but at present people are eager to have a better job outside their country. Now another trend has also developed in under-developed or developing countries that well to do people aspire to leave his country for the western countries, like Canada, USA, Australia for better living as immigrants.

Migration from Bangladesh began as early as the 1940s, mainly to Great Britain for settlement and again in 1960s, for employment purpose. But an unprecedented mass migration to the oil-rich Middle East took place in the mid 1970s. Due to unemployment and poverty at home and job opportunities and higher wages abroad, Bangladeshi people tried to look to other places of the world for work. At present Bangladesh migrants are working in Asia, the Middle East, North Africa, North America and Europe (Islam and Nuruzzaman, 2000: 87).

NOTES AND REFERENCES

1. Abramova, S.U. (1979) : Ideological, Doctrinal, Philosophical, religious and Political aspects of the African Slave Trade, The African Slave Trade from fifteenth to the nineteenth century Reports and papers of the meeting of experts organized by UNESCO at Port-au-Prince, Haiti, 31 January to 4 February, 1978.

2. Kamruddin Ahmad, (1978) : *Labour Movement in Bangladesh,* Inside Library, Dhaka.
3. *Bengal District Gazetteers of Calcutta,* 1907.
4. *Bengal District Gazetteers of Calcutta,* 1907.
5. *Bengal District Gazetteers of Jalpaiguri,* 1911.
6. Bhowmik, Sharit (1981) : *Class Formation in the Plantation System,* People's Publishing House (p) Ltd., New Delhi.
7. G. M. Broughton, (1924) : *Labour in Indian Industries,* Humphrey Milford Oxford University Press, London.
8. *Census of India,* 1911, Vol., V, Bengal, Part-1, Report.
9. *Census of India,* 1921, Part-1, Report, Superintendent, Govt. Printing, India, 1924.
10. Coupland, Sir Reginald (1933), *The British Anti-Slavery Movement,* Oxford University Press, London.
11. *Eastern Bengal and Assam, District Gazetteers, Jalpaiguri,* 1911.
12. Tushar Kanti Ghosh, (1987) : *Tea Gardens of West Bengal,* B. R. Publishing Corporation, Delhi.
13. Shahidul Haque, (2002) : *BISS Journal,* Bangladesh Institute of International and Strategic Studies, Dhaka.
14. Industrial Labour in India (1938) : *ILO Studies and Reports, Seris,* A., (Industrial Relations) No. 44, Geneva.
15. M. Rafiqul Islam and Nuruzzaman Md., Development Review, the *Bi-Annual Publication of the Academy for Planning and Development,* Vol. 14, January & June 2002, Number 1 & 2.
16. S. W. Panandikar (1933) : *Industrial Labour in India,* Longmans, Green & Co. Ltd., Bombay.
17. *Report on the Administration of Bengal, 1932-33.*
18. Stanton Russell, (1997) : *Migration Patterns of U.S. Foreign Policy Interest, Threatened Peoples Threatened Borders World Migration and US Policy* (ed) Michael S. Teitelbaum and Myron Weiner, Universal Book Traders, Delhi.
19. Panchanan Saha, (1978); *History of Working Class Movement,* Peoples Publishing House, New Delhi.
20. *The Statesman Year Book, 1918,* ed. Sir John Scott Ketti, Macmillan and Co. Ltd. London.
21. *The World Book of Encyclopedia* (1992), Vol. 17, World Bank Inc., Chicago, USA.
22. www.religioustolerance.org/sla his.htm.

10

Microfinance Initiatives and Self Help Groups in North Bengal Tourism: Prospects and Challenges

R. Ranjit

Introduction

In September 2000, the member states of the United Nations unanimously adopted the Millennium Development Goals (MDGs). The MDGs commit the international community to a common vision of development - one in which human development and poverty reduction have the highest priority. The objective of the MDGs is to serve as guideposts and focus the efforts of the world community on achieving significant, measurable improvements in poor people's lives. The goals grew out of the agreements and resolutions of various development conferences organized by the UN in the 1990s.

The poor have physical assets food, clothing, housing-and financial assets, such as income or savings, with which to acquire basic necessities. Access to financial services enables the poor to increase income and smooth consumption flows, and thus expand their asset base and reduce their vulnerability. Empirical evidence shows that, among the poor, those who had organized themselves in to SHGs and participating in mictofinance programs with access to financial services were able to improve their well-bring-both at te individual and household level-much more than those who did not have access to financial services.

North Bengal in one of the socially and economically backward regions of India. A large number of Self-help groups have been formed in North Bengal and these have taken up a wide range of activities. Considering the natural advantages of the region, tourism is one of the activities which has the maximum potential for employment and income generation.

North Bengal

North Bengal forms one of the three divisions of West Bengal. It consists of six districts namely Darjeeling, Jalpaiguri, Coochbehar, North Dinajpur, South Dinajpur and Malda. The North Bengal division has international boundaries with Nepal, Bhutan and Nepal while it border Indian states like Sikkim, Assam and Bihar. The region has heterogeneous cultural and ethnic mix which people of different races and religons living in harmony.

The landscape, history and cultures of each district have a distinct character. While Darjeeling has great Himalayan ranges passing through it, Jalpaiguri, lying in the sub-Himalayan foothills, present a rich biodiversity with dense forests, varied fauna and flora. Coochbehar is a city of old palaces of Koch kings, with temples and large water bodies. North and South Dinajpur are basically agricultural plains. But like Malda South Dinajpur has its own importance from the archaeological point of view.

What are SHGs?

Self Help Groups (SHGs) are informal associations of up to 20 women (their average size is 14) who meet regularly, usually once a month, to save small amounts (typically Rs. 10 to 50) a month. While they are formed with the encouragement of NGOs and other self-help promoting agencies (SHPAs) such as government agencies and the banks, they are expected to select their own members, and are therefore sometimes called affinity groups. After saving regularly for a minimum of six months, and using the funds to lend small amounts to each other for interest, which is ploughed back into group funds, and satisfactorily maintaining prescribed records and accounts, they become eligible to be "linked" by the local bank branch under a NABARD-sponsored programme called the SHG-Bank Linkage Programme. Inspired by the success of the NABARD experiment, the Government of India in the Ministry of Rural Development started the SGSY program.

The objective of the Swarnjayanti Gram Swarozgar Yojana (SGSY) is to bring the assisted poor families (Swarozgaries) above the Poverty Line by ensuring appreciable sustained level of income over a period of time. This objective is to be achieved by inter alia organising the rural poor into Self Help Groups (SHGs) through the process of social mobilization, their training and capacity building and provision of income generating assets. The SHG approach helps to the poor to build their self-confidence through community action. Interactions in group meetings and collective decision making enable them in identification and prioritization of their needs and resources. This process would ultimately lead to the strengthening and socio-economic empowerment of the rural poor as well as improve their collective bargaining power.

Activities of SHGs

Self help groups focus on meeting the credit requirements of its members through small loans. Mature groups with greater experience take up economic activities based on their skills, availability of markets and raw materials. The guidelines of schemes such as SGSY focus on identification of key activites - four or five activities in a block - and provide training, skill development and infrastructure support for these key activities.

In North Bengal, SHGs have taken up diverse activities. The more common activities are in the primary sector such as animal husbandry, dairy and poultry and other horticulture and agriculture based activities. Handicrafts and handlooms are also popular. However, tourism is one of the areas which have the maximum potential in North Bengal given its natural beauty and variegated culture and ethnic profile.

Tourism in North Bengal

With the growth in environmental awareness and the number of nature lovers, eco-tourism has become a buzzword in the tourism sector. Eco-tourism has the advantage of being environment friendly and relying on local resources and local employment and is particularly attractive for developing economies. Several islands economies in the Caribbean Pacific and Indian Ocean are primarily dependent on eco-tourism as the main source of national income. With Darjeeling already having a brand name with recognition value across the globe, the whole region comprises Darjeeling hills with Terai and the Dooars is capable of becoming a premier destination for nature lovers from across the World. The region also has several heritage sites, the most famous of which is the Darjeeling Himalayan Railways, declared a "World Heritage" by the UNESCO. Added to this, is the sheer beauty of uniformly trimmed tea gardens undualting over gently slopes surrounded by hills and forests and criss-crossed by hilly rivers.

Culturally Jalpaiguri and Darjeeling disticts show intense cultural diversity-apart from the plains-people, tribals from Chotonagpur plateau, primitive tribes of Toto, Rava, Mech as well as the Tibetan, Nepalese and Bhutanese communities live in harmony in this region.

Tourist flow in the Region

As already discussed, inspite of abundant natural resources starting from the mighty Himalayas in the north and the Bay of Bengal in the south, West Bengal so far could attract an insignificant portion (about 3%) of the total annual tourist flow of the country.

Northern Tourism Zone primarily comprising Darjeeling, Jalpaiguri, Cooch Bihar, Uttar Dinajpur and Dakshin Dinajpur and including Siliguri is already attracting a large number of tourists both from within the country and abroad. Trend in tourist arrival in West Bengal and Dooars (including Siliguri) is presented below in Table-1.

Table - 1 Trend in Tourist Arrival in West Bengal & North Bengal

	West Bengal			*North Bengal (including Dooars Region)*		
	Domestic	*Foreign*	*Total*	*Domestic*	*Foreign*	*Total*
1998	46.45	1.95	48.40	17.92	0.40	18.32
1999	47.03	1.99	49.02	18.38	0.42	18.80
2000	47.37	1.97	49.34	18.66	0.41	19.07
2001	49.43	2.84	52.27	21.10	0.57	21.67
2002	88.44	5.29	93.73	25.31	0.66	25.97
2003	113.00	7.06	120.06	30.37	0.76	31.13

Source: Department ofTourism, Govt. of West Bengal

It may be observed that North Bengal received about 26% of total tourist flow in West Bengal.

Projected Tourist Flow

It may be assumed that in the developing scenario, North Bengal region will be able to attract at least 10% additional tourists of the total tourist flow in the state and the share of foreign tourists will increase from the present level of 2-3% to 8%. Accordingly, based on the projected volume for tourist to West bengal, as estimated by WEBCON in the 20-Year Tourism Perspective Plan for the state of West Bengal (Master Plan), the projected volume for tourists to North Bengal region is worked out as below.

Table -2 Projected Tourist Flow to North Bengal Tourism Zone

(In lakh nos.)

Year	*West Bengal*	*North Bengal*	*Jalpaiguri*
2003	120.06	31.13	2.49
2007	137.07	50.95	5.10
2012	206.46	76.39	8.40
2017	370.06	136.92	16.43
2022	593.81	219.71	32.96

Source : WEBCON Estimate

There is ample scope of increasing the number and frequency of visits of the tourists in this region by creating attractions as well as developing adequate tourism infrastructure of international standard. It is also important to develop viable integrated circuits covering the prime attractions of the region. Of course, adequate publicity and awareness campaign, both within and outside the country through effective media planning, is no less important.

Requirement of Accommodation

The accommodation availability in and around Darjeeling/ Terai/ Dooars region is as follows-

Table - 3 Existing Accommodation in North Bengal

Accommodation Type	*No. of Beds*
Pvt. Sector Star Category	1052
Pvt. Sector Non-Star Category	6100
Govt. Accommodation	935
Total :	8087

Source: Field Survey by WEBCON

As an example of one district in the region, of the total accommodation (excluding Government accommodation but including Tourist lodges of WBTDC) available in North Bengal, about 16.5% are in Jalpaiguri district only. Major destination-wise availability of accommodation in the district is given vide table-4 below.

Table-4 Existing Accommodation in Major Destinations in Jalpaiguri District

Sl. No.		*No. of Beds Available*				
		Tourist Lodge	*Forest Bunga-lows*	*Pvt.Sector Hotels/ Guest Houses*	*Others (including Youth Hostels)*	*Total*
1.	Jalpaiguri Town	32	--	424	--	456
2.	Alipurduar Town	-	-	160	--	160
3.	Malbazar	20	--	30	20	70
4.	Chalsa	-	--	104	--	104
5.	Madarihat	57	12	10	102	181

6.	Lataguri	-	-	200	--	200
7.	Murti	-	16	--	--	16
8.	Other Places	-	102	--	--	102
	Total	109	130	928	122	1289

Note:

In Govt. sector, only Tourist Lodges under WBTDC are taken into consideration for estimation purpose. Other Govt. accommodations like Circuit House, PHE Guest House, Irrigation Guest House, Municipal Guest House. PWD Guest House and Zilla Parishad Guest House, etc. have not been included as these are mainly for Govt. touring officials and not for general tourists.

There is no 5-star hotel in Jalpaiguri. Except Sinclairs Hotel at Chalsa which is a 4-star category resort, all accommodations are, in general, of budget type mostly catering to the low-and and mid-end tourists. There are 3 tourist lodges in Jalpaiguri run by WBTDC, Govt. of West Bengal, one each at Jalpaiguri town, Malbazar and Madarihat. These apart, there are 24 forest bungalows having 130 bed capacity scattered in the forest area throughout the district. It is worth-mentioning that important hub like Alipurduar and destinations like Lataguri and Chalsa are mostly dependant on private accommodation. Therefore, Alipurduar definitely deserves a tourist lodge and a tourist office. Although there is a forest bungalow at Murti, the tourist potential of the place may further be extented by constructing a Tourist Lodge. Since Lataguri area already has fairly good accommodation capacity in private sector, any further capacity augmentation may not match with the limited carrying capacity of the Gorumara forest.

Requirement of Additional Rooms

Development of tourism would definitely generate demand for accommodation facilities in the region. Based on the projected flow of tourists (excluding day-trippers) and the standard Room Factor the future requirement of rooms is estimated as below.

R = Room Factor = 1/d x s x 1/c x 1(1+k)

D = No. of Working Days = 365

S = Average Duration of Stay = 2 days
C = Ideal average occupancy = 65%
K = Double occupancy factor = 80%

Thus, R= Room Factor = 1/365 x 2 x 100/65 x 100/180=0.004683

Estimated requirement of accommodation in the district is furnished in table-5 based on the projected tourist flow and the Room Factor.

Table - 5 Estimated Requirement of Accommodation in Jalpaiguri District

Year	*Available Beds*	*Requirement of Accommodation No. of Rooms (No. of Beds)*	*Additional Requirement (No. of Beds)*
2007	1289	2388 (4776)	3487
2012	4776	3934 (7868)	3092
2017	7868	7694 (15388)	7520
2022	15388	15435 (30870)	15482

Varieties of Tourism

There are many varieties of tourism which differ in form of activities and natural beauty showcased. These may be classified in to the following categories:

1) Eco-tourism
2) Heritage tourism
3) Cultural tourism
4) Religious/pilgrimage tourism
5) Get-away tourism
6) Highway tourism and Way side facilities
7) Rural and ethnic tourism
8) Business tourism
9) Adventure tourism
10) Tea tourism
11) Picnic spots
12) Other activities including educational, health and cultural tourism

We analyse some of the above categories and examine their suitability for SHG based activity and opportunities thereof.

Eco-tourism

According to the World Tourism Organisation (WTO), 'tourism that involves travelling to relatively undisturbed natural areas with the specified object of studying, admiring and enjoying the scenery and its wild plants and animals, as well as any existing cultural aspects (BOTH of the past and the PRESENT) found in these areas is Eco-tourism. Many tourist destinations in the Jalpaiguri fall under this category. Out of the 5 National Parks (covering an area of 1692.65 Sq. Kms) and 16 Wild Life Sanctuaries (covering an area of 1103.48 Sq. Kms) in the state, Jalpaiguri has 2 NPs viz. Buxa (117.10 Sq. Kms.) and Gorumara (79.45 Sq. Kms) and 3 WLSs viz. Chapramari (9.60 Sq. Kms.), Jaldapara (216.51 Sq. Kms.), Buxa (368.99 Sq. Kms) in addition to one Tiger Reserve i.e. Buxa Tiger Reserve (760.87 Sq. Kms). As per available records, total forest cover of the district is 1790 Sq. Kms. Moreover, about 700 Sq. Kms. of land in the district is under Tea Plantation. Taking all together, the total green cover of the district may be worked out to 2490 Sq. Kms. which is about 40% of the total geographical area (6245 Sq. Kms.) of the district. Bio-diversity of these protected forest areas, which attracts nature-lover tourists in the district, is depicted in the following table (Table 6.).

Table - 6

Bio-Diversity in the Protected Areas of Jalpaiguri District

Sl. No.	*National Parks/ WLS*	*Area in Sq.km.*	*Major Flora*	*Major Fauna*
1	Buxa NP	117.10	Sal, Simul, Siris Khair, Champ, Sidha,Toon,Lali Lampate, Mandane, Katus Teak, Orchids.	Tiger, Leopard (Black Panthar also) Elephant Clouded Leopard, Himalayan Black Bear, Barking Deer, Gaur Pangolin, Python, Raptors

				Black-necked Crane and other birds and Moths. Butterflies etc.
2	Gorumara NP	79.45	Tropical moist deciduous Sal forests associa-ted with Odal, Lali, Katus, Dil enia, Simul-Siris Khair, Tera grass land.	Great Indian Rh-inoceros, Leopard Elephant, Sloth, Sloth Bear, Hog, Sambar, Python, Turtle, Migratory Birds, Peafowl, Indian Pied Horn-bill.
3.	Chapra-mari WLS	9.60	Predominant Sal mixed forest Lali, Chilaune, Kanch-anan. Bahera, Kawla, Dilenia, Mallotus, etc.	Elephant, Gaur, Leopard, Sambar, Barking Deer, Rh-esus and Assamese Macaque, Hornbill lesser Adjutant Stork
4.	Jaldapar	216.51	Terai Grass land, reverine forest, Sal Forests, Simul Bad-Khair, Sosoo, Sidha Gamar, Mallotus, Kawla, Dilenia, Ficus.	Great Indian One-Horned Rhino, Tiger Gaur, Elephant, ger, Leopard, Sloth Bear, Otter, Bengal Florican, King Cobra
5.	Buxa WLS	368.99	A part of Buxa Tiger Reserve same as Buxa National Park, Buffer area.	Elephant, Leopard, Gaur, Spotted Deer, Sambar, Jungle Cat, Fishing Cat, Birds.

Source : State Forest Report, Directorate of Forest, Govt. of W.B.

The prominent eco-tourist spots are Gorumara, Chapramari, Murti, Badaganj, Kuttimari, Madarihat, Holong, Chilapata, Kodol Basti, Kunjanagar, Bhutan Ghat, Jayanti, Nimati and Raimatang Forest Range. However, all these spots are not well known and the facilities in all the places are not up to the mark. Most well-known and popular Eco Tourist spots are Madarihat, Holong, Gorumara and Murti. The entire tourism industry is virtually dependent on these forests, which have their natural limitations to mass tourism in the forest areas.

Opportunities for Self Help Groups

Most of the forest guest houses are located close to forest villages that have many Self help groups formed from members of the Forest Protection Committees and others. Provision of catering and guide services can be outsourced to these groups once they have sufficient training and skills in these areas. SHGs can also form cultural troupes which can earn a steady income through performance given to the boarders in these guest houses. Providing ethnic cuisine and sale of handcrafts are other avcnues for income generation.

Heritage Tourism

North Bengal has a number of interesting historical monuments, which bear rich heritage value. Many of these monuments are located in little known places and most of them are in poor shape due to lack of proper attention. Upkeep of these monuments will help them develop as viable Heritage Tourism sites. Examples of such historical sites are Baikunthapur Rajbari and Buxa Fort. There are some other lesser-known spots whose potential may be exploited for development of regional level tourism.

Opportunities for Self Help Groups

Many of the heritage tourist sites are lying in ruin despite the historical importance attached to these places. Archeological Survey of India is in the process of restoring several of these historical sites. The existing schemes of the Government for infrastructure can be utilized building accommodation and developing roads, drinking water supply and waste management system. These facilities can then be handed over to Self help groups for operation and maintenance.

Cultural Tourism

North Bengal is a confluence of a number of ethnic groups. About 19% of the total population of the Jalpaiguri district, for example, belong to various tribal communities like Kurukh-Oraon, Sadani or Sardri, Madhesi, Munda, Santhali, Boda, Mecn, Rabha, Malpahari and Toto who will preserve their linguistic identity, own culture, songs and dances. Similar cultural diversity exists in the other districts. Rich tribal culture of the Totas, Ravas, Mechs, Tamangs and Nepalese has made the region suitable for developing culture-based tourism.

To promote Cutural Tourism in Jalpaiguri, the district authorities hold annual fairs at Jalpesh every year. Several other minor fairs are also held in different parts of the division. However, due to inadequate facilities and lack of marketing efforts, these fairs are little known and have only local influences. Jalpesh's annual fair is gaining popularity day by day and at present is the largest event in the Jalpaiguri district. Other similar fairs and sporting events may be organised regularly to bring the region into the tourism map of the country.

Opportunities for Self Help Groups

To develop cultural tourism in the region, the traditional culture of the local communities needs more attention and support so that they may fulfil the inquisitiveness and interest of the tourists both from international and national levels regarding the uniqueness of traditional culture of the land. There several LAMPS which are groups of women in the tribal areas and they are most suited to meet the requirements of the domestic and foreign tourists.

Religious/ Pilgrimage Tourism

There are a number of religious shrines in the district. These tourist spots have limited local influences. Annual fairs and festivals are held at Jalpesh, Bateswar, Jatileshwar etc. Other important religious places of local influence in the district are Debi Choudhurani Mandir, Bhabani Pathak Mandir, Mahakal Temple, Makrapara TG Kali Mandir, Kalu Sahaber Masjid, etc.

Opportunities for Self Help Groups

All the religious spots of the region mostly have local influence except some such as Jalpesh where there is regional influence also. However, proper maintenance and upkeep may increase the inflow of regional tourists to the division. Self help groups have several opportunities in this sector. For example items used in pujas or religious offerings such as flowers, incense sticks and sweets can be supplied by the groups. There could be dedicated stalls for this purpose. The more resourceful groups can even consider running guesthouses or dharmshalas in these localtions.

Getaway Tourism

People living in the crowded and busy metropolis like Kolkata want to escape from the stress, air and noise pollution once in a while. Hence Getaway Tourism is becoming more and more popular. The resorts of Deolo, Mirik, Lava, Lolegaon, Islampur, Balurghat, Malbazar, Madarihat, Chalsa, Alipurduar, are rapidly developing into important Getaway Tourism Centres in the region. The other virgin places like Lataguri and Falakata have the potential to develop into resorts with provisions for necessary infrastructure.

Opportunities for Self Help Groups

There is a need for augmenting quality accommodation facilities suitable for mid-end tourists in most of the potential places particularly at Chalsa and Alipurduar, since these places are going to be important hubs in future. Scope for self-help groups to make a headstart in these areas is immense. In the new potential areas, Self help groups can exploit the early bird advantage and establish either business with generous financing available from financial institutions and subsides provided under SGSY and other schemes.

Highway Tourism and Wayside Facilities

Major elements of Highway Tourism, interalia, include -

1. Adequately wide and well maintained roads built to international standard for speedy smooth journey by motor vehicles.
2. Composite wayside facilities/motels on road sides at regular intervals to make the road journey pleasant and comfortable.

3. Road signage at important road junctions/diversions for guiding the tourists/travellers to the desired destinations.
4. Safety and security during road journey.
5. Wayside facilities required by tourists/visitors would include rest houses and recreation areas with toilet facility, limited accommodation provision for short stay, restaurant and snackbar, public telecom (PCO), medicine shop, tourist information centre, vantage points and motorist service areas with proper landscaping in keeping with the ambience of the sorrounding areas. Provision for fuel filling station either within the complex or close to it and highway police outpost are also desirable. A standard centre of wayside facilities needs about 3/4 acres of land on the wayside.

   Frequency of such wayside facilities will be such that an average limit for spacing is about one hour's travel time. The average distance between two composite wayside facilities should be around 50/60 km.
6. Considering the above factors a number of sites/locations have been identified in the region for development of composite wayside facilities. The proposed locations in Jalpaiguri district for instance are as follows.

Sl No.	*Name of Proposed Locations*	*Block*
1	Fatapukur on SH-12A	Rajganj
2	Nature Park-cum-Wayside facilities at Batabari More on NH-31	Meteli
3	Damdim More on NH-31	Mal
4	Nagrakata, on NH-31	Nagrakata
5	Binnaguri on NH-31	Dhupguri
6	Dhupguri on NH-31	Dhupguri
7	Falakata on SH-12A	Falakata
8	Eastern side of Torsa River on SH-12A	Alipurduwar-I
9	Barabisha on NH-31	Kumargram duwar
10	Parmalangi on NH-31	Kalchini
11	Jaigaon	Kalchini

Modernisation and Regulation of Dhabas

Standard WSF on the highway in the district is almost non-existent. Dhabas are now rendering wayside facilities to the trans-port operators as well as tourists. In between any two composite WSFs and at or near important district and rural road junctions small dhabas may operate and provide facilities to the local travellers. But the Dhabas generally lack in the following essential services:

a) Desired sanitary conditions within and outside the Dhaba
b) Properly hygienic eating places for tourists and Microfinance Initiatives and Self Help Groups
c) Adequate parking lots for trucks/buses/cars.

Considering these, a moderately designed model Dhaba should have-

a) Clean kitchen area
b) Lounge- cum-seating area for tourists
c) Resting-cum-dining area for track/bus/car drivers
d) Separate clean toilets for ladies and gents
e) Parking lots for at least 20 heavy vehicles and 20 light vehicles

Opportinities for Self Help Groups

There is need to develop highway tourism throughout the district at regular intervals with standard facilities to facilitate movement of tourists. A policy should be evolved to install signposts/signage system at all road junctions/ diversions and also at an interval of 10 km. or so. Self help groups are ideal for running clean and efficient dhabas and way side facilities. For this purpose, subsidies can be obtained from Total Sanitation campaign. SGSY and other centrally sponsored schemes for development of essential facilities.

Rural/Ethnic Tourism

Tourism growth potential can be harnessed as a strategy for Rural Development. The development of a strong platform around the concept of Rural Tourism is definitely useful for a country like India, where almost 74% of the population resides in its 7 million villages. Across the world the trends of industrialisation and development have had an urban centric approach. Alongside, the stresses of urban lifestyles have led to a "counter-urbanisation" syndrome. This has led to growing interest in the rural areas. At the same time this trend of urbanisation has led to falling income levels, lesser job opportunities in the rural areas leading to an urbanisation syndrome in the rural areas. Rural Tourism is one of the few activities which can provide a solution to these problems. Besides, there are other factors which are shifting the trend towards rural tourism like increasing levels of awareness, growing interest in heritage and culture and improved accessibility, and environmental consciousness. In the developed countries, this has resulted in a new style of tourism of visiting village settings to experience and live a relaxed, natural and healthy lifestyle. This concept has taken the shape of a formal kind of Rural Tourism.

Any form of tourism that showcases the rural life, art, culture and heritage at rural locations, thereby benefiting the local community economically and socially as well as enabling interaction between the tourists and the locals for a more enriching tourism experience can be termed as rural tourism. Rural tourism is essentially an activity, which takes place in the countryside. It is multi-faceted and may entail farm/ agricultural tourism, cultural tourism, nature tourism, adventure tourism, and eco-tourism. As against conventional tourism, rural tourism has certain typical characteristics viz, it is experience oriented, the locations are sparsely populated, it is predominantly in natural environment, it meshes with seasonal and local events and is based on preservation of culture, heritage and traditions. Select rural areas may be specially developed to provide hospitality services to stressful city dwellers within the natural and ethnic settings of the places concerned. Some villages in the district like Totopara and Rava Basti have potential for development for this purpose.

Opportunities for Self Help Groups

There is good scope for developing Rural Tourism Centres (RTCs) in the district through state Tourism Department under

RTC schemes of the GOI. Rural tourism is the best option for Self help groups based in rural areas. Houses belonging to the group members can be renovated and made suitable for the tourists to stay. Alternatively, cottages within the village may accommodate the tourists. Living in the pristine surroundings of the rural Bengal among the rustic folk, enjoying the ethnic cuisine and taking in the scenic beauty around would be a unforgettable experience for most travellers. However, the minimum creature comforts and facilities ought to be provided so as not to deter any but the diehard traveller.

Tea Tourism

The Tea Plantation Industry of Bengal is famous across the Microfinance Initiatives and Self Help Groups World. In fact, Darjeeling tea is known as a premium brand in the Western countries and Japan. Tea has been the backbone of the economy in North Bengal especially in the districts of Jalpaiguri and Darjeeling in addition to being a major foreign exchange earner for the country. With the exploside growth in population and the cyclical downturn in the tea industry, the time has come to look at tea gardens with a fresh perspective and explore sources of revenue apart from the traditional produce namely made tea. Tourism is one of the activities, which has maximum potential for employment and revenue generation in the tea industry.

Tea Gardens in Jalpaiguri & Darjeeling: The region comprising of the Dooars along with Terai and Darjeeling hills have a large number of tea gardens. There are 158 tea gardens in Jalpaiguri district and 115 in Darjeeling district. The total area under tea plantation in Jalpaiguri is 69.974 ha while in Darjeeling it is 26,509 ha. Total production of tea in Jalpaiguri is one. 43,060 MT while in Darjeeling it is 29,368 MT. The tea garden contains several attractions, which may be listed as below:

1) *Tea Garden Stay:* The Natural beauty of rows and rows of neatly trimmed tea bushes interspersed with lush green shade trees needs no elaboration. While tea is consumed the World over, it is only the rare foreign tourists who has any idea of what a tea bush looks like

and where it comes from. Tea is grown in only few countries World over and the prospect of living within a tea estate would be an attractive proposition in itself.

2) *Culture:* The tea estates in Darjeeling and Jalpaiguri districts represent a rich cultural and ethnic diversity. A large percentage of the tea garden workers had been brought here by planters in the late 19th Century and the early 20th Century from many places like Chotanagpur Plateau, Nepal and Bhutan. Some of the natives of the region have also joined the work force but their percentage is comparatively less. Many tribes such as Rava, Mech and others live in the tea estates. Over the decades, several cultural art forms have evolved some of them in splendid isolation far away from their original homes. Tourists would be fascinated by the wide array of folk art, music and dance available in the tea gardens.

3) *The Tea Making Process* : Tourists would also be captivated by the whole process of tea making from the plucking to the final packaging. The sight of women workers plucking two leaves and a bud and carrying these bundles on their backs from early morning would be a sight to behold. Similarly, the manufacturing process consists of the following steps would also be quite interesting. For example, CTC tea is made by the following process:

   Withering of green leaves by spreading thinly on trays for 10 to 20 hours.

   Rolling by machines for bruising the leaves and rupturing the cells and making them curled and twisted.

   Fermentation-by spreading about 2 inches deep upon low tables until they assume the coppery colour (taking about 5 hours to complete the process)

   Drying done by firing by machines immediately after fermentation.

   Further they may also visit Tea Auction Centres in Siliguri and Jalpaiguri

4) *As Retreats/ Resorts*: Tea gardens have good connectivity with reasonable internal roads. The Rest Houses and

Bungalows made in the colonial era have a large number of artifacts coming down from the British time. The tea gardens would be an ideal location for centres for Yoga therapy, meditation, Ayurvadic treatment and religious retreats. This aspect needs further marketing in the area.

5) *As part of an Integrated Circuit:* As the tea gardens fall within the region which has lots of hills and mountains as well as wildlife sanctuaries, natural parks and the Buxa Tiger Reserve. Stay in a tea garden can be a part of integrated tourism circuit. Existence of these natural attractions provides for a tremendous untapped potential for development of tourism circuit with the tea estates as the focal points.

6) *Adventure Spots:* The region has rich avenues for adventure spots. While water rafting can be done at Kalijhora on river Teesta while canoeing would be ideal at Jaldhaka and Jiti confluence at the Jaldhaka water sport centre. Kayaking, paddle boating and speed boating are some of the other water spots that are possible. Angling in the several small rivers and rivulets, which criss-cross the region would be attractive for several foreign tourists. Cycling inside the tea gardens can also be considered, as the terrain would provide tremendous challenges to all groups of cyclists.

7) *Golf:* Jalpaiguri district along with adjoining areas of Siliguri have a well-developed infrastructure for Golf. Golf has developed over the years due to presence of several Army and Air Force contonments in the region. Most of the European Clubs established by British Planters boasted of well-maintained Golf links and the tradition has been carried on till today by avid golfers from the ranks of tea estate managers, retired and serving armed forces officers and few enthusiasts among the civil servants. Some of the better-known Golf Courses are the Bengdubi Golf Course, which belongs to the Indian Army, the Nagrakata Golf Course, maintained by the Nagrakata Golf Club, Chalsa Golf Course, owned by the Chalsa Polo Club, Ranicherra Golf Course of the Western Dooars Planters' Club and the Central Dooars

Planters' Club near Binnaguri. Even now, several Japanese, Thai and Bhutanese players can be seen practicing in some of these courses. Golf being a favourite sport of foreign tourists, this aspect of tea tourism needs greater publicity. It may also be possible to have dedicated Golf package tour in which Golf enthusiasts would have the opportunity of playing Golf in different tea garden locations in the Dooars, Terai and the Darjeeling hill areas.

8) *Ethnic Activities:* Jalpaiguri district, as discussed before, is home to several ethnic tribes and communities. Many of the ethnic tribes live in forests and villages in and around tea gardens. They have a unique life style and culture, which would be of interests to tourists. The ethnic cuisine of these areas, which consists of several delicious and exotic dishes, would be another draw. The traditional practices, way of life and social relation can be showcased by organizing tourists' haats in these villages. It is, however, important to ensure that the tribal way of life is in no way disturbed due to tourist activities. Further, the maximum benefit from these activities should accrue to the tribal themselves.
9) *Nature Activity:* Horse and Pony riding and safari on elephant back can be arranged within the tea garden areas. While elephant rides are being organized within some of the wildlife sanctuaries, this can be introduced in the tea gardens as well. Bird watching is another interesting activity. The tea gardens of Jalpaiguri and Darjeeling are home of several migratory birds that come in a large number during particular seasons. Arrangements for watching birds from elevated desks built on trees connected with rope and bamboo can provide both adventure and views of nature from a close proximity. There are several breathtaking views of sunrise and sun set which can be viewed from the green tea estates and adjoining forests. These can also be viable tourist spot.

Some of the major potential sites for tea tourism are as follows:

Samsing Tea Estate:

Samsing Tea Garden is located in an area of unparallel natural beauty. The existing manager's bungalow can be developed into an eco-resort. There is a beautiful stretch of land on the banks of river Murti, between the hills of Darjeeling district and the Samsing Tea Garden. There are already some initiatives being taken for low cost eco-tourism, but this needs to be further developed to achieve the full potential. The tea garden also has excellent road connectivity from Siliguri and Bagdogra. It is also well connected with other attractions with the Dooars such as Chalsa, Murti, Damdim, Chapramari, Jaldapara and Garumara.

Accommodation at the Samsing Tea Estate at present is not sufficient for any large-scale tourist inflow. Extra accommodation facilities need to be created immediately and large stretches of land are readily available for the purpose. The condition of the internal road is very poor and this needs urgent improvement.

Water supply and other constraints in the area require attention. The main water sources of the tea garden are deep tube-wells while the workers' colony of the garden is dependent on a Jhora, these are not sufficient. There is a scheme for drawing water from Murti River to meet the need of the garden, which can be implemented to cater to the tourists' requirement. Power supply is of poor quality and the garden usually depends on the generator sets as backup power system. There is a plan for generating hydro electricity from the Murti River that can be explored further. Solid Waste Management and the treatment of wastewater effluent would also require attention when the tourist influx increases.

Hilla Tea Estate in Nagrakata

The Hilla Tea Estate owned by West Bengal Tea Development Corporation, is located on the banks of river Jaldhaka and Jiti. The Estate is spread over 300 acres of land set against the picturesque background of Bhutan hills. The Nagrakata Tea Research Association and Nagrakata Golf Club are situated in the vicinity. The Hilla Tea Estate has got tremendous potential for development of eco-tourism without hampering any estate activity. Being a Government Tea Estate, it would also be an ideal place for implementing Government sponsored schemes for development of tea tourism. Hilla can become a model, replicable by other privately owned tea gardens.

The Hilla Tea Estate is located at distance of 72 KM from Siliguri town, 82 KM from Bagdogra Airport and 9 KM away from Nagrakata town. The present connecting road is barely motor able. The road needs to be upgraded, strengthened and widened to at least 5.5 meters wide with a bituminous layer. Hilla Tea Estate is also well connected by road to other tourist places like Garumara, Jaldapara and Chapramari.

There is no accommodation available at Hilla Tea Estate at present and these will have to be created and Government land is available for the purpose. The water supply system needs renovation and up gradation as the present system is only sufficient to meet the demands of the workers' colony. There is electicity connection in the tea garden but this needs to be augmented and the quality of supply improved for tourists. The drainage and sewerage system would require a major overhaul for the purpose of tourism.

Batabari Tea Estate

Batabari Tea Estate falling within the Matiali block is uniquely located in close proximity to forests, rivers and tea estates. The Murti River flows in close vicinity to the garden while Garumara National Park and the Murti Bungalow are just beside it. Already there are several resorts coming up in the area and this can be an ideal location for a weekend get-away.

One of the biggest advantages of the area is the approach road, which is the well -maintained National Highway 31. It is also located very close to Railway Station at Chalsa. Water supply and accommodation will have to be created in the garden.

Damdim Tea Estate

Damdim is located on NH 31 from which important tourist destinations like Garubathan, Lava, and Lolegaon in Kalimpong

Sub-Division of Darjeeling district are very close by. The tea garden is located about 44 KM away from Siliguri town. The Murti Bungalow and Murti River are about 22 KM from thhis place. Accommodation at present is not available in this area. It needs to be developed though there are some backup facilities at Mal Tourist Lodge, Sinclairs Resort and the Forest Bungalow in Murti. The approach road is in good condition. The main water sources in this area are open dug wells. Apart from this Jhoras also can act as alternative water source.

Bridging Infrastructural Gaps

A review of the conditions in the various tea gardens shows that there are major infrastructural gaps, which need to be plugged for tea tourism to become a success. Availability of accommodation is a major bottleneck Provisions of accommodation poses of peculiar difficulty-on the one hand, it would be unwise to invest in construction of a large number of rooms without being certain of tourists' demand, while on the other hand, it would not be possible to effectively know or cater to tourists' demand without some accommodation. The middle path would be to build a few rooms with adequate facilities, observe the demand and add rooms and facilities thereafter. The present guidelines of the Government of West Bengal in the L& LR Department are also rather time consuming and need further simplification if accommodation is to be constructed in any large number.

Physical infrastructure is also in a poor shape. Although some tea gardens are fortunate to be located beside National and State Highways, most tea gardens are connected by roads, which are in a bad condition. The internal roads in the tea gardens are also barely motor able. Road connectivity would require vast improvement if tea tourism is to take off. Availability of water supply is a major problem in the region as a whole. During the lean season, there is a lack of adequate drinking water supply in the area. When the tourists enter the tea gardens, the pressure on the existing water sources would multiply manifolds and therefore alternative water supply source would have to be organized. Availability and quality of electricity is another important bottleneck. The region suffers from periodic load-shedding and poor quality of power. The situation would have to be rectified if the tourists are to be attracted in a large number.

Opportunities for Self Help Groups

There are several Self help groups consisting of tea garden workers and their families. The different services required by tea tourism can easily be provided by these groups.

Picnic Tourism

Day visitors to the places of leisure and entertainment including picnickers, not spending even one night at the tourist spots are strictly not tourists as per the definition of WTO.

However, such picnic and entertainment places like parks and gardens add to the attractiveness of nearby tourist places and provide important sub-products and also generate lot of direct and indirect employment to the local people or the host community. Some places having scenic beauties are often identified Picnic Spots. These spots may be developed by the local Gram Panchayats by providing facilities like drinking water, toilet, landscaping, boating in available water body, etc (for which reasonable fees are to be charged from the visitors) and handed over to the local Self Help Groups (SHG) for regular management. Prominent picnic spots in the districts are Bankona, Daikhata, Kulti, Khuskhuia Park, Raimatang Forest Village, Nimati Forest Range, Pana Forest Range etc. Necessary guidance in this regard may be obtained from the Directorate of Parks and Gardens, Department of Forests, Government of West Bengal.

Opportunities for Self Help Groups

Picnic spots are being run as a profitable business by several self help groups in the region. The SHG women can be given more training in environmental awareness and preservation on nature. This will help in making their business more sustainable and eco-friendly.

Conclusion

In the above paragraphs we saw several ways in which SHGs can take part in the burgeoning tourism activities in the region and reap a handsome harvest. This will fulfil the need for diversification of the traditional activities of women which were confined to animal husbandry and handicrafts. It is hoped that with greater participation of women in tourism promotion the region will see an upsurge both in the quality of services and in the employment potential of the area. This will require close and harmonious working of the government, the non governmental sector and the private sector. Particular attention is required for skills training and capacity building. At the same time, infrastructure development will require adequate attention if the full potential of the tourism sector is to be realized.

NOTES AND REFERENCES

Bella, Abzug, and Susan. Davis, 1998. "India" Mapping Progress: Assessing Implementation of the Beijing Platform.

Samirendra Nath Dhar, and Soumitra Sarkar, 2006 "Self -help groups: a Micro financial approach to poverty reduction and establishment of human rights for rural women". *South Asian Journal of Human Rights,* Serial Publications, New Delhi; S.K. Ghosh 1989. *Indian Women through the Ages.* Ashish Publishing House, New Delhi.

L. Mayoux 1998a, Participatory Learning for Women's Empowerment in Micro-Finance Programmes: Negotiating Complexity, Conflict and Change. *IDS Bulletin,* Vol.29, No. 4, pp.39-50.

L. Mayoux 1998b, Women's Empowerment and Micro-Finance Programmes: Approaches, Evidence and Ways Forward. DPP Working Paper No. 41.

L. Mayoux 1999b, From Access to Empowerment: Gender Issues in Micro-Finance. In CDS Virtual Conference.

K. McKee 1989, Microlevel Strategies for Supporting Livelihoods, Employment and Income Generation of Poor Women in the Third World: The Challenge of Significance. World Development, Vol.17, No. 7 pp.993-1006.

N. McNamara & S. Morse 1998, Donors and Sustainability in the Provision of Financial Services in Nigeria. IDS Bulletin, Vol.29, No.4, pp. 91-101.

Micro-Credit Summit 1997, Declaration and Plan of Action. Available from: http//www.microcreditsummit.org/declaration.htm (Accessed on: 18.08.99).

C.O.N. Moser 1993, *Gender Planning and Development: Theory, Practice and Training*, Routledge, London.

P., B. Oakley, Pratt and A. Clayton 1997 Outcomes and Impact: Evaluating Change in Soical Development. *INTRAC*, Oxford.

S.R. Osmani 1989, Limits to the Alleviation of Poverty through Non-Farm Credit. *The Bangladesh Development Studies*, Vol. XVII, No. 4, pp. 1-19.

L.N.K. Osmani 1998, Impact of Credit on the Relative Well Being of Women: Evidence from the Grameen Bank. *IDS Bulletin*, Vol.29, No. 4, pp.31-40.

Pitt & Khandker 1995, Household and Intrahousehold Impacts of the Grameen Bank and Similar Targeted Credit Programmes in Bangladesh. In a Workshop on 'Credit Programmes for the Poor Household and Intrahousehold Impacts and Programme Sustainability', Dhaka, Bangladesh.

J. Price 1992, Women's Development: Welfare Projects or Political Empowerment?. Amesterdam Conference, Mimeo.

R. Ranjit 2006. "Tourism in Darjeeling hill areas - A multivariate approach". S.B. Chatterjee & Sons. Kolkata

Manab Sen, and Ashok, Sircar, 2006 "Self Help groups & Microfinance in West Bengal" Loka Kalyan Parishad and CARE-CASHE, West Bengal.

A. Sen 1990, *Development as Freedom*. Oxford University Press, Oxford.

Anne Tinker, 1996. Improving Women's Health in India. Development in Practice Series. The World Bank. Venkateswaran, Sandhya. 1995. *Environment, Development and the Gender Gap*. New Delhi: Sage Publications.

WEBCON. 2004 "Tea Tourism Development Plan in North Bengal" Department of Tourism, Government of West Bengal.

WEBCON. 2005 "Tourism Development cum Investment Plan in Jalpaiguri" District Magistrate, Jalpaiguri, Government of West Bengal.

11

Evaluating Anti-Poverty Programmes in Dakshin Dinajpur District

Anil Bhuimali

Introduction

In rural India there exists massive poverty; because majority of the rural masses fail to attain a well-being considered to be a reasonable minimum by the standards of the society. In the analysis of poverty, we consider 'poverty line' as the most important measure and the person who falls below this line is considered as 'poor'. All the measurements of poverty line are done on the basis of income or consumption expenditure. This may not be right measure of poverty (Sen, 1985; Dutta (2012); Banerjee & Latif, 2008). In explaining the concept of standard of living and poverty, Professor Sen (1985) specifically mentions that to measure poverty properly it needs to include education and health parameters along with income or consumption expenditure. The income of the rural masses the poor, in particular exhibits greater variability than current consumption. Naturally, current consumption has been considered to be more authentic indicator of the current standard of living. To see the socio-economic status of the rural masses we have taken Dakshin Dinajpur district as our sample district from where 14 villages-seven villages from rural Balurghat and seven villages from rural Gangarampur have been taken for our detailed investigation. We have utilized both the primary as well as secondary data in order to see the actual status of the poor in the context of poverty alleviating measures by the government of India.

Our Study

To ascertain the socio-economic status of people in rural areas we have taken data on literacy, status of residential building, land holding of the households, sanitary facilities available, meal status, engagement of family members in the agricultural activities, households' engagements in anti-poverty programmes etc. We have ultimately considered 'meal status' (two square meals in three months, six months, nine months and 12 months) of the sample households as the measure of poverty. On the basis of meal status, we have measured the proportion of poor. Apart from this, we have examined the literacy, government aid received, status of residential buildings, migration, etc. to judge the socio-economic status of the rural people of a backward district of North Bengal region of West Bengal. The educational status of the sample villages as well as the GPs under Balurghat subdivision has been presented in tables 1, 2, 3, 4, 5, 6, 7, 8, and 9.The following map shows the sample villages of rural Balurghat.

Table -1: Literacy: Village Patiram

Income (Rs)	Illiterate			Up to X			MP			Above XII			Total
	M	F	T	M	F	T	M	F	T	M	F	T	
Up to 2000	85	85	170	56	45	101	-	-	-	01	01	02	273
2001-3000	30	18	48	15	12	27	-	01	01	-	-	-	76
3001-4000	04	02	06	03	04	07	01	-	01	-	-	-	14
Above 4000	02	02	04	02	05	07	01	-	01	04	02	06	18
Total			228			142			03			08	381

Source: Field survey, 2007

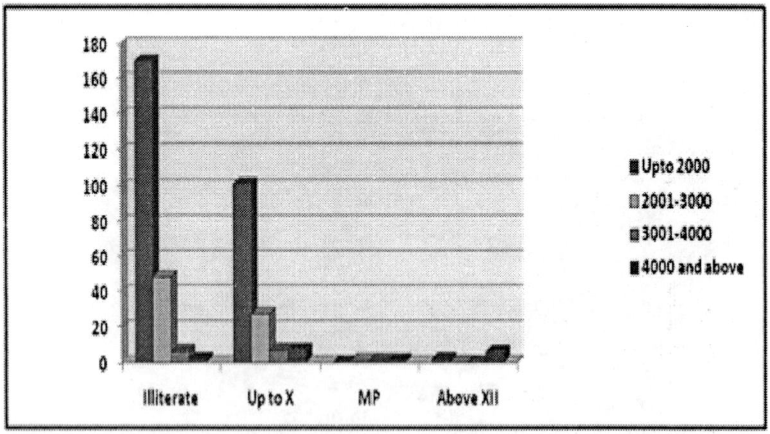

Table -2 Literacy: Village Dakshin Para and adjacent area

Income (Rs)	Illiterate			Up to X			MP			Above XII			Total
	M	F	T	M	F	T	M	F	T	M	F	T	
Up to 2000	49	70	119	58	59	117	06	10	16	01	-	01	253
2001-3000	13	14	27	8	17	25	04	01	05	02	01	03	60
3001-4000	02	-	02	02	02	04	-	-	-	-	-	-	06
Above 4000	-	-	-	-	-	-	-	-	-	-	-	-	-
Total			148			146			21			04	319

Source: Field survey, 2007

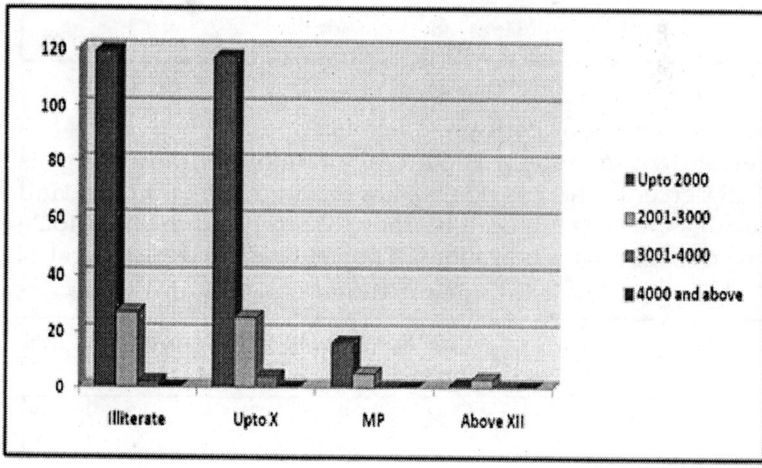

Table-3: Literacy: Patiram GP

Village	*No. of Persons*	*Literate Total*	*Illiterate Total*
Patiram	381	153(40.15)	228(59.84)
Dakshin Para & the Adi. Area	319	171(53.60)	148(46.40)
Total	700	324(46.28)	376(53.71)

Source: Field survey, 2007

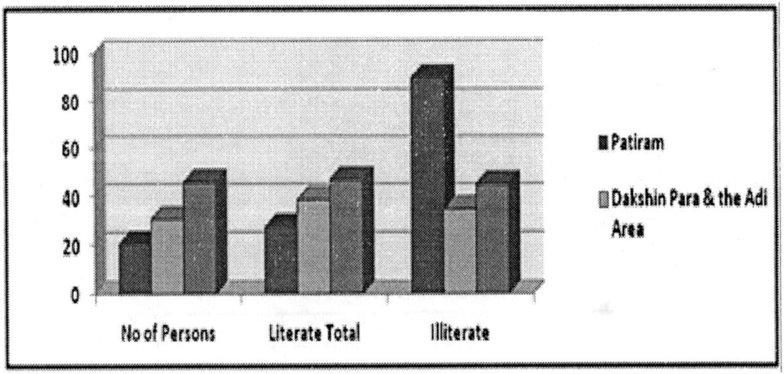

The literacy of Patiram GP consisting of 700 persons has been shown in table-3. The literacy rate of Patiram village is 40.15 percent whereas it is 53.60 percent in Dakshinpara and the adjacent area. Overall literacy rate in Patiram GP is 46.28 percent. This means that about 54 percent people were illiterates.

Table- 4: Literacy: Village Gobindapur

Income (Rs)	*Illiterate*			*Up to X*			*MP*			*Above XII*			*Total*
	M	F	T	M	F	T	M	F	T	M	F	T	
Upto 2000	38	38	76	46	52	98	03	02	05	-	-	-	179
2001-3000	07	09	16	07	08	15	-	-	-	1	1	02	33
3001-4000	-	-	-	02	04	09	-	-	-	-	-	-	09
Above 4000	-	-	-	-	-	-	-	-	-	-	-	-	-
Total		92			122			05			02		221

Source: Field survey, 2007

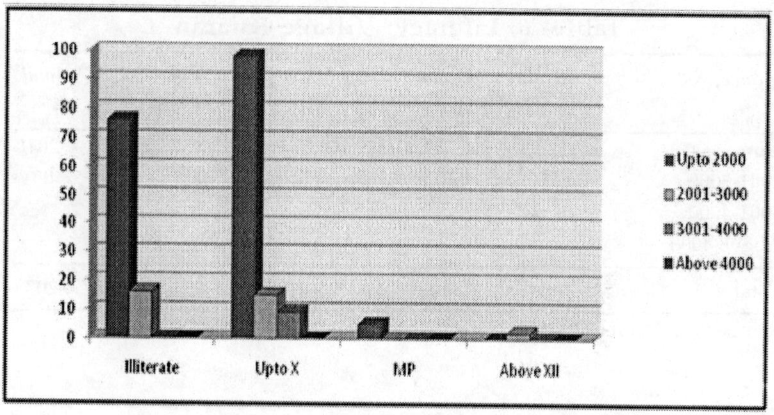

Table-5: Literacy: Village Mayamari

Income (Rs)	*Illiterate*			*Up to X*			*MP*			*Above XII*			*Total*
	M	*F*	*T*	*M*	*F*	*T*	*M*	*F*	*T*	*M*	*F*	*T*	
Upto 2000	22	19	41	27	29	56	04	02	06	-	-	-	103
2001-3000	02	06	08	12	11	23	02	-	-	01	-	01	32
3001-4000	02	02	04	04	04	08	-	-	-	-	01	01	13
Above 4000	-	-	-	-	-	-	-	-	-	-	-	-	-
Total		53			87			06			02		148

Source:Field survey, 2007

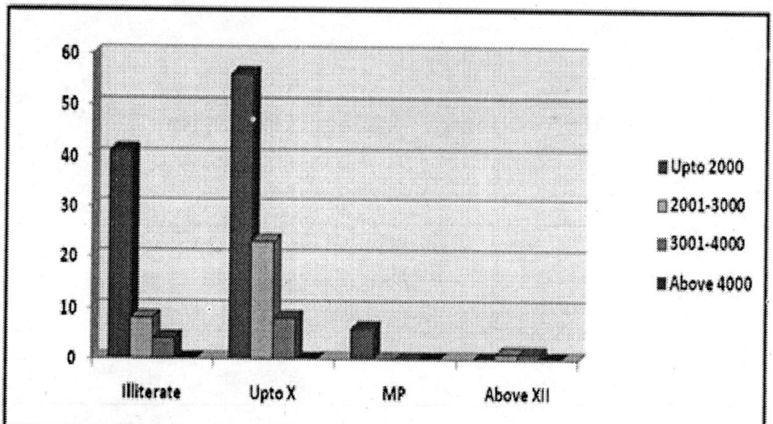

Table- 6: Literacy: Village Kuaran

Income (Rs)	*Illiterate*			*Up to X*			*MP*			*Above XII*			*Total*
	M	*F*	*T*	*M*	*F*	*T*	*M*	*F*	*T*	*M*	*F*	*T*	
Upto 2000	47	52	99	43	39	102	03	-	03	-	-	-	204
2001-3000	-	-	-	-	01	01	01	-	01	01	-	01	03
3001-4000	-	-	-	-	-	-	-	-	-	-	-	-	-
Above 4000	-	-	-	-	-	-	-	-	-	-	-	-	-
Total		99			103			04			01		207

Source:Field survey, 2007

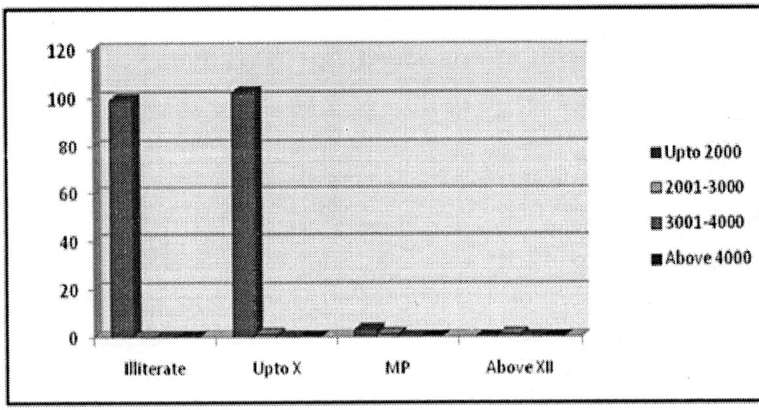

Table-7: Literacy: Village Chakvrigu

Income (Rs)	*Illiterate*			*Up to X*			*MP*			*Above XII*			*Total*
	M	*F*	*T*	*M*	*F*	*T*	*M*	*F*	*T*	*M*	*F*	*T*	
Upto 2000	47	37	84	55	73	128	04	02	06	-	-	-	218
2001-3000	03	05	08	05	10	15	01	02	03	02	-	02	28
3001-4000	03	02	05	06	04	10	01	02	03	03	-	03	21
Above 4000	03	-	03	05	09	14	01	02	03	-	-	-	20
Total		100			167			15			05		287

Source: Field survey, 2007

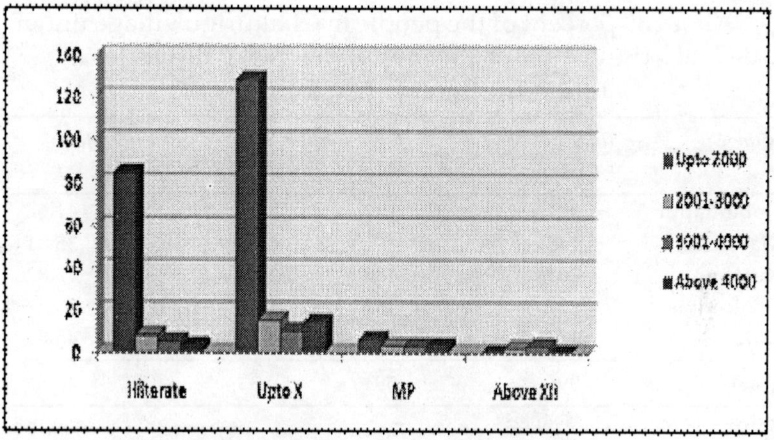

Table-8: Literacy: Village Dakra

Income (Rs)	*Illiterate*			*Up to X*			*MP*			*Above XII*			*Total*
	M	*F*	*T*	*M*	*F*	*T*	*M*	*F*	*T*	*M*	*F*	*T*	
Upto 2000	25	36	61	41	31	72	-	-	-	-	-	-	133
2001-3000	-	-	-	-	-	-	-	-	-	-	-	-	-
3001-4000	-	-	-	-	-	-	-	-	-	-	-	-	-
Above 4000	-	-	-	-	-	-	-	-	-	-	-	-	-
Total		61			72								133

Source:Field survey, 2007

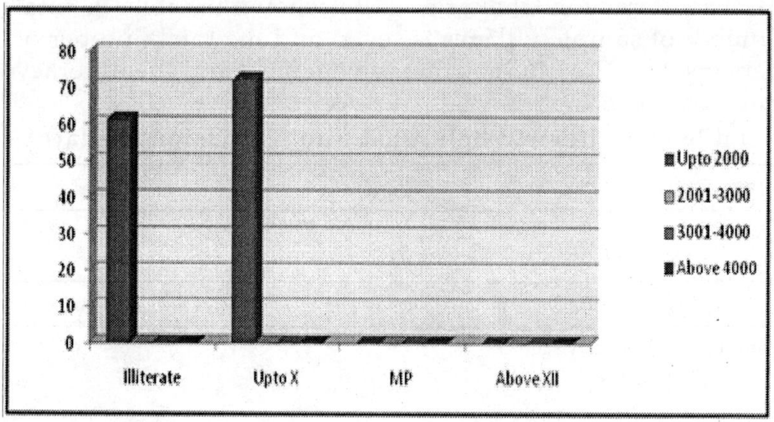

About 35 percent of the people in Chakurigu village under GP Chakvrigu of Balurghat subdivision are illiterates.

Table-9: Literacy: Chakvrigu GP

Village	*Total no. of Persons*	*Literates*		*Illiterates*	
		Total	*%*	*Total*	*%*
Gobindapur	221	129	58.37	92	41.62
Mayamari	148	95	64.18	53	35.81
Kuaron	207	108	52.17	99	47.82
Chakvrigu	287	187	65.15	100	53.47
Dakra	133	72	54.13	61	45.86
Total	996	591	59.33	405	40.66

Source: Field Survey, 2007

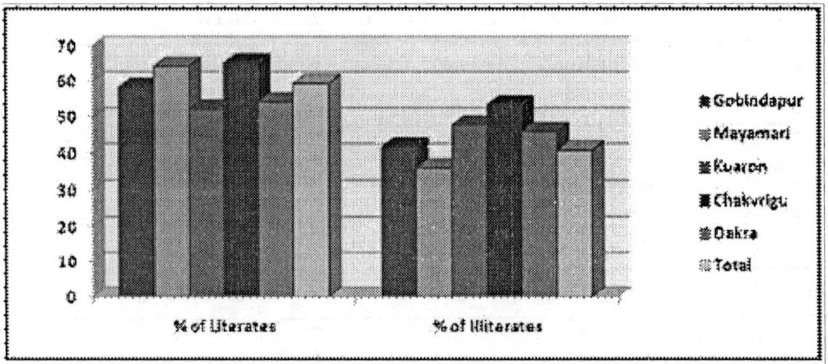

The literacy in Chakvrigu GP is shown in table -9. Total number of sample villages is seven and the total number of persons 996. The Literacy rate is 59 percent and the illiteracy rate 41 percent.

Table -10: Literacy: Balurghat Sub – Division (Sadar)

GP	*No. of Persons*	*Literates*	*Illiterates*
Chakvrigu	996	591 (59.33)	405 (40.66)
Patiram	700	324 (46.28)	376 (53.71)
Total	1696	915 (53.95)	781 (46.05)

Source: Field Survey, 2007

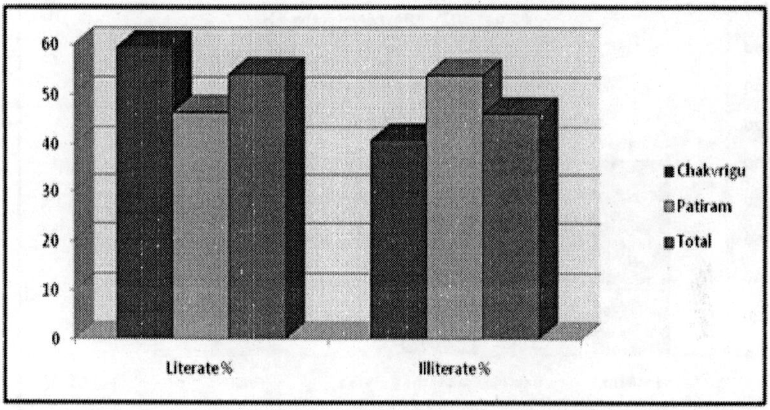

Table- 10 represents the overall literacy and illiteracy of the sample villages under Balurghat subdivision. Overall literacy rate is 46 percent and the illiteracy rate is 54 percent. It is a shame to us all that even today more than 50 percent of rural population remains illiterate in spite of so many steps adopted by the central and state governments to reduce/ eliminate poverty.

Tables 11,12,13,14,15,16,17,18,19,20,21,22,23,24, and 25 exhibit the government aid enjoyed and wage-employment received by the villagers (Sample households of Patiram GP & Chakvrigu GP of Balurghat subdivision) migration and BPL or proportion of poor of the sample villages of Balurghat subdivision.

Table-11: Government Aid Received: Patiram GP

Village	*No. of Households*	*Govt. Aid Received (No. of Households)*
Patiram	100	03 (3)
Dakshin Para & the Adi. Area	54	08 (34.4)
Total	154	11 (7.1)

Source: Field Survey, 2007

Note: Figures in the parentheses indicate percentage to total.

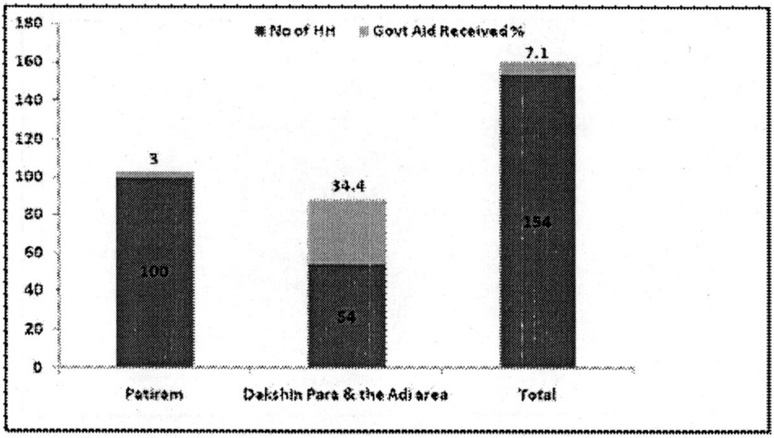

Table-11 shows that a few number of villagers under Patiram GP received Government aid during 2007. It shows that on average, only 7 (seven) percent of the villagers came under the government aid.

Table -12: 100 days work: Patiram GP (During 2007)

Village	*No. of Households*	*No. of Man days*
Patiram	100	27
Dakshin Para & the Adi. Area	54	18
Total	154	45 (12)

Source: Field Survey, 2007

Note: Figures in the parentheses indicate per person man-days.

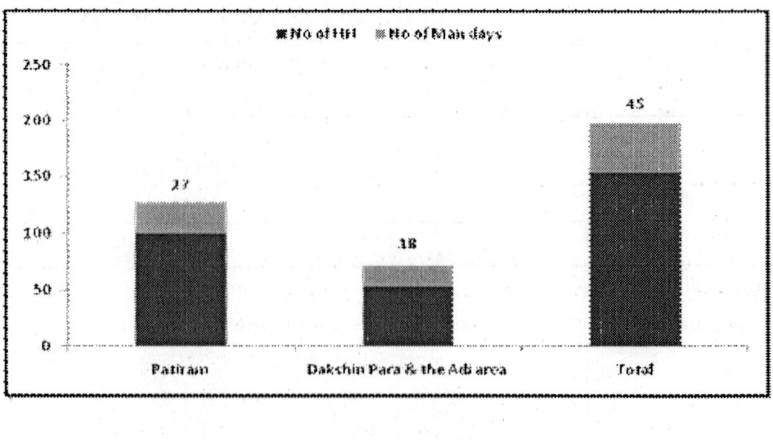

The data presented in table -12 shows that only 12 man days had been created in Patiram GP in 2007. This programme is known as the 'food for work' programme. This was started on November 14, 2004 in 150 most backward districts of India.

Table-13: Government Aid Received: Chakvrigu GP

Village	*No. of Households*	*No. of Man days (per person)*
Gobindapur	50	04
Mayamari	40	06
Kuaron	50	NIL
Chakvrigue	75	NIL
Dakra	27	02
Total	242	12 (10)

Source: Field survey, 2007

Note: Figures in the parentheses indicate per person man-days.

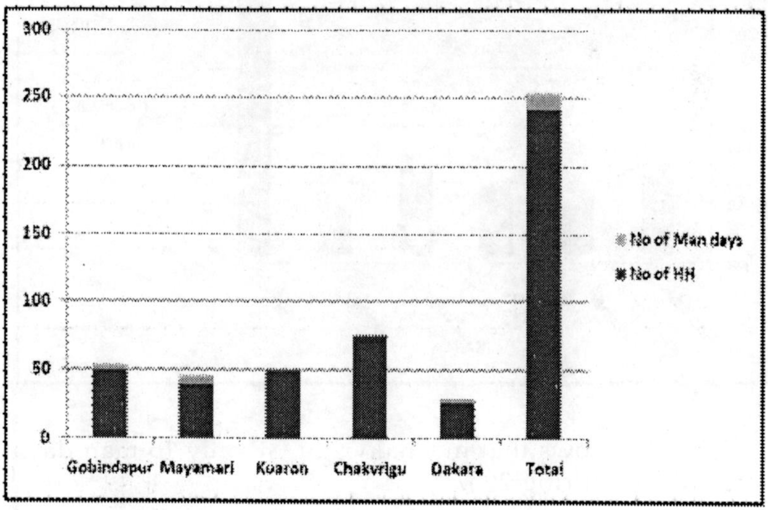

The table -13 shows that only 12 families received government aid during 2007. Only about 10 families received government aid during 2007 in Chakvrigu GP.

Table- 14: 100 days work: Chakvrigu GP (During 2007)

Village	*No. of Households*	*No. of Man days (per person)*
Gobindapur	50	12
Mayamari	40	14
Kuaron	50	05
Chakvrigue	75	08
Dakra	27	07
Total	242	46 (15)

Source:Field survey, 2007

Note: Figures in the parentheses indicate per person no. of man-days created.

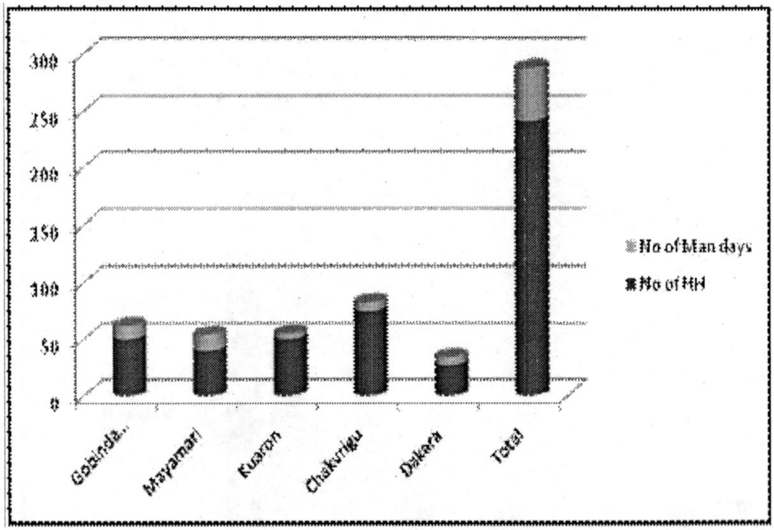

Table-14 shows that in Chakvrigu GP only 15 man-days were created during 2007.

Government aid received and 100-days work got by the rural people of Balurghat subdivision are shown in tables-15 and 16, respectively. Table-15 shows that only 5 percent households received government aid and table -16 shows that only 13.5 man-days were created in Balurghat rural areas.

Table-15: Government Aid Received: Balurghat

GP	*No. of Households*	*Govt. Aid Received*
Patiram	154	11 (7.1)
Chakvrigu	242	12 (4.95)
Total	396	23(5.0)

Source: Field survey, 2007

Note: Figures in the parentheses indicate percent to total.

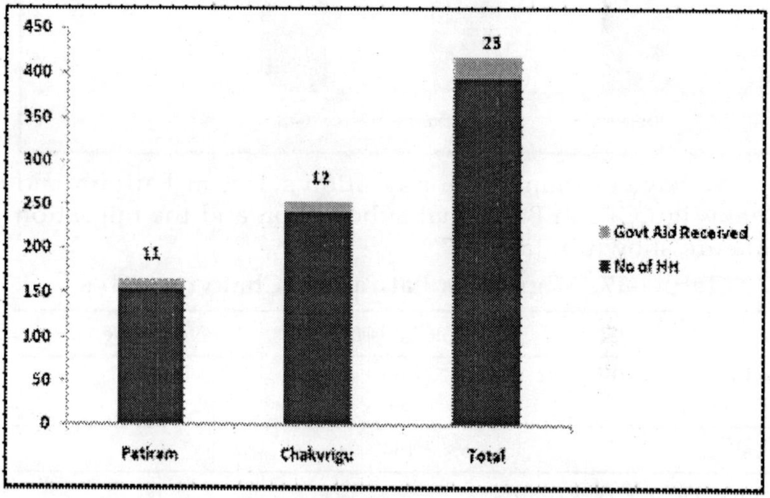

Table-16: 100 Days work: Balurghat sample villages

GP	*No. of Households*	*No. of Man days (per person)*
Patiram	154	12
Chakvrigu	242	15
Total	396	13.5

Source:Field survey, 2007

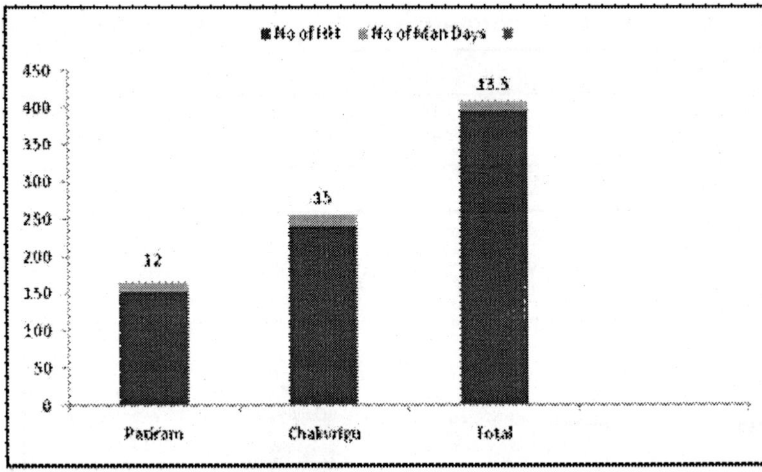

We have examined the migration status at Patiram and Chakvrigu GPs in Balurghat subdivision and the migration data are shown in table-17.

Table -17: Migration: Patiram & Chakvrigu GPs

GP	*No. of Households*	*No. of Migrants*
Patiram	100	17
Chakvrigu	54	16
Total	154	33

Source: Field Survey, 2007

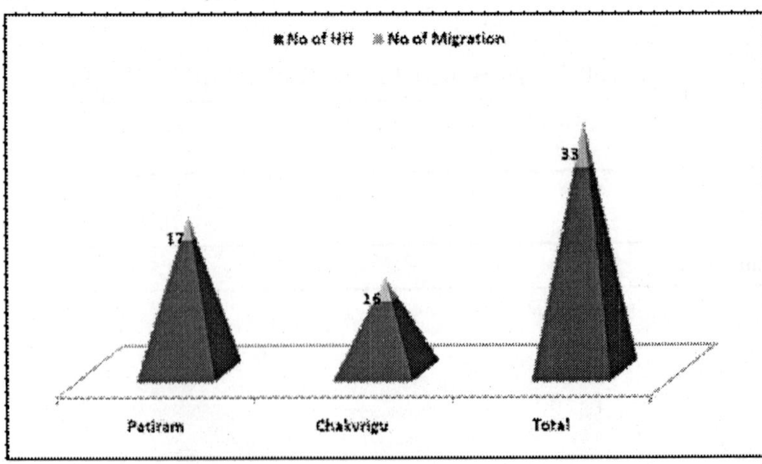

From our survey we found only 17 persons migrated from Patiram villages during 2007 and there were 16 persons who migrated from Chakvrigu villages. But all such migrations were temporary migration. The time period during which they did migrate was 3 to 6 months. Certainly, the migration of at least one member from a family improved the economic status of the household; but at the same time the people migrated & returned back to their home with fatal disease.

We noticed that about 100 families from where at least one person migrated to Delhi, or Haryana, or Kerala had improved their residential buildings (partially pucca) with toilet facilities along with personal tube well. Along with this, each and every child of such families was regularly attending school. The dropout rate was almost nil. The illiteracy rate which we found (about 45 percent) was among the elders and seniors of the villagers.

Table-18: Meal Status: Village Gobindapur

Land Holding (in acre)	*Two square meals taken* Three months	Six Months	*No of Persons* Throughout the year	*Total*
0-.33	-	38	01	39
.34- 1.0	-	04	05	09
1.01 -2.00	-	-	02	02
Above 2.00	-	-	-	-
Total	-	42	08	50

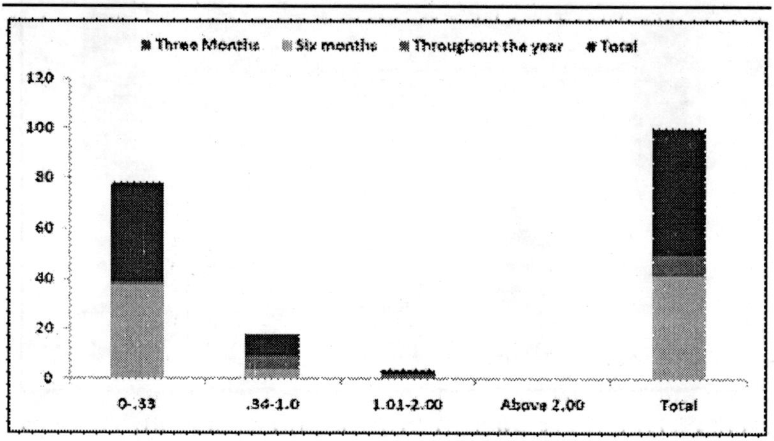

Examining the meal status of Gobindapur shown in table 18, we can see that 84 percent people cannot take two square meals throughout the year. They are really the poorest of the poor. Only in terms of food intake, also we can estimate poverty. Meal status of the sample households(village-wise,GP -wise,and the sample households in the Balurghat subdivision as a whole has been shown in tables 6.22,6.23,6.24,6.25,6.26,6.27,6.28 and 6.29 respectively.

Table-19: Meal Status: Village Mayamari

Land Holding (in acre)	*Two square meals taken* Three months	*Six Months*	*No of Persons Throughout the year*	*Total*
0-.33	02	28	-	30
.34- 1.0	-	-	09	09
1.01 -2.00	-	-	01	01
Above 2.00	-	-	-	-
Total	02	28	10	40

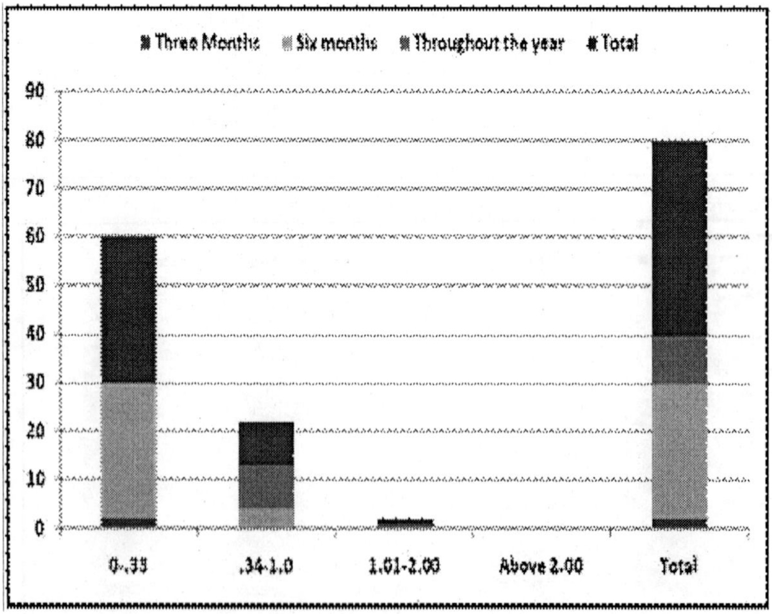

Table-20: Meal Status: Village Kuaran

Land Holding (in acre)	*Two square meals taken* *Three months*	*Six Months*	*No of Persons Throughout the year*	*Total*
0-.33	23	22	05	50
.34-1.0	-	-	-	-
1.01-2.00	-	-	-	-
Above 2.00	-	-	-	-
Total	23	22	05	50

Table-21: Meal Status: Village Chakvrigu

Land Holding (in acre)	*Two square meals taken* *Three months*	*Six Months*	*No of Persons Throughout the year*	*Total*
0-.33	06	58	07	71
.34-1.0	-	-	-	-
1.01-2.00	-	-	-	-
Above 2.00	-	-	04	04
Total	06	58	11	75

Table-22: Meal Status: Village Mayamari

Land Holding (in acre)	*Two square meals taken* *Three months*	*Six Months*	*No of Persons Throughout the year*	*Total*
0-.33	07	19	-	26
.34- 1.0	-	-	01	01
1.01 -2.00	-	-	-	-
Above 2.00	-	-	-	-
Total	07	19	01	27

Table-23: Meal Status: Village Patiram

Land Holding (in acre)	Two square meals taken Three months	Six Months	No of Persons Throughout the year	Total
0-.33	17	50	27	94
.34- 1.0	-	-	02	02
1.01 -2.00	-	-	03	03
Above 2.00	-	-	01	01
Total	17	50	33	100

Table-24: Meal Status: Village Dakshin para and adjacent area

Land Holding (in acre)	Two square meals taken Three months	Six Months	No of Persons Throughout the year	Total
0-.33	16	22	03	41
.34- 1.0	01	05	03	09
1.01 -2.00	-	-	03	03
Above 2.00	-	-	01	01
Total	17	27	10	54

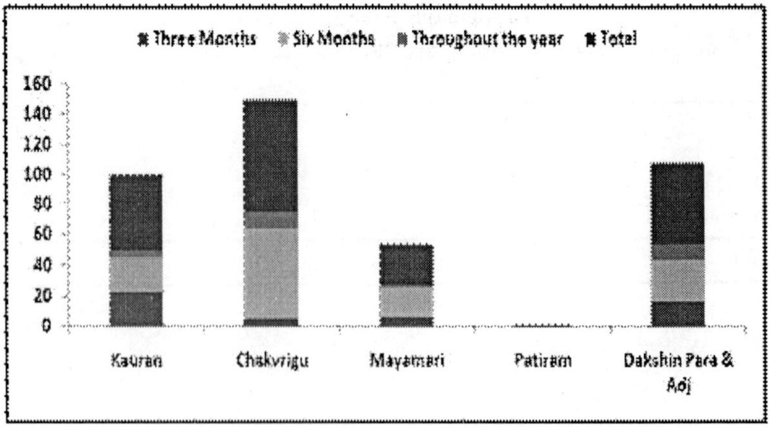

Table-25: BPL Status: Balurghat subdivision

Village	*Poor*	*(%)*	*Non-poor*	*(%)*	*Total*
Gobindapur	42	(84%)	08	(16%)	50
Mayamari	32	(75%)	10	(25%)	40
Kuaron	45	(90%)	05	(10%)	50
Chakvrigu	64	(85.33%)	11	(14.6%)	75
Dakra	26	(96.29%)	01	(3.7%)	27
Patiram	67	(67%)	33	(33%)	100
Dakshin Para & the Adi. Area	44	(81.48%)	10	(18.51%)	54
Total	318	(80.34%)	78	(19.66%)	396

Source: Field Survey, 2007

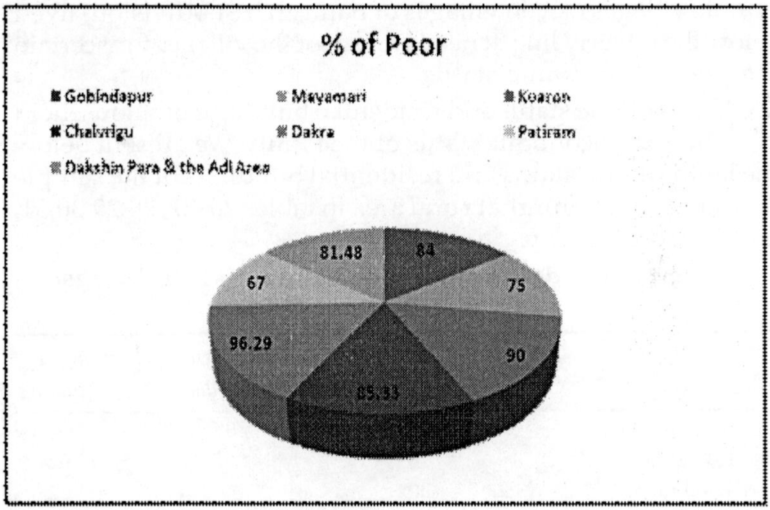

We have indentified the BPL status of survey villages under Balurghat subdivision and presented this in table-6.29. We surveyed seven villages. Total number of respondents was 396, of which 318 belonged to BPL category. We now count the proportion of poor in the sample villages under Balurghat subdivision. The formula for calculating proportion of poor is as follows.

$P_0 \quad P_N N$

Here

$P_0 \quad 396^{318} \quad 0.803$

Where Po = Proportion of Poor

P_N = Total number of Poor

N = Total Population

This means that more than 80 percent of people of the sample villages (seven villages of Balurghat Subdivision) lived below the poverty line. It needs revisit of the villages to ascertain the present economic status.

Landholding status and residential buildings of a household also show the economic status of the family. We present below the landholding status and residential buildings of the sample households of Balurghat rural area in tables 26, 27, 28,29,30,31, and 32, respectively.

Table-26: Land Holding and Residential Buildings: Gobindapur

	Land Holding and Residential Building		
Land Holding (in acre)	*No. of Households*	*Kachha*	*Pucca*
Up to .33 (acre)	39	39	-
.34- 1.00 (acre)	09	07	02
1.01 -2.00 (acre)	02	-	02
Above 2.00 (acre)	-	-	-
Total	50	46	04

Source:Field Survey, 2007

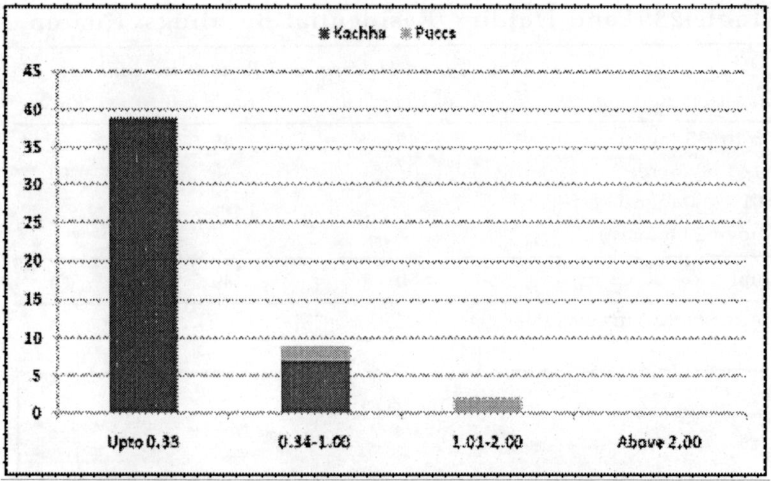

Table –27: Land Holding Residential Buildings: Mayamari

Land Holding (in acre)	Land Holding and Residential Building No. of Households	Kachha	Pucca
Up to .33 (acre)	29	28	01
.34- 1.00 (acre)	10	09	01
1.01 -2.00 (acre)	01	-	01
Above 2.00 (acre)	-	-	-
Total	40	37	03

Source:Field Survey, 2007

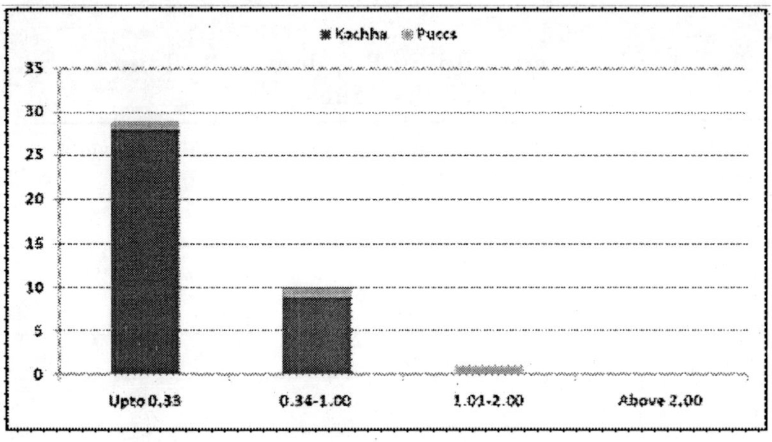

Table-28: Land Holding Residential Buildings: Kuaron

Land Holding (in acre)	*Land Holding and Residential Building* No. of Households	Kachha	Pucca
Up to .33 (acre)	49	49	-
.34- 1.00 (acre)	01	-	01
1.01 -2.00 (acre)	-	-	-
Above 2.00 (acre)	-	-	-
Total	50	49	01

Source:Field Survey, 2007

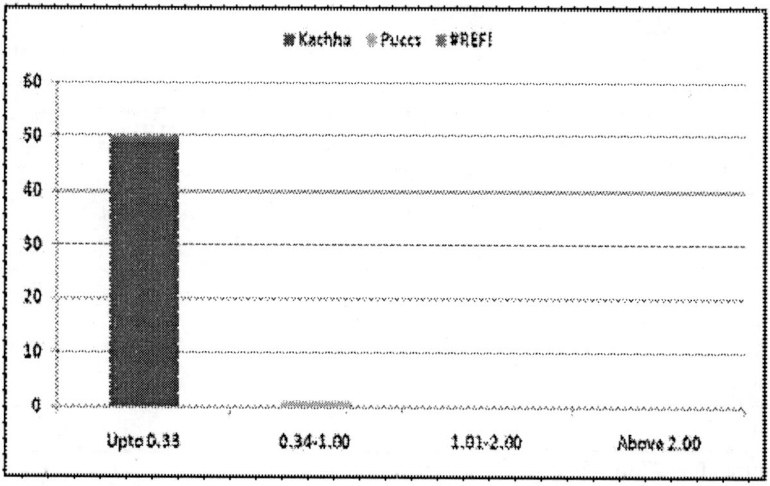

Table-29: Land Holding Residential Buildings: Chakvrigue

Land Holding (in acre)	*Land Holding and Residential Building* No. of Households	Kachha	Pucca
Up to .33 (acre)	69	69	-
.34- 1.00 (acre)	04	04	-
1.01 -2.00 (acre)	01	-	01
Above 2.00 (acre)	01	-	01
Total	75	73	02

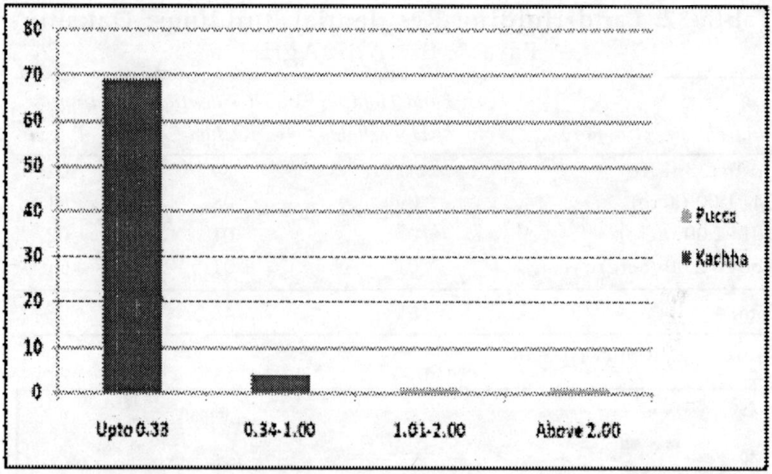

Table-30: Land Holding Residential Buildings: Dakre

	Land Holding and Residential Building		
Land Holding (in acre)	*No. of Households*	*Kachha*	*Pucca*
Up to .33 (acre)	26	26	-
.34- 1.00 (acre)		01	-
011.01 -2.00 (acre)	-	-	-
Above 2.00 (acre)	-	-	-
Total	27	-	-

Source:Field Survey, 2007

Table-31: Land Holding Residential Buildings: Kuaron

	Land Holding and Residential Building		
Land Holding (in acre)	*No. of Households*	*Kachha*	*Pucca*
Up to .33 (acre)	89	81	11
.34- 1.00 (acre)	05	03	01
1.01 -2.00 (acre)	04	-	03
Above 2.00 (acre)	02	-	01
Total	100	84	16

Source:Field Survey, 2007

Table-32: Land Holding Residential Buildings: Dakshin Para & the Adi. Agri.

	Land Holding and Residential Building		
Land Holding (in acre)	*No. of Households*	*Kachha*	*Pucca*
Up to .33 (acre)	41	39	02
.34- 1.00 (acre)	09	08	01
1.01 -2.00 (acre)	03	01	02
Above 2.00 (acre)	01	01	01
Total	54	48	06

Source: Field Survey, 2007

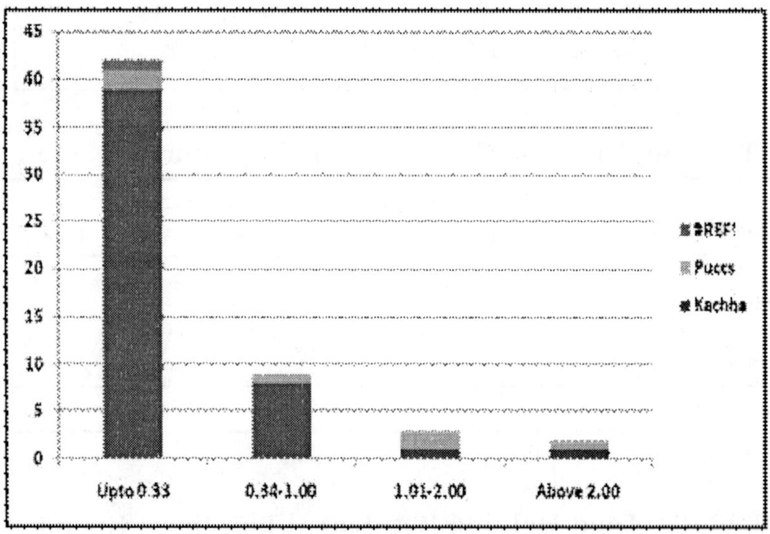

Our Survey – II: Our second survey relates to two GPs under Gangarampur subdivision of Dakshin Dinajpur District. This covers some important parameters of sample villages, such as land holding, status of residential building, meal status, government aid received by the households, food for work benefit (100-days work), migration, educational status of the members of households etc. The villages surveyed under Gangarampur subdivision are relatively more rural and remote than those of the Balurghat villages. The results collected and tabulated have been displayed in tabular forms. The literacy status (village -wise, GP-wise and Gangarampur subdivision as a whole (total samples) is shown in tables 33, 34. 35, 36. 37, 38, 39, 40, 41, and 42 respectively.

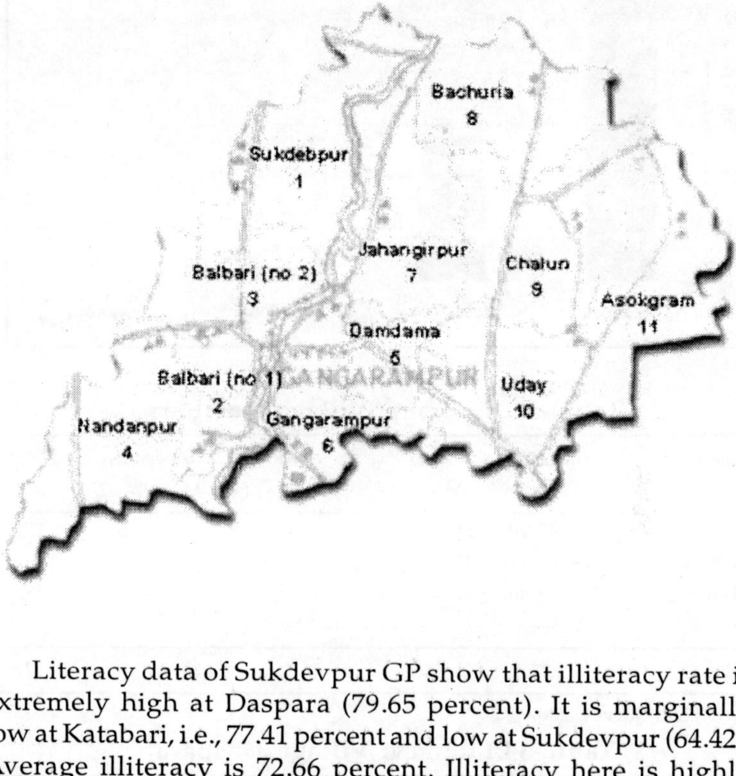

Literacy data of Sukdevpur GP show that illiteracy rate is extremely high at Daspara (79.65 percent). It is marginally low at Katabari, i.e., 77.41 percent and low at Sukdevpur (64.42). Average illiteracy is 72.66 percent. Illiteracy here is highly positively correlated with poverty. The census data, 2011 show that in Sukdevpur GP there were 62.66 percent BPL status people. Our survey reveals that it was 63 percent in 2007. In the whole of Gangarampur subdivision, the illiteracy rate was more than 50 percent (52.79 percent).

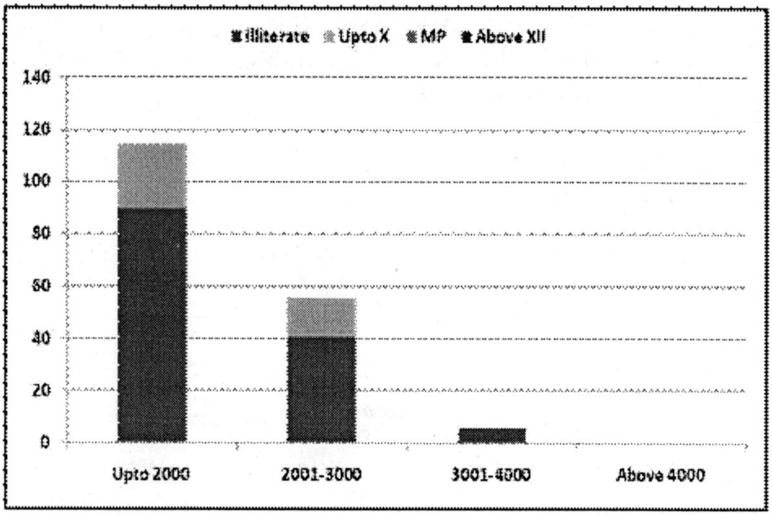

Table-33: Literacy: Village Katabari

Income (Rs)	*Illiterate*			*Up to X*			*MP*			*Above XII*			*Total*
	M	*F*	*T*	*M*	*F*	*T*	*M*	*F*	*T*	*M*	*F*	*T*	
Upto 2000	43	47	90	11	14	25	-	-	-	-	-	-	115
2001-3000	19	22	41	07	08	15	-	-	-	-	-	-	56
3001-4000	03	03	06	-	-	-	-	-	-	-	-	-	06
Above 4000	-	-	-	-	-	-	-	-	-	-	-	-	-
Total		137			40								177

Source: Field Survey, 2007

Table-34:Literacy: Village Daspara

Income (Rs)	*Illiterate*			*Up to X*			*MP*			*Above XII*			*Total*
	M	*F*	*T*	*M*	*F*	*T*	*M*	*F*	*T*	*M*	*F*	*T*	
Upto 2000	84	83	167	15	10	25	01	6	01	01	-	01	194
2001-3000	06	08	14	08	06	14	01	04	05	01	-	01	34
3001-4000	02	01	03	-	-	-	-	-	-	-	-	-	03
Above 4000	-	-	-	-	-	-	-	-	-	-	-	-	-
Total		184			39			06			02		231

Source: Field Survey, 2007

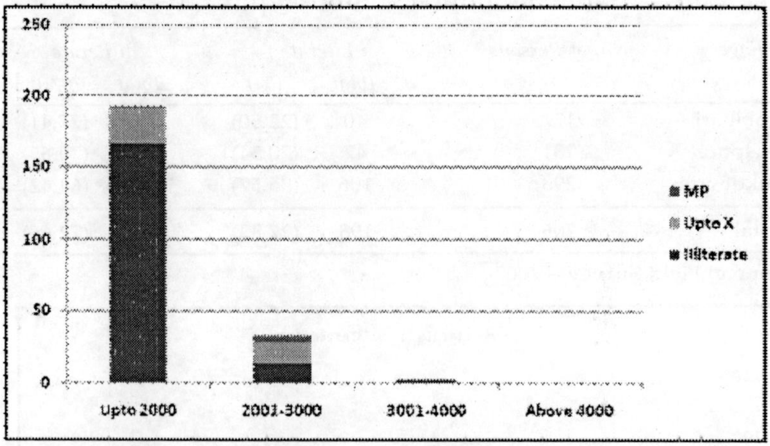

Table-35: Literacy: Village Sukdevpur

Income (Rs)	*Illiterate*			*Up to X*			*MP*			*Above XII*			*Total*
	M	*F*	*T*	*M*	*F*	*T*	*M*	*F*	*T*	*M*	*F*	*T*	
Upto 2000	95	75	140	36	36	72		01	01		01	01	214
2001-3000	26	26	52	12	19	31		01	01				84
3001-4000	-	-	-	-	-	-	-	-	-	-	-	-	-
Above 4000	-	-	-	-	-	-	-	-	-	-	-	-	-
Total		192			103			02			01		298

Source: Field Survey, 2007

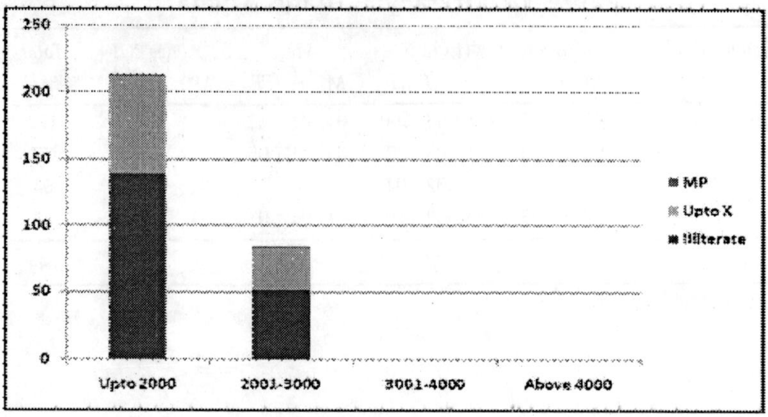

Table-36: Literacy: Sukdevpur GP

Village	*No. of Persons*	*Literate*		*Illiterate*	
		Total	*(%)*	*Total*	*(%)*
Kotabari	177	40	(22.50)	137	(77.41)
Daspore	231	47	(20.34)	184	(79.65)
Sukdevpur	298	106	(35.57)	192	(64.42)
Total	706	193	(27.33)	513	(72.66)

Source: Field Survey – 2007

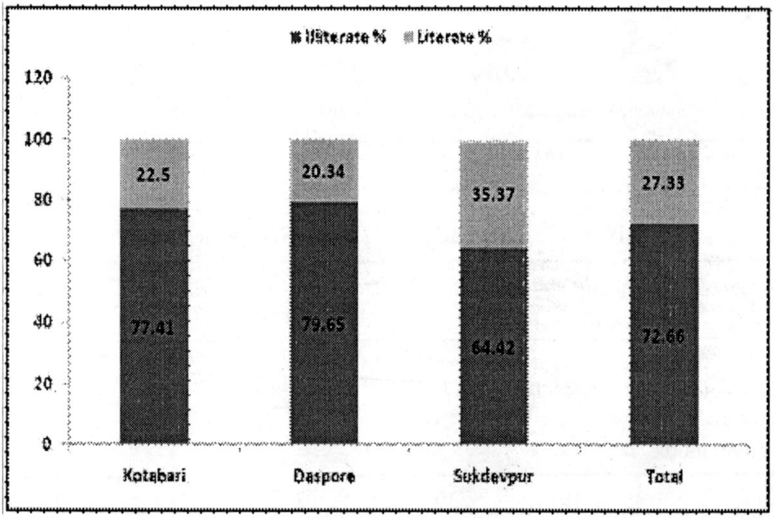

Table-37: Literacy: Village Ausha

Income (Rs)	*Illiterate*			*Up to X*			*MP*			*Above XII*			*Total*
	M	*F*	*T*	*M*	*F*	*T*	*M*	*F*	*T*	*M*	*F*	*T*	
Upto 2000	25	52	77	47	53	100	01	01	02	-	-	-	179
2001-3000	03	07	10	14	08	22	04	01	05	-	-	-	37
3001-4000	-	-	-	02	02	04	-	-	-	-	-	-	04
Above 4000	02	01	03	10	09	19	01	01	02	-	-	-	24
Total		90			145			09					244

Source: Field Survey, 2007.

Table-38: Literacy: Village Pulinda

Income (Rs)	*Illiterate*			*Up to X*			*MP*			*Above XII*			*Total*
	M	*F*	*T*	*M*	*F*	*T*	*M*	*F*	*T*	*M*	*F*	*T*	
Upto 2000	93	106	199	87	77	164	05	01	06	01	-	01	370
2001-3000	15	15	30	06	07	13	02	01	03	-	-	-	46
3001-4000	03	03	06	08	08	16	01	01	02	-	-	-	24
Above 4000	04	04	08	03	02	05	02	01	03	01	-	01	17
Total		243			198			14			02		457

Source: Field Survey, 2007

Table-6.43:Literacy: Village Panchagram

Income (Rs)	*Illiterate*			*Up to X*			*MP*			*Above XII*			*Total*
	M	*F*	*T*	*M*	*F*	*T*	*M*	*F*	*T*	*M*	*F*	*T*	
Upto 2000	19	24	43	12	07	19	-	-	-	-	-	-	62
2001-3000		01	01	01		01	-	-	-	-	-	-	02
3001-4000	-	-	-	-	-	-	-	-	-	-	-	-	
Above 4000	-	-	-	-	-	-	-	-	-	-	-	-	
Total		44			20								64

Source:Field Survey, 2007

Table-39:Literacy: Village Panchagram

Income (Rs)	*Illiterate*			*Up to X*			*MP*			*Above XII*			*Total*
	M	*F*	*T*	*M*	*F*	*T*	*M*	*F*	*T*	*M*	*F*	*T*	
Upto 2000	10	16	26	13	14	27	-	01	01	-	-	-	54
2001-3000	02	02	04	04	07	11	-	-	-	-	-	-	15
3001-4000	-	-	-	-	-	-	-	-	-	-	-	-	-
Above 4000	-	-	-	-	-	-	-	-	-	-	-	-	-
Total		30			38			01					69

Source: Field Survey, 2007

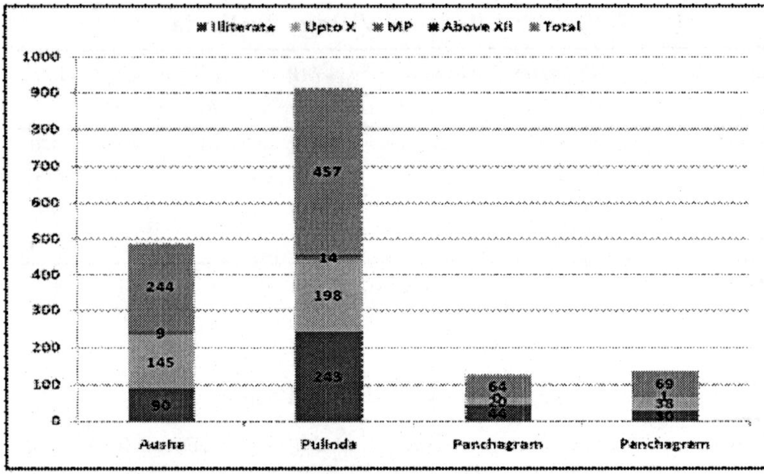

Table-40:Literacy: Uday GP

Village	*No. of Persons*	*Literate*		*Illiterate*	
		Total	*(%)*	*Total*	*(%)*
Ausha	244	154	(63.11)	90	(736.89)
Pulinda	457	214	(46.82)	243	(53.18)
Panchagram	64	20	(31.25)	44	(68.75)
Itagichak	69	39	(56.52)	30	(43.48)
Total	834	427	(51.19)	407	(48.81)

Source: Field Survey – 2007

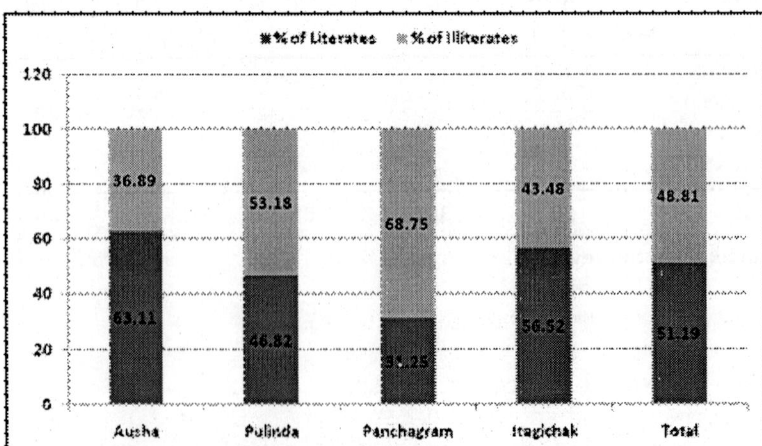

Table-41:Literacy: Gangarampur Sub: Division

GP	*No. of Persons*	*Literates*		*Illiterates*	
		Total	*(%)*	*Total*	*(%)*
Uday GP	834	427	(51.10)	407	(48.81)
Sukdevpur	706	386	(54.67)	320	(45.33)
Total	1540	813	(52.79)	727	(47.21)

Source: Field Survey – 2007

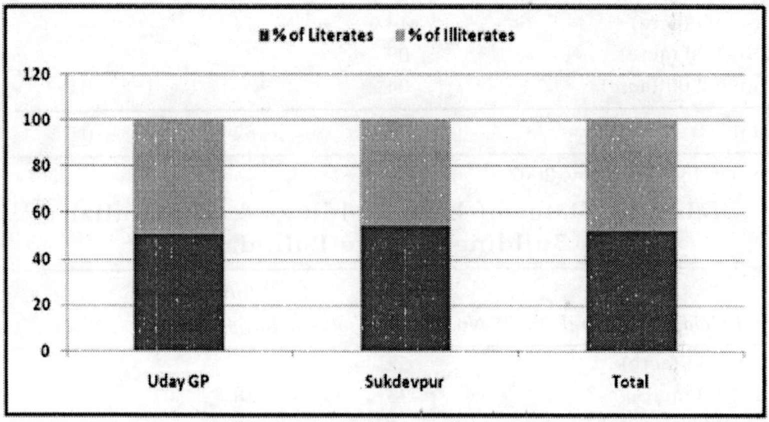

During our entire survey in 2007, we have clearly noticed that most of the sample villagers do not have access over land, financial resources, knowledge and other assets along with levels of literacy. They also have inadequate access over health facilities. They do not have piped drinking water nor do they have sanitary facilities (excepting a few).

We begin our analysis with the discussion of access to land (land-holding status) and the status of residential buildings. Data collected on land-holding status (land for building residence and cultivated land) show that about 68 percent of the sample households possess land up to .33 acre. They don't have access over cultivated land and a few of them have cultivated land over tiny plots which are not economically viable and thus not remunerative. In this category (households having land less than .33 acre), also landless vested land-holders belong. In the whole of our sample villages under Gangarampur subdivision, the total numbers of households received vested land are only 12.The land holding status and the status of residential buildings have been shown in tables 42,43,44,45,46,47, and 48 6.47,6.48, respectively.

Table-42: Status of Land Holdings & Residential Building: Village Ausha

Land Holding (in acre)	*No. of Households*	*Resd. Building* *Kachha*	*Pucca*
Up to .33 (acre)	29	29	-
.34- 1.00 (acre)	14	14	-
1.01 -2.00 (acre)	09	09	-
Above 2.00 (acre)	04	-	04
Total	56	52	04

Source: Field Survey, 2007

Table-43: Status of Land Holdings & Residential Building: Village Pulinda

Land Holding (in acre)	*No. of Households*	*Resd. Building* *Kachha*	*Pucca*
Up to .33 (acre)	52	52	-
.34- 1.00 (acre)	28	28	-
1.01 -2.00 (acre)	15	15	-
Above 2.00 (acre)	05	05	-
Total	100	100	-

Source: Field Survey, 2007

Table-44: Status of Land Holdings & Residential Building: Village Panchagram

Land Holding (in acre)	*No. of Households*	*Resd. Building* *Kachha*	*Pucca*
Up to .33 (acre)	14	14	-
.34- 1.00 (acre)	07	06	01
1.01 -2.00 (acre)	-	-	-
Above 2.00 (acre)	-	-	-
Total	21	20	01

Source: Field Survey, 2007

Table-45: Status of Land Holdings & Residential Building: Village Hajichak

Land Holding (in acre)	*No. of Households*	*Resd. Building* Kachha	Pucca
Up to .33 (acre)	18	18	-
.34- 1.00 (acre)	01	01	-
1.01 -2.00 (acre)	02	01	01
Above 2.00 (acre)	-	-	-
Total	21	20	01

Source: Field Survey, 2007

Table-46: Status of Land Holdings & Residential Building: Village Katabari

Land Holding (in acre)	*No. of Households*	*Resd. Building* Kachha	Pucca
Up to .33 (acre)	35	35	-
.34- 1.00 (acre)	11	10	01
1.01 -2.00 (acre)	01	-	01
Above 2.00 (acre)	01	-	01
Total	48	45	03

Source: Field Survey, 2007

Table-47: Status of Land Holdings & Residential Building: Village Daspara

Land Holding (in acre)	*No. of Households*	*Resd. Building* Kachha	Pucca
Up to .33 (acre)	51	51	-
.34- 1.00 (acre)	17	16	-
1.01 -2.00 (acre)	03	-	04
Above 2.00 (acre)	02	-	02
Total	73	67	06

Source: Field Survey, 2007

Table-48: Status of Land Holdings & Residential Building: Village Sukdevpur

Land Holding (in acre)	*No. of Households*	*Resd. Building* Kachha	Pucca
Up to .33 (acre)	84	84	-
.34- 1.00 (acre)	12	11	1
1.01 -2.00 (acre)	04	1	3
Above 2.00 (acre)	-	-	-
Total	100	96	04

Source: Field Survey, 2007

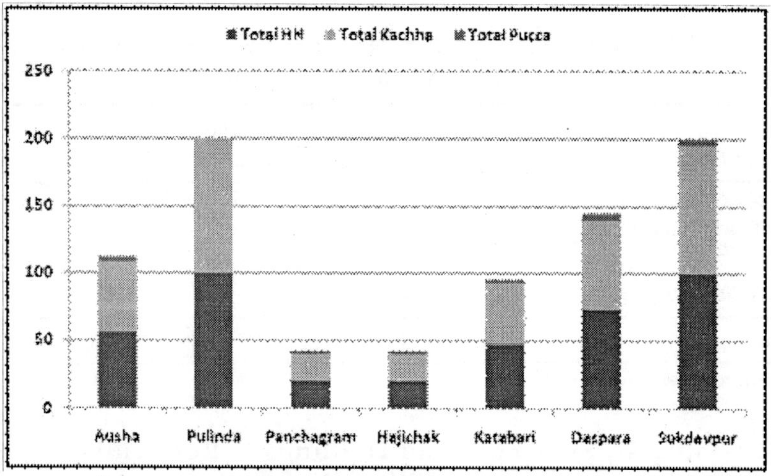

Identifying the poor is very time consuming and painstaking if that is done on the basis of income earned or consumption expenditure made by a person. For this reason, most of the developing countries use 'proxy means tests' to identify the 'poor'. In a proxy means tests, each family gets scored on the basis of a small number of variables essential for the family's minimum standard of living(Dutta,2013). These are like the ownership of land, kind of home, i.e. whether the house is *pucca* or *kucha*, meal status i.e. whether a person does have two square meals, a day. Also some measures of earning capacity such as the education and training of the adults, type of jobs they hold etc. Some other indices are also taken into consideration. These are called behavioral responses to poverty i.e. whether the children are in school or working, whether they are working in times of playing, etc.

In identifying the BPL population in the rural areas the identification either suffers from 'inclusion error' or 'exclusion error'. In inclusion error it happens 'over identification' of the BPL population i.e. there are some persons who are ineligible to become poor have got BPL card. In the case of 'exclusion error 'some persons who are really poor have not been considered as poor and thus not been placed in the BPL list.

Our survey results on government aid received by the beneficiaries, 100-days work enjoyed, migration took place, meal status of the sample households & BPL status have been shown in tables 49,50,51,52,53, 54, 55, 56, 57,58,59,60, 61,62,63, 64,65, and 66.

.Official BPL status (data supplied by the Department of Panchayat and Rural Development, Government of West Bengal, 2009) has also been shown in table -6.68,respectively.

Table-49: Govt. Aid Received: Uday GP

Village	*Total no. of Households*	*No. of households received aid*
Ausha	56	07
Pulinda	100	08
Panchagram	21	01
Hajichak	21	02
Total	108	18

Source: Field Survey-2007

Table-50: 100 Days Work: Uday GP

Village	*No.of House Holders*	*No. of Days Worked (Per Person)*
Ausha	56	30
Pulinda	100	35
Panchagram	21	10
Hajichak	21	12
Total	108	87(18)

Source: Field Survey, 2007

Note: Figures in the parentheses indicate per person man-days.

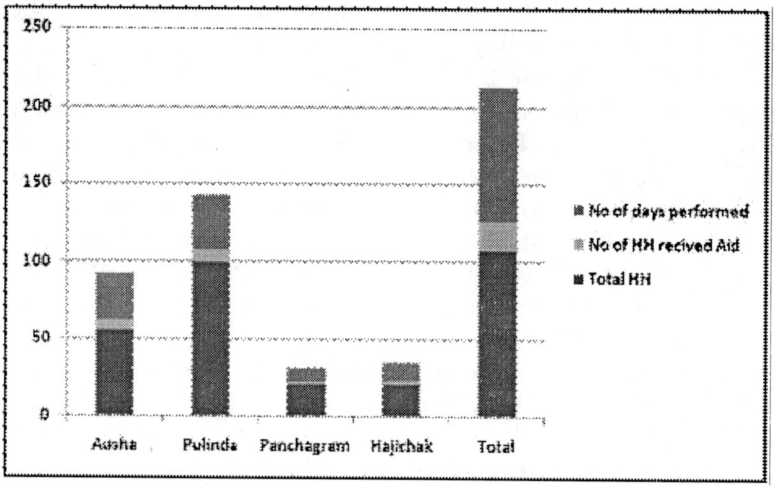

Table-51: Govt. Aid Received Sukdevpur GP

Village	*No. of Households*	*Govt. Aid Received*
Katabari	48	01
Daspara	73	07
Sukdevpur	100	09
Total	221	17

Source: Field Survey-2001

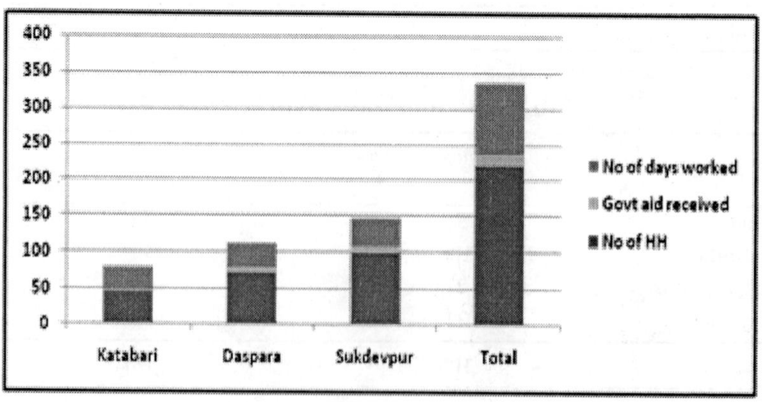

Table-52: 100 Days Work: Sukdevpur GP

Village	*No. of House Holds*	*No. of Days Worked (per person)*
Katabari	48	30
Daspara	73	32
Sukdevpur	100	38
Total	221	100 (21.5)

Source: Field Survey-2001.

Table-53: Migration

Name of GP	*Total households*	*No. of Migration*
Uday	108	35
Sukdevpur	221	17
Total	329	42

Source : Field Survey, 2007

Table-54: Government Aid Received: Gangarampur

Name of GP	*Total no. of households*	*No. of households received aid*
Uday	108	18
Sukdevpur	221	17
Total	329	35

Note: Figures in the parentheses indicate per person man-days.

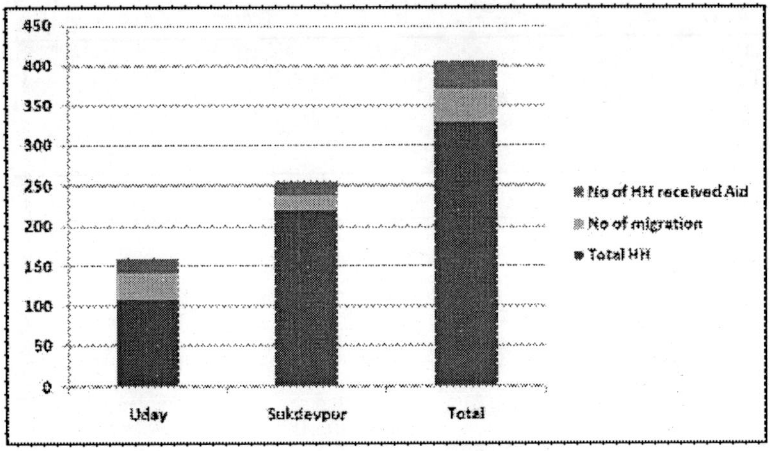

Table- 55: 100 Days Work: Gangarampur

Name of GP	*Total no. of households*	*No. of days worked (per person)*
Uday	108	18
Sukdevpur	221	21.5
Total	329	20.5

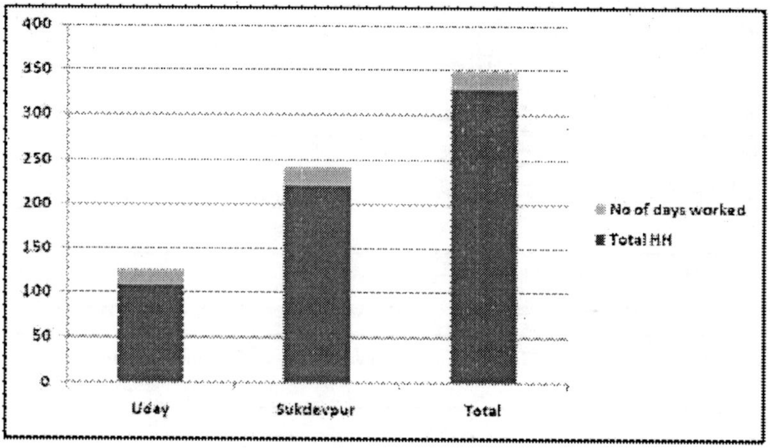

Table-56: Meal status: Ausha

	Two square meals taken			*No of Households*
Land Holding (in acre)	*Three months*	*Six Months*	*Throughout the year*	*Total*
0-.33	12	16	01	29
.34 – 1.0	-	12	02	14
1.01 – 2.00	-	-	09	09
Above 2.00	-	-	04	04
Total	12	28	16	56

Source: Field survey, 2007

Table-57 : Meal Status: Pulinda

Land Holding (in acre)	Two square meals taken: Three months	Six Months	Throughout the year	No of Households Total
0-.33	19	41		60
.34 – 1.0	-	13	02	15
1.01 – 2.00	-	-	06	06
Above 2.00	-	-	08	19
Total	19	54	16	100

Table-58: Meal Status: Panchagram

Land Holding (in acre)	Two square meals taken: Three months	Six Months	Throughout the year	No of Households Total
0-.33	-	14	-	14
.34 – 1.0	-	-	05	05
1.01 – 2.00	-	-	02	02
Above 2.00	-	-	-	-
Total	-	14	07	21

Table-59: Meal Status: Hajichak

Land Holding (in acre)	Two square meals taken: Three months	Six Months	Throughout the year	No of Households Total
0-.33	01	11	07	19
.34 – 1.0	-	-	01	01
1.01 – 2.00	-	-	01	01
Above 2.00	-	-	-	-
Total	01	11	09	21

Table-60: Meal Status: Katabari

Land Holding (in acre)	Two square meals taken: Three months	Six Months	Throughout the year	No of Households Total
0-.33	12	18	06	36
.34 – 1.0	03	02	05	10
1.01 – 2.00	-	-	01	01
Above 2.00	-	-	01	01
Total	15	20	13	48

Table-61: Meal Status : Village Daspara

	Two square meals taken			*No of Households*
Land Holding (in acre)	*Three months*	*Six Months*	*Throughout the year*	*Total*
0-.33	04	45	02	51
.34 – 1.0	-	07	10	17
1.01 – 2.00	-	-	03	03
Above 2.00	-	-	02	02
Total	04	52	17	73

Table-62: Meal Status: Sukdevpur

	Two square meals taken			*No of Households*
Land Holding (in acre)	*Three months*	*Six Months*	*Throughout the year*	*Total*
0-.33	06	67	-	73
.34 – 1.0	-	-	20	20
1.01 – 2.00	-	-	07	07
Above 2.00	-	-	-	-
Total	06	67	27	100

Table-63: BPL Status : Gangarampur Sub Division

Village	*Poor*	*(%)*	*Non-Poor*	*(%)*	*Total (%)*
Ausha	40	(71.43)	16	(28.57)	56
Pulinda	63 (63)	27 (27)	100		
Panchagram	14	(66.66)	07	(33.33)	21
Hajichak	12	(57.14)	09	(42.85)	21
Katabari	35	(72.91)	13	(27.08)	48
Daspara	56	(76.71)	17	(23.28)	73
Sukdevpur	63	(63)	27	(27)	100
total	283	(67.54)	116	(27.68)	419

Source: Field Survey, 2007.

The proportion of poor in the rural Gangarampur is calculated as follows.

PN 283

PO .... = ... = 0.675

N 419

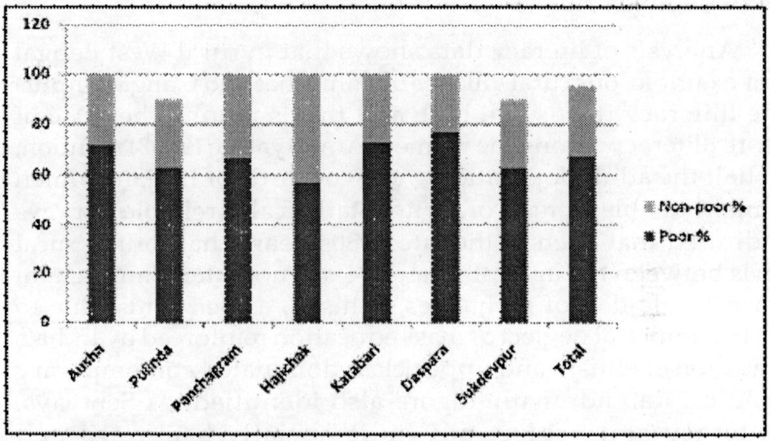

Table-65:Official BPL Status: Dakshin Dinajpur

Name of GP	*Population*	*BPL*	*%*
Chakvrigue	26,890	8,978	33.38
Patiram	35,821	10,377	28.96
Uday	14,168	8,345	58.90
Sukdevpur	23,347	14,631	62.66
Total	1,00,226	42,331	42.23

Source: Census of India, 2011 Dept. of Panchayat and Rural Development Govt. of West Bengal, 2009 Dakshin Dinajpur District.

Table-66:Official BPL: Dakshin Dinajpur District, 2009

Name of Block	*Population*	*BPL (2004)*	*%*
Balurghat	4,02,158	153776	38.23
Hili	83,754	48248	57.60
Kumarganj	169102	75593	44.70
Tapan	250504	108414	43.27
Gangarampur	293845	97278	33.10
Bangghihari	68665	51737	75.34
Kushamomdi	198752	74774	37.62
Harirampur	209496	87911	41.96
Total	16,76,276	6,97,731	41.62

Source: Census, 2011, Deptt. Of P & RD, Dakshin Dinajpur.

Conclusion

Analysis of literacy data shows that in rural West Bengal (for example, our rural villages of Balurghat and Gangarampur) the illiteracy rate is still high and this is more so because of more illiteracy among the women. Amartya Sen (2003) mention, ".. half the adult population and two-thirds of Indian women remain unable to read or write. Statistically reliable surveys indicated that even in the late 1980s nearly half of the rural girls between the ages of 12 and 14 did not attend any school for a single day of their lives". This is, as Sen hints, due to British imperial neglect of mass education reinforced by India's tradition of elitism and upper-class dominated contemporary politics. Rabindranath Tagore also identified, as Sen says, illiteracy and neglect put India socially backward and economically underdeveloped (Sen, 2005).

On the basis of food intake (two sqauer meals a day), we have estimated BPL population in Balurghat and Gangarampur rural areas. We have also calculated proportion of poor for both the areas. The proportion of poor is extremely high i.e., it is 0.803 in rural Balurghat and in rural Gangarampur it is 0.675. This may perhaps be due to the fact that there are more job opportunities in rural Gangarampur than Balurghat. The rural Gangarampur is agriculturally developed with the vast expansion of multiple cropping (three crops in a year) and larger productivity rate than agriculture in rural Balurghat. We have noticed a huge illiteracy among the rural masses ,more than 45 percent. This is more among the women and girl children. A large number of child labour we have noticed in agricultural activities especially during the sowing and harvesting seasons. While comparing BPL population data (our data with official data) we particularly found a huge gap. Huge variation in poverty is found in Chakvarigu and Patiram, while the gap has been minimum in Uday and Sukdevpur GPs. Overall poverty gap is about 25 percent (our results : 67.54 percent, official results: 42.23 percent).

Data collected and presented in tabular forms tell us that the government aid received by the rural households is very negligible. In rural Balurghat only about 5 percent households received government aid and in rural Gangarampur this amount is only 10.6 percent. Overall amount of Government aid received by rural households of the Dakshin Dinajpur District was only 8.7 percent. This amount of aid, we think, cannot improve the economic status of rural poor.

As regard the implementation of 100 days work we also find that only 13.5 man-days were created in rural Balurghat and that 20.5 in rural Gangarampur. Overall man -days created in rural Dakshin Dinajpur were only 17 days (per person).

NOTES AND REFERENCES

1. M.S. Ahluwalia, "Rural Poverty and Agricultural Performance in India", *Journal of Development Studies,* 22, 1977.
2. Abhijit V Banerjee : "Why Fighting Poverty is Hard", Massachusetts Institute of Technology, September, 2008.
3. Pranab K Bardhan, (1973): " On the Incidence of Poverty in Rural India of the Sixties", Annual Number, Feb'1973.
4. A. Bhuimali, (2003) 'Gandhian Economics and Globalisation': *International Journal of Nov-violence - In- Action,* Vol-1, No-2, July, 2003.
5. A. Bhuimali, 'In Search of a Model Rural Cooperative Credit Society for India', *Indian Journal of Social Development,* Vol. 2, No. 2, 2002.
6. A. Bhuimali, 'Relevance of M.K. Gandhi's Idea of Self-Sufficient village Economy in the 21st Century', Abstract published in the Conference Volume of Indian Society of Gandhi an Studies XXIVth Conference Volume, 2001.
7. A. Bhuimali, 'Science & Humanity: Some Critical Issues', in A.Puspa Rajan (ed.) A value Crisis on the Way Out, Department of Inter-religious Studies, Madurai, Kamraj University, 2002.
8. A. Bhuimali, *Rural Cooperative and Economic Development,* Sarup and Sons, 2003.
9. A. Sen, (2005): *The Argumentative Indian,* Allen Lane.
10. A.K., Sen, *Choice of techniques,* Oxford University, 1962.
11. Amartya Sen, (1987): *The Standard of Living,* Published by Press Syndicate of the University of Cambridge.
12. Amartya Sen, (2006) : *Identity and Violence. 'The Illusion of Destiny'.* Allen Law, Published by the Penguin Group.

12.

The Community–Forest Relationship: Evidences from Joint Forest Management in North Bengal

Salil Mukherjee

Introduction:

In recent years there has been increased forest degradation. At present 9.4 million hectares of forest disappeared every year during the period 1990 and 2000. India's existing forest are primarily concentrated in three regions : the central forest belt with it's nexus in the Chhotanagpur plateau of Orissa, Bihar and Madhya Pradesh; the northsouth belt of the Western Ghats and the Himalayan band stretching from the north to the northeast. Forests are an important source of food specially for the local community those who settled in and around the forest. Reportedly, 60 percent of non-timber forest product (NTFP) is consumed as food or as a supplement by forest dwellers. In a survey of 216 household (Tribal and Caste), it was found that, of the 122 uses of plants or their parts listed by the people, the maximum were food (44) followed by fuel (39) and medicinal purposes (18). [Malhotra et al 1991]. Besides this forests provide multiple services to the multiple users. The demand for these services from the forest is also increasing at a rapid rate. 70 percent of the rural and 50 percent of the urban people use fuel wood for cooking purposes. Forest meets nearly 80 percent of the rural energy requirements (according to India's submission at UNCED). Apart from subsistence fuel wood needs, 'headloading' of fuel wood is also an important source of income for many poor families. Thus their dependence on fuel wood is likely to continue for several more years. A host of policy measures had been taken from time to time for conservation of forest bio-diversity (see Aneexure). But even after the persuasion of such long drawn policies in several years; till now we are facing two prominent questions :—How forest can be conserved? For whom the forest is?

Now over a decade or two these questions ponder the domain of policy makers and thinkers over the world. Policy makers have gradually come to accept the view that in conservation efforts, a participatory approach is essential for success, rather than based on solely government initiatives (Malhotra and Poffenberger 1989, Poffenberger 1990). We expect forest is for all as it not only influence the local stakeholders but also the globe through different indirect benefits. The point of duscussion of our paper is on the allegation of energy experts and foresters to the local community for the degradation and destruction by means of fuel wood extraction. This paper addresses these issues in four sections. In section II, discussion will be made on the present demographic features of two districts of North Bengal, Jalpaiguri and Darjeeling in terms of the fuel consumption pattern of the primary stakeholders. In the III section, discussion will be made on the community-forest relationship and will try focus on some motivating factors which can contribute towards successful Joint Forest Management (JFM) programme in North Bengal. In section IV summary will be made on the above two sections prescribing some desirable changes that can be adopted in the implementation of successful JFM programme.

SECTION II. STUDY AREA AND SOME REFLECTIONS

The northern, sub-Himalayan districts of North Bengal namely, Jalpaiguri and Darjeeling is concerned as one of the biological hotspot in the world; —The narrow ('chicken neck') region of North Bengal—starting from South Dinajpur to Jalpaiguri district, has a great political importance. This part is surrounded by a numbers of other states along with three neighbouring countries : Bengladesh, Nepal and Bhutan. Several studies show that its close proximity to three international borders is an important factor in attracting a large number of legal or illegal migrants, driven from their home by both natural disasters and man made problems. Fuel wood collection and trade act as a safety net for many of these displaced people, who often arrive in North Bengal with almost nothing. Fuel wood business was found to be the main source of income for 10 percent of rural households in these districts. Around 72000 tons of fuel wood per week, some 45 percent of total fuel wood supply is monetised, traded in the primary and secondary markets of North West Bengal (Dr. Ram Prasad et al 1999).

Table 2.1

Fuel wood dependence in the two districts of North Bengal

District	*Total Population (million)*	*Forest in sq. k.m.*	*Forest as a % of area*	*Percent of Household dependent*
Darjeeling	1.3	1445	45.9	88
Jalpaiguri	2.8	1580	25.4	86

Table 2.1 above reflects the dependency of this two districts of North Bengal on fuel wood to meet their energy requirement. There is a significant chance of conflict between the forest department and local communities regarding defacto access of forest resources. Consequently blaming and counter blaming to each other may lead to possible mismanagement. Forests are considerably rich in North Bengal till the date and if there is no external interference, it can sustain the people living on it over a longtime horizon.

From Table 2.2, which is based on survey of 12 sites in North Bengal by CREATE, it is clear that except two sites, forest per capita is quite high all most on all sites. Dependency on forest can be visualized from col. no. 9. So it is quite wrong at this moment to blame and treat the local community as the biggest threat to forest. Most of the needs for forest wood are

Table 2.2
Forest Condition of North Bengal

Site	*Density*	*Mean DBH*	*Mean height*	*Total area*	*Vol. FW m³*	*Supply /ha*	*F.wood m³*	*Demand /ha*	*No. of user*	*F.wood /capita*	*Forest/ capita*
Lataguri	139	0.42	19.04	3963	2840071.88	71665	1143.78	0.29	324	3.53	8765.62
Jayantia	300	0.32	17.7	10123	3475159.67	837.22	8958.30	0.88	1041	8.61	8141.30
Kalpokhri	472	0.21	9.59	382.9	119645.71	312.51	343.48	0.90	26	13.21	4601.70
Fapri	236	0.2	12.02	28.47	524520.87	184.25	1812.83	0.64	976	1.86	537.42
Khuntimari	48	0.56	21.61	2500	1263577.79	505.43	9350.19	3.74	1400	6.68	902.56
Bungkulung	178	0.15	11.73	469.8	35992.28	76.94	2125.23	4.54	632	3.36	56.95
Rampuria	187	0.23	11.26	178.1	309360.44	173.66	2226.24	12.50	175	12.72	176.78
Dadgrama	62	0.55	25.97	577.5	438725.79	759.70	35611.64	16.67	1504	23.68	291.71
Niamti	337	0.21	13.25	3629	1110220.60	305.93	108629.66	29.93	3388	32.06	327.69
Simanatar	40	0.12	7.74	257.8	1680.22	6.52	1323.34	5.13	156	8.48	10.77
Poobong	27	0.2	9.13	118.1	1843.57	15.60	4469.17	37.83	606	7.37	3.04
Sulka Para	96	0.3	12.7	1443	249322.32	172.73	632627.46	438.29	1769	357.62	140.94

met by way of twigs and branches rather than logs. Sustainable use of forest resources can not lead to deforestation. Introduction of JFM also provides access to forest resources subject to fulfilment of certain duties on the part of the local people. The present status of JFM programme in North Bengal is given below (Table 2.3 & 2.4)—

Table 2.3

Site Matrix

Site	*Forest type*	*Location*	*Distance from market*	*Management*
Nimati	Tiger Reserve	Plains	Near	Wild life
Jainti	Tiger Reserve	Plains	Far	Wild life
Sulkapara	National Park	Plains	Near	Wild life
Lataguri	National Park	Plains	Near	Wild life
Salugarah	Reserve Forest	Plains	Near	Territorial
Dabgram	Reserve Forest	Plains	Far	Territorial
Khutimari	Reserve Forest	Plains	Near	Territorial
Kalpokhri	National Park	Hills	Far	Wild life
Simanatar	Reserve forest	Hills	Near	Territorial
Bunkulung	Reserve Forest	Hills	Far	Territorial
Rampuria	Wildlife Sanc.	Hills	Far	Wild life
Poodong	Reserve forest	Hills	Near	Territorial

Table 2.4

User Groups in Relation to JFM

User Group	*Site*	*Status of JFM*
Nimati-Domohani FPC	Nimati	Registered functional
Nimati-Domohani Non FPC	Nimati	Users are non-members
Rava FPC		Nimati Registered defunct
N. Jhora Tea Garden	Nimati	Users being non-Members
Jayanti EDC		Jainti Unregistered functional
Bhutiya Basti EDC	Jainti	Registered functional
Hazipara EDC	Sulkapara	Registered functional
Dangapara EDC	Sulkapara	Registered functional
Tondu Tea Garden	Sulkapara	Users are non-members
Bichabhanga EDC	Lataguri	Registered functional
Fafri FPC	Salugarah	Registered defunct
Jaldumur FPC	Dabgram	Registered defunct

Kalpokhri	Kalpokhri	Non-JFM usergroup
Simanatar	Simanatar	Non-JFM usergroup
Bungkulung FPC	Bunkulung	Registered functional
Bungkulung Non FPC	Bunkulung	Users are non-members
Poobong FPC	Poobong	Unregistered functional
Rampuria EDC	Rampuria	Registered functional
Madhya Salbari FPC	Khutimari	Registered defunct

The ground realities of successful implementation of JFM in South Bengal rather than in North Bengal are different. Two important causes may be mentioned behind that, firstly forest resource is already scarce in South Bengal when JFM was introduced but the situation is not so much worse here and secondly, the benefits distributed from JFM are ad-hoc in nature and not conducive in generating collective action in long term perspective that JFM aimed for.

In the following section, focus will be given on some problems in the existing JFM structure in terms of forest-community relationship, which may act as constraints towards successful implementation of JFM programme in North Bengal.

SECTION III. A. COMMUNITY FOREST RELATIONSHIP AND SUSTAINABILITY OF RESOURCE USE

The JFM programme introduced in North Bengal is not space-specific. The programme is a success in South Bengal and the officials hoped the same for North Bengal. This does not happen, as ground situation is different. May be projected the problem in the following manner.

n_i $\quad$ n_j

n_i = No. of person engaged in timber collection for trade

n_j = No. of person engaged in fuelwood and NTFP for consumption and sale

$(n_i \cap n_j)$ = No. of person engaged in all the activity

$(n_i U n_j)$ = Total No. of local community

All the activities are de-facto. The introduction of JFM under such circumstances will certainly curtail the de-facto benefits. So, in the post JFM period, by participation in JFM programme, there has to be a balance between sacrifice and reward across the all stakeholders to make the programme sustainable. The whole issue of sustainability should be addressed from a general equilibrium of frame work. The solution probably lies in developing a proper incentive—disincentive structure of all the stakeholders towards utilization of resources. The exchange relationship of four major stakeholders can be represented through a schematic diagram popularized by Chakraborty et al (2001).

Communities dependent on forest for livelihood—totally or partially (C);

The Rest of the community (R);

The Forest Department (FD); and

The Rest of the Government (G).

Flow of incentives across the stakeholders

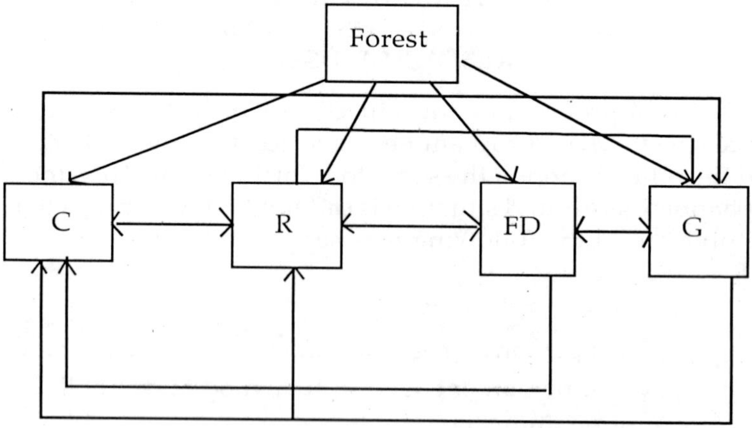

The above relationship can be shown under through a Service-Benefit matrix among the stakeholders

Benefits

	C	R	FD	G	F
C	0	Employment non-forest consumption goods.	Employment, technical services	Grants	De facto de jure benefits
R	Labour	0	Forestry resources	Grants	Intangible environment benefits
FD	Labour & protection	Revenue	0	Grants	Resources
G	Tax	Tax	Revenue	0	Intangible environment benefits
F	Protection	-	-	-	0

Indian experience suggest that C has been the perennial loser in the exchange process involving forestry resources. In the process, the inhabitants of those resource rich regions remained resource-poor themselves. Obviously, the incentives-disincentives structure resulting out of the existing 'State-property-right regime' can not ensure sustainable use of the forestry resources (Chakrabarty 2001).

B. Condition for Participation :

The term 'participation' refers to a process, through which stakeholders' influence and share control over development initiatives and the decisions and resources, which affects them (World Bank). This definition of participation rarely holds in the existing participatory institution. Generally, we observed different types of participation in a decision making process a la their underlying institutional structure. As Kothari et.al. pointed out this includes a whole range of situation from one extreme in which official/private agencies predominantly retain control but consult with local communities in planning or implementation; to the other extreme in which communities are completely in control (Kothari et al, 1998). But in any type of participatory institution individuals will participate and this participation will sustain it : (Mukherjee and Sarkar 2002).

$$E(Rj)t\ E\ (Cj)t\ (1)$$

$$R_j/(1+r)^t \geq C_j/(1+r)^t; \ -(2)$$

Where, $R_j \Rightarrow$ Reward; $C_j \Rightarrow$ Sacrifice; $r \Rightarrow$ individuals rate of discount/opportunity costs; $t \Rightarrow$ time.

Condition (1) states that an individual can look into a cooperation plan either in long run perspective or in short run perspective. At any point of time expected benefit from cooperation may be less than the expected costs of cooperation. However, in that case if condition (2) holds that individual will decide to participate. There may be another case when an individual enters into a contract of cooperation anticipating some quick gains. In that case they will not be interested about the sustainability of cooperation.

So participation can be either active or passive. The problem of sustainable management lies with the passive participation. Now at this stage, active participation of community is essential for sustainability of JFM. To convert the passive to active participator, the concept of Mr. A. Maslow, a psychologist in profession, who developed a widely acclaimed conceptual framework may be applied for understainding human motivation. His theory based on hierarchy of human needs, which is represented below :]

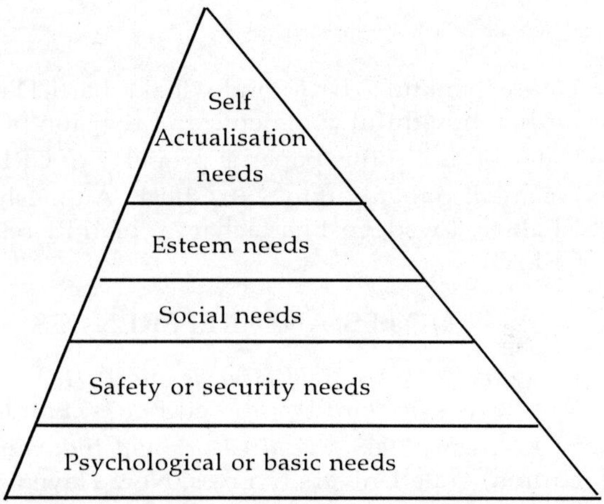

According to him, to motivate people in active participation in any field of work, First, basic needs, e.g. food, shelter etc., Second, security needs, e.g. in terms of employment or monetary security and Third, social needs, e.g. belongingness to society, to be satisfied. Out of this five level of human needs, when someone reaches towards attainment of social needs, only then one can be motivated properly in active participation—and can contribute in the successful implementation of JFM programme in North Bengal.

SECTION IV : CONCLUSION

Building truly participatory institutions requires several measures. JFM has little chance of success where benefits are not distributed equitably among various members of the community. The response of the local communities for participation in the management of renewable natural resources so far depended entirely on the mangnitude and pace of economic return to them. JFM will remain ineffective unless the socio-economic upliftment of the local community is taken up with right earnest. Healthcare, sanitation, and drinking water are basic needs which should be fulfilled first of all. Next, infrastructure to develop cottage industries based on NTFP should be provided. Suitable eco development project can be promoted and finally, the development of eco tourism can play an important role in motivating people in collective action process to make JFM a successful one.

Note :

1. We are thankful to Dr. Milindo Chakrabarti, Director, CREATE for his thoughtful comments and revision of earlier drafts.
2. Data set use in this paper is property of CREATE.
3. We are also thankful to S. R. Ghosh, Animesh Sarkar, Sarala Khaling, Joysdeep Bhattacharya, of IFRI research team at CREATE.

NOTES AND REFERENCES

1. B. Agarwal, 1986, *Cold Hearths and Barren Slopes : The Fuel Wood Crisis in Third World,* Zed Books, London.
2. K. J. Arrow, 1963, *Social Choice and Individual Values* (2nd edition), Yale University Press, New Haven, Conn.
3. A. Aziz and D. D. Arnold, (eds.), 1996, *Decentralize Governance in Asian Countries,* pp. 13-33, Sage Publication, London, p. 14.
4. B. Barry and R. Hardin, eds., 1982, *Rational Man and Irrational Society? : An Introduction and Sourcebook*. Beverly Hills : Sage.
5. G. S. Becker, 1976, *The Economic Approach to Human Behavior,* University of Chicago Press, Chicago.
6. H. Blair, 1986, "Social Forestry : Times to Modify Goals?" *Economic and Political Weekly,* Vol.-XXI, No. 30, pp. 1317-321.
7. M. Chakrabarti, 2001, "Towards An Operational Definition of Sustainability", paper presented to the seminar on 'Poverty and Sustainable Development' organised by the UNESCO Chair, University of Montesquieu-Bordeaux IV-UNESCO Paris, 22nd & 23rd Nov. 2001.
8. M. R. Chakrabarti, Mukherjee & Atanu Sarkar, 2002, "Joint Forest Management in North Bengal, India : Condition for Institutional Sustainability, paper accepted in XII World Forestry Congress to be held in Qubec, during September, 2003.
9. CREATE, 2002, "Heterogeneity and Collective Action : Evidence From Joint Forest Management in North Bengal", Paper Presented at IFRI Network Meeting, Nairobi.
10. R.L. Coase, 1960, "The Problem of Social Cost". *Journal of Law and Economics* 3 (October).
11. R. Courant, and F. John, 1965, Introduction to Calculus and Analysis, Vol. 1, Interscience Publishers, New York.
12. N. Frohlich, and J. A. Oppenhimer, 1999, "Kenneth J. Arrow,

Welfare Aggregation, and Progress in Political Theory", In Competition & Cooperation, Alt, J.E., Levi, M., E, Ostrom, (eds.), Russell Sage Foundation, New York.

13. M. Gadgil and R. Guha, 1993, *This Fissured Land : An Ecological History of India,* Oxford University Press, New Delhi.

14. R. E. Goodin, 1999, "Rationality Redux : Reflections on Herbert A. Simon's Vision of Politics" In *Competition & Cooperation,* Alt, J.E., Levi, M. and E., Ostrom (eds.), Russell Sage Foundation, New York.

15. A. K. Gulati, 1990, "Community Forestry or Social Forestry for Rural Development—A Critical Review", *Indian Forester,* Vol. 116, No. 9, pp. 687-92.

16. R. Jeffery, & N. Sundar (eds.), 1999, *A New Moral Economy for India's Forests?*, Sage Publications, New Delhi.

17. B. D. Jones, 1999, "Bounded Rationality, Political Institutions and The Analysis of Outcomes" In *Competition & Cooperation,* Alt, J.E., Levi, M., E, Ostrom, (eds.), Russell Sage Foundation, New York.

18. L. L. Kiser, & E. Ostrom, 1982, "The Three World of Action: A Metatheoretical Synthesis of Institutional Approaches", In Ostrom, E. (ed.), *Strategies of Political Inquiry,* Sage Publications, New Delhi.

19. A. Kothari et. al. (eds.), 1996, *People And Protected Areas,* Sage Publications, New Delhi.

20. A. Kothari, et. al. (eds.), 1998, *Community and Conservation,* Sage Publications, New Delhi.

21. M. Lee 1994, Institutional Analysis, Public Policy and The Possibility of Collective Action in Common-Pool-Resources: A dynamic Game Theoretic Approach, Department of Political Science, Indiana University, Bloomington.

22. K. C. Malhotra, & M. Poffenberger, 1989, "Forest Regeneration through Community Protection : The West Bengal Experience". Ford Foundation, New Delhi.

23. K. C. Malhotra, D. Deb, M. Dutta, T.S.Vasulu, G. Jadav & M. Adhikari, 1991, "Role of NTFP in Village Economy. A Household Survey in Jamboni Range, Midnapore District, West Bengal. Mimeo. Institute for Biological Research and Development, Calcutta.

24. R. Mukherjee and A. Sarkar, 2002 "Individual Choice and Sustainability of Participation : Reflections from Joint Forest Management in North Bengal" Paper presented in the National

Seminar at Tufangang Mahavidyalaya on 24th & 25th Sept. 2002.

25. MoEF, 1995, List of National Park and Sanctuaries of India, Ministry of Environment and Forest, Government of India, New Delhi.
26. M. Olson, 1965, *The Logic of Collective Action, Public Goods and the Theory of Groups,* Harvard University Press, Cambridge.
27. E. Ostrom, 1990, *Governing the Commons,* Cambridge University Press, Cambridge.
28. E. Ostrom, et.al. (eds.), 1994, *Rules, Games and Common-pool Resources,* The University of Michigan Press, Michigan.
29. V. Ostrom 1997, *The Meaning of Democracy and the Vulnerability of Democracies,* The University of Michigan Press, Michigan.
30. M. Poffenberger 1990, "Forest management partnership. Regenerating India's Forest. Workshop on sustainable forestry, New Delhi, Ford Foundation, New Delhi.
31. Ram Prasad, P. Bhattacherjee, B. Joshi, 1999, "Fuel wood collection and Trade as a survival strategy in North West Bengal", *Wood Energy News.* Vol. 14, No. 2.

Annexure-I

Chronology of Key Policies and laws concerning conservation of Forest Bio-diversity

Year	*Policy/Laws (Competent Authority)*
1848	Timber Ordinance No. 24
1885	Forest Ordinance No. 10
1907	Do No. 16
1929	First Authoritative forest policy statement
1937	Fauna & Flora protection Ordinance No. 2
1964	Amendment Act No. 44
1970	Amendment Act No. 1
1993	Amendment Act No. 49
1953	National Forest Policy
1969	UNESCO Biological Programme
1975	UNESCO Man and Biosphere Programme
1982	Mahaweli Environment Project
1988	National Heritage Wilderness Areas Act No. 3
1990	National Policy for Wildlife Conservation
1995	National Forest Policy

13

Green Tourism in North Bengal: An Ecological Analysis

Dr Suman Mukherjee & Palash Dey

Introduction:

Green Tourism is a kind of approach to tourism meant to make the development of tourism ecologically supportable in the long term. The very importance of Green Tourism lies in its motives to conserve the resources and increase the value of local culture and tradition. Green Tourism is a responsible tourism intending to generate employment and income along with alleviating any deeper impact on environment and local culture. Green Tourism or environmentally responsible tourism is a new concept. The origins of present day Green Tourism lie in the nature and outdoor tourism. Green Tourism is not simply about showing tourists attractive landscapes. It is about inculcating a deeper love for diverse nature and its mysteries through innovative educational means while providing livelihood alternatives to people who depend on that eco system for a living. It is also about producing minimal impact on the environment in remote natural areas. In 1989 "Hague Declaration on Tourism" advocated rational management of tourism so that it can contribute to the protection and preservation of the national and cultural environment, keeping in view the contradicting relationship between environment and tourism. Most of the researches have agreed that environment friendly tourism should aim at merging with the eco-system natural as well as social. West Bengal is rich in wild life. About 13.38% of the state's total area is covered by forests. Altitudinal, physiographic and climatic variations have contributed to diverse eco-systems, habitat and wild life forms in the state. 15 wild life sanctuaries, 5 National Parks, 3 Tiger Reserves provide excellent habitats for the states varied wild life. There are four National Parks in North Bengal-- *a)* Neora Valley National Park in Kalimpong District, *b)* Singalila National Park in Darjeeling District, *c)* Jaldapara National Park in Alipurduar District and *d)* Garumara National Park is situated in Jalpaiguri District. A fundamental requirement for Green Tourism to be practiced is control on access to an area. National Parks and Wild life Sanctuaries are the most amenable to regulate access and thus most suitable as Green Tourism destinations. However the present paper first provides the present status of Green Tourism activity in North Bengal. Then it proceeds to summarize a critical account of the impact of Green Tourism activity on the ecology and environment of the area.

Objectives of the Present Study:

The present paper embraces the following objectives:

- To explore the status of Green Tourism in Darjeeling, Kalimpong, Jalpaiguri, Alipurduar and Cooch Behar District
- To study about Green Tourism
- To know about the Characteristics and Principles of Green Tourism
- To understand the relationship between Green and Eco-Tourism
- To understand the Possibilities of Implementing Green Tourism in North Bengal
- To study the Challenges while Implementing sustainable Green Tourism
- To analyze the ecological impacts of Green Tourism on the study area

The Study Area:

Darjeeling and Kalimpong in Hill Region: Darjeeling and Kalimpong conjures visions of snow peaks, serenity of vibrant green hills steeped in splendor, a land of breathtaking beauty crowned by the majestic Himalayas. Darjeeling and Kalimpong are one of the most magnificent hill resorts in the world. This heavenly retreat is bathed in hues of every shade. Flaming red rhododendrons, sparkling white magnolias, miles of undulating hillsides covered with emerald green tea bushes, the exotic forests of silver fir - all under the blanket of a brilliant azure sky dappled with specks of clouds, compellingly confounds Darjeeling as the 'Queen of Hill Stations'. The crest of Kanchenjunga shining in the first dawn light truly supports the title.

Jalpaiguri, Alipurduar and Cooch Behar in Dooars Region: The place where nature has kept its doors open. Derived from the word 'doors' (doors to Bhutan), this region, located in the district of Jalpaiguri, Alipurduar and Cooch Behar, forms a gateway to the hill stations of North Bengal, Sikkim, Bhutan & North-Eastern states. The dense natural forests, interwoven with lush green tea gardens, criss-crossed by Teesta, Raidak, Torsha, Jaldhaka, Kaljani and other rivers. The study area is also enriched with several distinctive species of fauna and flora. Thus, Jalpaiguri, Alipurduar and Cooch Behar with its rich natural endowments can provide regional growth impulses through the promotion of Green Tourism activity.

The Concept of Green Tourism:

Green Tourism is defined as environmentally friendly tourism activities with various focuses and meanings. In a broad term, Green Tourism is about being an environmentally friendly tourist or providing environmentally friendly tourist services.[1] Green Tourism means sustainable, equitable, community based endeavor for improving living standard of indigenous host communities.[2] From 1990 Green Tourism combined with Community Tourism concepts has become a new trend in India. West Bengal is also a hot spot in the map of the movement and here also private organizations are the key players. Here conservation of nature and environment is one of the main features of the project. The slogan of the Green Tourism and Community Tourism activists is: "Linking protected areas with the people's livelihood by giving them ownership through tourism is the first step towards conservation".[3] Green tourism is a term that can be applied to any form of tourism that relates to the natural environment and cultural heritage of an area or that undertakes good environmental management (or green) practice. There are three methods included by which a tourism practice would have to demonstrate practices for preventing or minimizing impacts to the environment if it were to be considered a green operations as follows:

a. The wise use of resources such as raw materials, water and energy.
b. The prevention of pollution (air, land, and water).
c. The protection and where possible the enhancement of biodiversity.[4]

The Key Elaements of the Green Tourism:

- Existence of National Park/Sanctuary/Nature as prime attraction.
- Should be ecologically, socially, culturally, and economically sustainable.
- Should have participation of the local stakeholders.
- Should be a low profile venture.
- Should be capable of forging partnership with the existing tourism industry.[5]

Characteristics of Green Tourism:

- Green Tourism tries its utmost to maintain the importance of local culture and tradition
- Green Tourism is informatory, as it doesn't only let tourist know about the destinations but also it helps locals knowing about the culture and civilization of tourists.
- This kind of tourism is aimed to conserve the resources of destinations where one is visiting to Green Tourism

seeks deeper involvement of locals, which provide local people an opportunity and make their living. Above all, Green Tourism stresses pointedly upon integrity of the tourist places.

Principles and Policy of Green Tourism:

The Ministry of Tourism has come up with a set of policies and guidelines for the development of Green Tourism in pursuance of the Government policy. These have been formulated after analyzing the documents of various national and international organizations working in this field. A selective approach, scientific planning, effective control and continuous monitoring has to be adopted, to help preserve, retain and enrich our worldview and life-style, our cultural expressions and heritage in all its manifestations[6]:

- It should involve local community and lead to economic development of the area.
- It should identify the likely conflicts between resource use for tourism and livelihood of local inhabitants and attempt to minimize such conflicts.
- The type and scale of tourism development should be compatible with the environment and socio-cultural characteristics of the local community.
- It should be planned as part of the overall area development strategy, ensuring sectoral integrations.
- Educates the traveler on the importance of conservation (natural resources, biodiversity).
- Avoids negative impacts that can damage or destroy the integrity or character of the natural environment.
- Direct revenues to the conservation of the natural areas and the management of protected areas.
- Increasingly relies on infrastructure that has been developed sensitively in harmony with the environment– minimizing use of fossil fuels, conserving flora and fauna.

Green Tourism Resources in North Bengal:

The major Green Tourism resources consist of what is known as the Protected Area Network.

- National Parks: *a)* Neora Valley National Park, *b)* Singalila National Park, *c)* Jaldapara National Park and *d)* Garumara National Park.
- Wildlife Sanctuaries: Mahananda, Chapramari wildlife Sanctuaries and Buxa Tiger Reserve.
- Ex-Situ Conservation Areas: Lloyd Botanical Garden and Padmaja Naidu Himalayan Zoological Garden.
- Wetland: Rasik Bill

Popular Green Tourism Destinations in North Bengal:

Neora Valley National Park: Neora Valley National Park[7] is situated in the Kalimpong District and was established in 1986. It spreads over an area of 88 km and is one of the richest biological zones in the entire Northeast. It is the land of the elegant Red Panda in the pristine undisturbed natural habitat with rugged inaccessible hilly terrain and rich diverse flora and fauna making this park an important wilderness zone. The National Park enjoys the distinction of being situated over one of the oldest Reserve Forest in India .Red Panda, Himalayan Thar, Tiger, Goral, Himalayan Black Bear, Wild Boar, Wild Dog and clouded Leopard and birds like Redstart, Whistling Thrush, Golden Headed Black Finch, Niltava, Yuhina are found in this National Park. State Forest Report, West Bengal, 2006-2007. State Forest Report, West Bengal, 2006-2007.

Singalila National Park: Singalila National Park[8] is a national park located on the Singalila Ridge at an altitude of more than 7000 feet above sea level, in the Darjeeling district of West Bengal. It is well known for the trekking route to Sandakphu that runs through it.

The park was declared a Wildlife Sanctuary in 1986, and was made an Indian National Park in 1992. The region had long been used as the trekking route from Manebhanjang to Sandakphu (the highest peak of West Bengal) and Phalut.

Flora:

Thick bamboo, oak, magnolia and rhododendron forest between 2000 and 3600 m cover the Singalila Ridge. There are two seasons of wildflower bloom - one in spring (March–

April) when the Rhododendrons bloom, and another in the post-monsoon season (around October), when the lower forests bloom (Primula, Geranium, Saxifraga, Bistort, Senecio, Cotoneaster and numerous orchids). Sandakphu is known as the "mountain of poisonous plants" due to the large concentration of Himalayan Cobra Lilies (Arisaema) which grow there.

Fauna:

Mammals: The park has a number of small mammals including the Red Panda, Leopard Cat, Barking Deer, Yellow-throated Marten, Wild Boar, Pangolin and the Pika. Larger mammals include the Himalayan Black Bear, Leopard, Clouded Leopard, Serow and Takin. Tigers occasionally wander into the area, but do not have a large enough prey base to make residence in these forests feasible.

Birds: The park is a birder's delight with over 120 species recorded including many rare and exotic species like the Scarlet Minivet, Kalij Pheasant, Blood Pheasant, Satyr Tragopan, Brown and Fulvous Parrotbills, Rufous-vented Tit, and Old World babblers like the Fire-tailed Myzornis and the Golden-breasted Fulvetta. The park is also on the flyway of many migratory birds.

Reptiles and Amphibians: The endangered Himalayan Newt frequents the region, and congregates around the lakes of Jore Pokhri and Sukhiapokhri and nearby lakes to reproduce. Jore Pokhri and Sukhiapokhri are within 20 km of the park boundary, and are protected wildlife sanctuaries.

Lloyd Botanical Garden: The East Himalayas represent an immense variety of flora and fauna. Plants and flowers abound in Lloyd Botanical Gardens,[9] Darjeeling-balmy alpine plants, geraniums, spectacular azaleas, rhododendrons, free forms and conifers.

Padmaja Naidu Himalayan Zoological Garden: In Darjeeling at the zoological park[10], one can have glimpses of high altitude wild life, like the Siberian Tiger, Himalayan black bear and pandas, while a nearby farm is breeding snow leopards.

Jaldapara National Park: Jaldapara National Park[11] (formerly Jaldapara Wildlife Sanctuary) is a national park situated at the foothills of the Eastern Himalayas in Alipurduar Sub-Division of Alipurduar district in West Bengal and on the bank of the Torsa River. Jaldapara is situated at an altitude of 61 m and is spread across 216.51 k (83.59 sq mi) of vast grassland with patches of riverine forests. It was declared a sanctuary in 1941 for protection of its great variety flora and fauna. Today, it has the largest population of the Indian one horned rhinoceros in the state, an animal threatened with extinction, and is a Habitat management area .The nearby Chilapata Forests is an elephant corridor between Jaldapara and the Buxa Tiger Reserve Nearby is the Gorumara National Park, known for its population of Indian Rhinoceros. Jaldapara Wildlife Sanctuary was established in 1941 for the purpose of protecting the Indian one-horned rhinoceros. In May 2012 it was declared a national park.

The forest is mainly savannah covered with tall elephant grasses. The main attraction of the park is the Indian one-horned rhinoceros. The park holds the largest rhino population in India after Kaziranga National Park in Assam. Other animals in the park include Royal Bengal Tigers, elephants, sambar, barking deer, spotted deer, hog deer, wild pigs, and bison.

Jaldapara is a paradise for bird watchers. It is one of the very few places in India, where the Bengal florican is sighted. The other birds to be found here are the crested eagle, Pallas's fish eagle, shikra, Finn's weaver, jungle fowl, peafowl (peacock), partridge, and lesser Pied Hornbill. Pythons, monitor lizards, kraits, cobras, geckos, and about 8 species of fresh water turtles can also be found here.

Many of the animals in the park are endangered, like the Indian one-horned rhino and elephants.

Tourism Activities: Rare one-horned Rhinoceros, the mighty Bison, Leopard, Spotted Deer, Sambar, Hog Deer, reptiles, huge wild Tuskers, Wild Boars and the rarest variety of animals and birds including plenty of Peacocks are the main attraction of this park. Elephant safaris through the Jaldapara forest in search of wild animals, is a memorable experience. Numerous watch towers here allow tourist to take a real close look at wildlife. Moreover the scintillating light and sound show at Jaldapara guest house adds a new dimension in Green Tourism.

Gorumara National Park: Gorumara National Park12 in northern West Bengal is located in the Jalpaiguri District of the Himalayan foothills, it is a medium-sized park with grasslands and forests. Gorumara was a reserve forest since 1895. The park was declared a Wildlife Sanctuary in 1949, on account of its breeding population of Indian Rhinoceros. It was declared an Indian National Park on January 31, 1994.It is primarily known for its population of Indian Rhinoceros. The park has been declared as the best among the protected areas in India by the Ministry of Environment and Forests for the year 2009.

Rasik Bill: Rasikbill[13] is a huge lake situated in the town of Tufanganj in Cooch Behar District of West Bengal. It is prominent bird viewing spot. Situated around a vast lake spreading more than 175 hectares territory, Rasik Bill Lake is encompassed by three dull and thick woods – Nagurhaat, Atasmochar and Bochamari. They are differentiated by Batikata a little trench. It is a great shelter of Green Tourism in the wild with stunning magnificence of its photo postcard landscape.

Major Attractions of Rasik Bill: The Lake itself is the splendor of the place. A beautiful crocodile rehabilitation centre, a deer park and a huge aquarium are major attractions of Rasik Bill. Sweet water fishes like Kutiputti and Borali (two popular varieties of fish of North Bengal) are found in the lake in abundance. The park with deer moving around and the fluttering of birds on the bank of the lake is nice place to make much of your leisure. There are also a python house, a leopard house and a Tortoise house to visit. Apart from all these Rasik Bill is famous for bird watching activities. Numerous local and migratory birds make their nests at Rasik Bill. Bird watching and boating in Rasik Bill is the most popular activity. Being in a boat on water amidst greenery of nature is an out of the world experience that takes you away from the cares and worries of earthly life. Known as the birding paradise one of the famous tourist activity of Rasik Bill is bird watching. Another famous thing to do while staying in the eco resort of Rasik Bill is sculling in the scenic lake. While boating in Rasik Bill, visitors can spot exotic water fowls like Pied Kingfisher, Wingeon Duck, and Small Blue Kingfisher. Apart from spotting exotic migratory birds there are many other attractions in Rasik Bill like large aquarium, a deer park, a crocodile rehabilitation center, a tortoise rescue center, a python centre and a Leopard Rescue Centre. Tourist can visit all these astounding places during their stay in Rasik Bill Eco-Resort.[14]

Popular Green Tourism Activities in North Bengal:

I) Forest & Wildlife Tourism: Traveling around the forest arena of this region aids tourists observe and interact with local plant and animal life in their natural habitats. The experience is beyond words and the intangible, psychological benefits of the visit are countless. Even those indifferent to forest life and nature will get the essence of these. Wildlife tourism is an element of many nations' travel industry centered on observation and interaction with local animal and plant life in their natural habitats. While it can include eco- and animal-friendly tourism, safari hunting and similar high-intervention activities also fall under the umbrella of wildlife tourism. Wildlife tourism, in its simplest sense, is interacting with wild animals in their natural habitat, either by actively (e.g. hunting/collection) or passively (e.g. watching/ photography). It has experienced a dramatic and rapid growth in recent years worldwide and many elements are closely aligned to Eco-Tourism and Green Tourism.

As a multimillion-dollar international industry, wildlife tourism is often characterized by the offering of customized tour packages and safaris to allow close access to wildlife.

a) Jatraprosad Watch Tower: The best way to watch wildlife at the park is to use powerful binoculars, with night vision facilities at night, from the numerous well-located watchtowers at the park. The watchtowers are:

- Jatraprasad Watch Tower: Named after a legendary elephant.
- Rhino Observation Point: Watch tower in front of the Gorumara forest bungalow.
- Chandrachur Watch Tower (Old Khunia Watch Tower): Near the Murti forest bungalow.
- Chukchuki Bird-watching Point: Good for birding.

b) Rhino Point Watch Tower: There are no ranger-led or otherwise four-wheel drive vehicle or elephant-back forays into the jungle. Hiking is permitted on metallic roads, but is slightly unsafe considering the population of elephants, gaur and rhinoceros present in the park. The park is closed in the Monsoon season from 16 June to 15 September. The best time to visit Gorumara is from November to March.

One can also visit the adjoining forest villages to get acquainted with the lifestyle and culture of the villagers. A live show of the ethnic tribal dance can be seen every evening in Budhuram Forest Village.

One can visit the Lataguri Nature Interpretation Centre for an interpretive exhibit of the local natural history.

c) Buxa Tiger Reserve: Buxa National Park[15], in the subdivision of Alipurduar, Alipurduar District, was set up in the year of 1982-83 at the north eastern corner of West Bengal bordering Bhutan and Assam. With an area of 759 sq km this picturesque reserve with its prodigious Terai, Bhabar as well as Hilly landscape, Criss crossed by numerous rivers and their tributaries, presents a breathtaking landscape. Buxa is rich with bio-diversity and has a great collection of rare orchids and medicinal plants. Because of inaccessible terrain some parts of Buxa hills in the Sinchula range are still unexplored. The veritable flora and fauna of these wet forests attracts tourists and nature lovers every year.

II) Natural History Museum Tourism: The Museum of Natural History, an institution devoted to environmental education, derives its strength principally from theme-based exhibition galleries, experiential resource centers such as Discovery Room, Activity Room, and educational and out-reach activities, with the intention to depict the country's rich natural heritage and natural history(Geology, Botany and Zoology). For a wildlife lover visiting a natural history museum is as much interesting as it is to go on a safari in a wildlife reserve. In a state like West Bengal, where diversity is rich, existence of such museums is a boon. Depicting many facets of the Indian wildlife these museums are established to impart awareness and to make people understand the importance of the environment and its resources.

a) Bengal Natural History Museum, Darjeeling: It started as a modest effort way back in 1903 when the then Governor of Bengal initiated creation of a small museum in the Botanical Gardens of Darjeeling.[16] A small building in the Botanical Garden was constructed at a cost of Rupees 14,000/- to display only the butterflies and birds of the area. However it was too small and not good enough for the students and researchers to study the whole bird and animal life in the region. Therefore a new building near Chowrasta was constructed in 1915 at a cost of Rupees 55,000/- to satisfy such requirement. In 1923, Bengal Natural Museum Society was formed that took charge of the management of the museum. It continued until 1976 after which the management was taken over by the Forest Department of the state of West Bengal. During the initial days of the museum, an amateur ornithologist Charles M Inlis was the Curator of the museum. He held the post for 26 years since 1923. During his time, he had put in immense effort and built up the museum with active support from many officials including E.O. Shebbeare, The Conservator of Forest (Bengal), G.E. Shaw, The Superintendent of Cinchona Plantation, and many others. Today the museum houses huge collection and specimens that include wide varieties of birds with nests and eggs, reptiles and fishes, mammals, insects and more. All these specimens are of real creatures that were captured and preserved. There is a special taxidermy unit in the museum which specializes in curing, staffing and rendering the birds and animals for display on the glass cabinets. This unit has been there right from the inception of the museum. Recently the Bengal Natural History Museum has been moved from its earlier location (which was only few minutes' walk from the town center at Chowrasta and in the premises of Wildlife Division-I of Darjeeling) to a newly constructed building at the compound where Darjeeling Zoo is located along with Himalayan Mountaineering Institute. There are two large sections of the museum. One is located at the ground level and the other at the basement. The early initiation offered a collection of butterflies and birds of the area, however today, the museum houses huge collection and specimens of varieties of birds with nests and eggs, reptiles and fishes, mammals and insects. All these specimens are real creatures that were captured and preserved. There is a special taxidermy unit in the museum which specializes in curing, staffing and rendering the birds and animals for display in the glass cabinets. The museum has two large sections, one at the ground level and the other at the basement. The first section is that of birds that have specimens like Himalayan Brown Wood Owls, Northern spotted owlet, Northern Brown Fish Owl, pheasants, fly catchers and woodpeckers that are placed in natural settings on the tree branches. There are over 820 specimens of birds belonging to more than 400 species of the area. The other side of the museum one can notice a large collection of birds' eggs. There are about 110 species of eggs, but all are not displayed due to lack of space. A nice collection of nests of various sizes, about 35 out of 76 species of snakes 57 species of fish specimen can be seen here in the museum. It has many rare and valuable books including 125 volume series of "The Fauna of British India". There is also a reading room here.

b) Forest School Museum, Kurseong: The Central Academy of Forest Education College is located in Kurseong, in the beautiful hills of Darjeeling district in the state of West Bengal. Established in 1927, this is the only Rangers' College in the country under the direct control of the Government of India.[17] This college is engaged exclusively in training Forest Range Officers from various states and Union Territories. The College Building was said to be constructed during late 19th Century. It along with its landed property (31.57acres) was once a property of St Mary's Seminary under the Catholic Mission of West Bengal (Society of Jesus) which was purchased by Government of India in 1974. A proposal for declaring the College building as a Heritage Building is under active consideration. The West Bengal Forest School Museum, located in the woods of the Dow Hill in Kurseong features some rare collections of animal skins, bones and hides, selection of models, photographs of certain fauna of the forest regions. The Museum is a two storey building. It contains animal skins, bones and hides and wooden products. It also has models of different dams, forest houses etc. And it has a skeleton. It's a large two-storied museum in Dow Hill that stores many exhibits of flora and fauna of the region. It has been recently renovated and restored.

Recent Trends in Green Tourism activities in North Bengal:

a) Garden-Fresh Travel: Tea-Tourism: When it comes to 'tea tourism'[18],Darjeeling and the Dooars areas of West Bengal surely win hands down. Darjeeling boasts of many beautiful and sprawling tea estates. One of the first names that come to the mind is the Glenburn Tea Estate that also has a tea nursery. Other tea estates which should be on any enthusiastic traveller's must-visit list in the Darjeeling include the, Makaibari, Happy valley and Puttabong Tea estate Those on a tea tour to Darjeeling can visit other tea estates like Margaret's Hope, Singbulli, Naxalbari, Longview, Sungma and Castleton. Tourist can simply spend time in the tea gardens and observe the method of plucking tea leaves done carefully by the workers there. Besides, tourist can also indulge in adventure activities like hiking and jungle safari in the woodlands surrounding these tea estates which feature hundreds of birds, floral diversity, and are almost all wildlife sanctums without the label. Tourist can marvel at the old growth teak and mahogany trees that are abundant here along with orchids of outstanding beauty. One can experience genuine bio-dynamic vegetable and herbs gardens here.

b) Tree House Tourism: Tree house recreation has of late made its mark as a much sought after alternative form of recreation.[19] The ideal location for introducing Tree House Tourism would be the lush green Dooars region of North Bengal which is rife with game and some of the most haunting wilderness trails – the Mahananda-Jaldapara-Gorumara-Buxa Wildlife circuit is definitely providing the tourists with not only scenic jungle vistas but also dramatic wildlife encounters with the creatures of the wild. The reserves teem with a bewildering variety of animals that snoop around adjacent villages and tea plantations. It is one of the last pockets left in India with a wild population of the elusive Indian One-Horned Rhinoceros. Native elephants and bisons too are found in plenty. Dhup Jhora Eco-resort is an example of tree house tourism in Jalpaiguri.

c) Adventure Tourism: Paragliding: Paragliding is the recreational and competitive adventure sport of flying paraglide: lightweight, free-flying, foot-launched glider aircraft with no rigid primary structure. Paragliding is an exciting adventure sport that lets tourists soar like a bird and fly among the clouds thus letting them seek the best of outdoors. Tourists can maneuver their way as they wish and in the end, they will be left with a lot of wonderful memories and one unforgettable experience. Kalimpong is tucked in the foothills of the vast Himalayan land towards the Northern most Bengal. With infinite landscapes and exciting nature views around, Kalimpong makes for one of the frontrunners in the list of places offering exciting adventure sports. No prize for guessing paragliding in Kalimpong! The city in the northeast is located on a daunting altitude which gives it an upper hand when travelers go short listing places for adventure sports. The vastness of North Bengal is such an allure that it leaves every adventurer tempted. From the list of adventures in the offering, paragliding in Kalimpong is, for sure, a nerve jostling activity.[20] A mere thought of soaring above the tea plantations and infinite valleys while marveling at seamless mountain views would make tourists soul delves into the vastness. April to June and October is the best time to visit Kalimpong for paragliding. During this period the weather conditions are just perfect thus making for an ideal situation for a good flight.

d) Adventure Tourism: River Rafting: Rafting and white water rafting are recreational outdoor activities which use an inflatable raft to navigate a river or other body of water. This is often done on white water or different degrees of rough water. Teesta River Rafting is the most popular adventure sport activity in Kalimpong, West Bengal.[21] Teesta River has become one of the most popular hotspots for White Water Rafting in eastern India and among the must include things during Kalimpong Tour. Teesta River with its green surroundings is the best choice for Rafting in Kalimpong. The Teesta river rafting has carved out deep ravines and gorges in Sikkim meandering through the hills with Kalimpong lying just off the river. This makes for quite an exciting and enthralling rafting experience. Ideally rafting can be done enroute, between Gangtok to Darjeeling, Gangtok to Kalimpong or Gangtok to Siliguri. The routes for non-swimmers are gentle and easy without much rapids involved. However for the swimmers and experienced clients, the routes are more adventurous with high grade rapids providing quite a thrill. The rafting trips for non-swimmers in Teesta River start mostly at Melli Bridge and culminate at Geil Khola in Kalimpong. This is a 12 km stretch which takes 1-2 hours. The rafting trip for Swimmers and experience clients starts at Tarkhola and ends at Melli. It is a 20 km stretch and takes 2-3 Hours. Another way is to go down to Teesta Bazaar, which is the main hub for rafting. Here you will find the River Rafting Center of GTA Tourism. They organize the rafting on Teesta River. The best time to raft on Teesta is from March to June and September to November.

e) Sport Fishing: Angling: Angling is a method of fishing by means of an "angle" (fish hook). Angling is the principal method of sport fishing. Catch and release fishing is increasingly practiced by recreational fishermen. Sport fishing in the rivers flowing through Kalimpong has the potential of attracting loads of anglers from outside.[22] The most popular spots for sport fishing are the confluences, where the Teesta meets other rivers. According to anglers, the best spot among the lot is Tribeni, which is the confluence of the Teesta and Rangeet. Doban at 27 Mile, where the Relli joins the Teesta, and the Teesta-Ravi Jhora confluence a few kilometers downstream are other spots frequented by the anglers. Sport fishing also takes place in the upper reaches of the Relli, Rishi and Mam rivers. The anglers use a hook, attached to a fishing line, which in turn is connected to a rod, to catch fish. The rods are usually fitted with a wheel that helps retrieve the catch. The hook is dressed with bait to lure the fish. Kalimpong is promoted as an angling destination; it would give a huge fillip to tourism. Among the most sought after angling spots are the places where the Teesta meets other rivers.

Green Tourism Initiatives in North Bengal:

The Government of West Bengal has also set up Green Tourism centres and Nature Interpretation centres at several places over North Bengal, which includes Barodabari, Lava, Paren, Lepchaghat, Rasik Bill, Lulegaon, Buxa, Gorubathan, Rongpo, Mongpong, Jaldhaka and Suntelikhola (Samsing).

The West Bengal Forest Development Corporations Limited runs 20 Green Tourism resorts, 17 in North Bengal and 3 in

South Bengal, in the following districts:

Darjeeling: Lepchajagat, Kalimpong, Lava, Lolegaon, Rangpo, Mongpong, Gorubathan, Samsing, Suntlekhola, Jaldhaka and Paren.

Jalpaiguri and Alipurduar: Murti, Barodabri (Malungi), Rajabhatkhawa and Rangamati.

The underlying objectives are to disseminate awareness for conservation of bio-diversity and inculcate a spirit of adventure among the young generation in particular. The Corporation has been trying to develop some good adventure and wilderness tourist resorts adjacent to forest areas taking advantage of the existing infrastructure wherever they exist.

The Green Tourism resorts at Lava, Lolegaon, Gorubathan, Samsing, Jaldhaka and Paren suffered heavy damages on 8.2.2011 during the political turmoil. Action to revive the defunct eco-resorts has been initiated. To make up for the Green Tourism capacity thus lost, the WBFDCL has set up tented accommodation at Jaldhaka and Suntlekhola (Kalimpong Division) and Rangamati (Buxa Tiger Reserve) during 2011-12 which are a hit with the visitors. At present, only 14 Eco-resorts of the WBFDCL (North Bengal: 12, South Bengal:2) with 301 beds (North Bengal:229 beds, South Bengal:72 beds) are available for tourists. The WBFDCL also runs a ropeway for tourists at Darjeeling in collaboration with M/S Conveyor & Ropeway Services Private Limited. A Museum maintained by the NTFP Division at Sukna near Siliguri is also a great attraction for the tourists.[23]

Nature Education and Wilderness Resort at Rasik Bill: West Bengal Forest Development Corporation (WBFDC) has built a Nature Education and Wilderness Resort in Rasik Bill. Rasik Bill Nature Education and Wilderness Resort is an Eco-Resort. There are 2 Non AC cottages and 2 eight bedded rooms in Rasik Bill Eco-Resort. Bounded by the tall wooded trees, visitors staying in Rasik Bill Eco-Resort can listen to the alluring chirpings of exotic birds. WBFDC Eco-Resort of Rasik Bill has become the abode nature lovers traveling in Cooch Behar. With its serene ambiance and great service, it is the best resort to stay in Rasik Bill.[24]

Ecological Impacts of Green Tourism:

Positive Impacts of Green Tourism: 'Biological diversity' is a broad term which encompasses the wealth of natural eco-systems with the remarkable variety of fauna, flora and microorganisms. Despite the variation, these forms of life are all closely connected and dependent on one another. Today biodiversity is under threat from several directions. According to United Nations Environment Program (UNEP), uncontrolled land conversion, climate change, pollution and other unsustainable human activities are causing biodiversity loss at a rate many times higher than that of natural extinction. Tourism can contribute positively to biodiversity conservation. Biodiversity also works like a magnet for tourism. So, there is a direct link between biodiversity and tourism with areas of unique natural beauty there is a direct link between biodiversity and tourism with areas of unique natural beauty attracting large number of visitors. A close relationship between Tourism and Biodiversity is asserted when the United Nations World Tourism Organization (UNWTO) and the Convention on Biological Diversity (CBD) term them as the natural allies. Biodiversity is thus one of tourism's greatest assets and fundamental to its long term sustained growth. Eco- tourism can be tool in promoting biodiversity conservation especially through education and interpretation.

Conservation Issues in Gorumara National Park: The major conservation focus of the park is to maintain a viable breeding community of Indian Rhinoceroses. However, the lack of large predators has caused significantly worrying skews in the populations of large herbivores in the park. The rhinoceros male: female ratio, usually 1:3, shot up to 1:1 - resulting in male dominance fights and deaths. The Gaur population also doubled in recent years, with risk of overgrazing.[25]

Conservation Issues in Singalila National Park: The major issues at the park are trash collection on trekking routes and ensuring minimal damage of flora by trekkers, as flora at such high altitudes tend to grow really slowly. Grazing of yak and cattle from neighboring villages can also be a problem. Forest fires can be a threat to the park, especially in spring when the accumulated debris from winter can be a hazard. A forest fire swept through the national park on March 6, 2006.

Even though the national park has a resident Red Panda population of only about 20-25 members, Project Red Panda (funded by the Central Zoo Authority) chose Singalila National Park for reintroduction of Red Pandas from its captive breeding program at the Padmaja Naidu Himalayan Zoological Park in Darjeeling, mainly due to reasons of proximity. Two females, Sweety and Milli, were released in November 2004. Milli was killed by a leopard, but Sweety adapted to the wild and gave birth to an offspring - the first such successful re-entry for Red Panda.[26]

Negative Impacts of Green Tourism: The Government of West Bengal has launched several schemes for exploiting the full potential of tourism industry in the state in accordance with the National Action Plan for Tourism, 1992. The environmental implications of the further growth of tourism industry in the state, however, need to be understood the most important direct effect that the Green Tourism industry brings on the environment is increased pressure on the carrying capacity of the eco-system in each tourist locality. Increased transport and construction activities lead to large scale deforestation and destabilization of natural landforms, while increased tourist flow leads to increase in solid waste dumping as well as depletion of water and fuel resources. Overflow of tourists to ecologically sensitive areas like Jaldapara, Gorumara and trampling, killing as well as excessive disturbance lead to destruction of rare and endangered species. Apart from these, noise pollution from vehicles and public address systems, water pollution, vehicular emissions, untreated sewage also have direct effects on bio-diversity, ambient environment and general profile of tourist spots.

The rapid growth rate of Green Tourism activity in North Bengal is inviting some negative impacts on the environment. Green Tourism attracts attention to natural treasures, thereby increasing the pressures upon them. Thus, increasing construction of resorts is causing loss to a number of plants. In fact heavy human use of open space adversely affects the biomass. Again the increasing use of wood as fuel and timber in a number of industrial products such as souvenir industry also leads to felling and cutting of trees.[27]

One of the most disturbing facts about eco-tourism is that it is mainly promoting the expropriation of wilderness areas, national parks, isolated tribal areas and even the areas having no trace of any permanent settlement. Tourists opting for such tourism often belong to the prosperous strata of society and are capable and ready to pay for everything they wish, so consumerism becomes focal theme here. Tour operators succumb to ever increasing demands made by visitors and to facilitate and entertain them. They build completely artificial landscape in the area like mega-resorts, luxury hotels as well as shopping centers. Such changes cost almost the entire eco-system dearly, many of flora and fauna species lose their natural habitat and in the long run this may even lead to species extinction. Tourism competes with other forms of development and human activity for natural resources, especially land and water. The use of natural resources subsequently leads to the transformation of ecological habitats and loss of flora and fauna. Land transformation for tourism development can directly destroy ecological habitats. The use of resources for tourism involves an 'opportunity cost' as they are denied to other sectors of economic development.

Conclusion

Green Tourism is a growing agenda for the future development of tourism. The growth in this agenda and increase in demand for green tourism are underpinned by many drivers including:

(1) The development of a world-wide societal consciousness about nature protection and appreciation, fuelled largely by the environment's higher media profile.

(2) A growing interest by individuals to 'reconnect' with nature and seek out experiences of a more spiritual thought provoking and physically challenging kind.

(3) Pressure in the workplace and the highly competitive lifestyles led by many in the developed world.

(4) Improved access to the countryside and more free time and disposable income for an increased number of people.[28]

In conclusion it can be mentioned that in West Bengal, Green Tourism has failed to achieve its goal. Biodiversity conservation has also neglected in the various National Parks of North Bengal. Unfortunately, much of what passes off for Green Tourism in North Bengal is a sad caricature of what it was originally meant to be. There is a terrific potential in Green Tourism to educate people, strengthen conservation measures and reduce ecological impacts. But only if we design our wildlife and eco-tourism with imagination and socio-ecological sensitivity, otherwise eco and wildlife tourism in North Bengal may very well be reduced to a monster in the green grab of an ecological savior. Green Tourism can contribute positively to biodiversity conservation in various National Parks and Wildlife Sanctuaries of North Bengal. Sustainable Green Tourism, one that establishes a suitable balance between the environmental, economic and socio-cultural aspects of tourism development, is a key to maximizing tourism's positive contribution to biodiversity at the local, national and global level. In the end, all Green Tourism-related activities should be well designed, executed and managed in an environment friendly manner so that the environment is not degraded.

NOTES AND REFERENCES

1) Debasis Bhattacharya, Ranjan Sarkar, Bhaskar Choudhury, 'Irresponsible Eco-Tourism Practices Flanking The Best National Park In India: A Multivariate Analysis', in *S.I.T Journal of Management*, Vol. 1. No. 1. June 2012. pp. 1 – 27, p-2.

2) Shwn-Meei Lee, Hiroshi Chris Honda, Gui Ren and Yu-Chen Lo, 'The Implementation of Green Tourism and Hospitality', in *Journal of Tourism and Hospitality*, Vol. 5. Issue.4.2016.pp.2-5.

3) Aftabuddin SK, Dr. Kadambari Jain, 'Green Tourism Practices in India-A Paradigm Shift in Sustainable Development', in *International Journal of Science, Technology and Management*, Vol.6, No.5, May 2017,pp.70-74.

4) Vinay Tandon, 'Eco-Tourism, Environmental Panacea or Poison?' in *Kurukshetra: A Journal on Rural Development*, vol-55, no-8, June, 2007, pp. 3-6, p-3.

5) State Forest Report-2006-2007, Dept. of Forest, Govt. of West Bengal, Chapter-16, p-117.

6) 'Eco-Tourism: To belt up the bewildering wilderness', in West Bengal Tourism Special Issue, Dept. of Information and Culture, Govt. of West Bengal, July-2004.
7) State Forest Report-2006-2007, Dept. of Forest, Govt. of West Bengal, Chapter-16 (Green Tourism in West Bengal), p-117.
8) *Ibid,* p-117.
9) 'Wild Beauty: The enchanting woodlands of Bengal', A Tourist Information Brochure published by Department of Tourism, Govt. of West Bengal, 2012. 'The East Himalayas: Simply out of this World', A Tourist Information Brochure Published by Department of Tourism, Govt. of West Bengal, 2012.
10) 'Darjeeling: The Queen of the Hills', A Tourist Information Brochure published by Department of Tourism, Govt. of West Bengal, 2019.
11) 'Green Dooars: In the Foothills of the Himalayas', A Tourist Information Brochure Published by Department of Tourism, Govt. of West Bengal, 2019.
12) 'Dreamland Dooars', A Tourist Information Brochure published by Department of Tourism, Govt. of West Bengal, 2012./ 'A Paradise on Earth: The Dooars', A Tourist Information Brochure Published by Department of Tourism, Govt. of West Bengal, 2008.
13) 'Once the Abode of Princes: Cooch Behar', A Tourist Information Brochure published by Department of Tourism, Govt. of West Bengal, 2018.
14) Information collected from the Official Website of West Bengal Forest Development Corporations: https://www.wbfdc.com/
15) 'Wild Beauty: The enchanting woodlands of Bengal', A Tourist Information Brochure published by Department of Tourism, Govt. of West Bengal, 2012.
16) 'Darjeeling: The Queen of the Hills', A Tourist Information Brochure published by Department of Tourism, Govt. of West Bengal, 2019.
17) 'Kurseong: Serene Beauty', A Tourist Information Brochure published by Department of Tourism, Govt. of West Bengal, 2019.
18) 'Garden Fresh Travel: Tea Tourism in Bengal', A Tourist Information Brochure Published by Department of Tourism, Govt. of West Bengal, 2012.
19) 'Dreamland Dooars', A Tourist Information Brochure published by Department of Tourism, Govt. of West Bengal, 2012./ 'A

Paradise on Earth: The Dooars', A Tourist Information Brochure Published by Department of Tourism, Govt. of West Bengal, 2008.

20) 'Sensational: Ecology and Adventure in Bengal', A Tourist Information Brochure Published by Department of Tourism, Govt. of West Bengal, 2008.

21) 'Kalimpong: Tryst with Nature', A Tourist Information Brochure Published by Department of Tourism, Govt. of West Bengal, 2019./ 'Sensational: Ecology and Adventure in Bengal', A Tourist Information Brochure Published by Department of Tourism, Govt. of West Bengal, 2008.

22) *Ibid.*

23) State Forest Report, Dept. of Forest, 2010-2011. Govt. of West Bengal, Chapter-15 (West Bengal Forest Development Corporation Limited), p-126.

24) Information collected from the Official Website of West Bengal Forest Development Corporations: https://www.wbfdc.com/

25) Madhusudan Karmakar, 'Eco-Tourism and Its Impact on Regional Economy-A Study of North Bengal', in *Tourismos: An International Multidisciplinary Journal of Tourism Volume* 6, Number 1, Spring 2011, pp. 251-270, p-256.

26) State Forest Report, Dept. of Forest, 2010-2011. Govt. of West Bengal, Chapter-11, p-98.

27) Ibid, p-92.

28) Shwn-Meei Lee, Hiroshi Chris Honda, Gui Ren and Yu-Chen Lo, 'The Implementation of Green Tourism and Hospitality', in *Journal of Tourism and Hospitality,* Vol. 5. Issue.4.2016.pp.5. port of the L.I.C – p.96.